THE
SPIRITUAL
CHILD

Also by Lisa Miller

The Oxford Handbook of Psychology and Spirituality (editor)

THE
SPIRITUAL
CHILD

THE NEW SCIENCE ON
PARENTING FOR HEALTH AND
LIFELONG THRIVING

LISA MILLER, PH.D.
with Teresa Barker

St. Martin's Press
New York

THE SPIRITUAL CHILD. Copyright © 2015 by Lisa Miller. All rights reserved. Printed in the United States of America. For information, address St. Martin's Press, 175 Fifth Avenue, New York, N.Y. 10010.

www.stmartins.com

The Library of Congress Cataloging-in-Publication Data is available upon request.

ISBN 978-1-250-03292-8 (hardcover)
ISBN 978-1-250-03291-1 (e-book)

St. Martin's Press books may be purchased for educational, business, or promotional use. For information on bulk purchases, please contact the Macmillan Corporate and Premium Sales Department at 1-800-221-7945, extension 5442, or write to specialmarkets@macmillan.com.

First Edition: May 2015

10 9 8 7 6 5 4 3 2 1

In love,
for Isaiah, Leah, and Lila

Contents

THE
SPIRITUAL
CHILD

Introduction

Science is a lens, a way of understanding just about anything, including, as it turns out, spirituality. Science is particularly powerful in deciphering things difficult to perceive with the naked eye, which has made it all the more valuable as we search for tangible evidence to explain our relationship with an essentially intangible realm.

I am a clinical psychologist and director of clinical psychology at Columbia University, Teachers College, and a leading scientist in the now booming field of spirituality and psychology, mental health, and thriving. My lab has conducted multiple research studies and published scores of research articles on spiritual development in children, adolescents, and families. Often when I give talks across the country, parents rush up with accounts of their children caring for younger siblings or elderly grandparents, talking to animals, or singing in prayer. "Children are so spiritual!" they'll say. Sometimes in difficult family moments or a crisis, children display wisdom and understanding far more on point than the surrounding aggravated or bereaved adults. These moments are but a glimpse into the deep foundational reality of childhood. As a scientist,

I know childhood spirituality to be a powerful truth that is incontrovertible yet strangely absent from our mainstream culture. That "children are so spiritual" is not merely anecdote or opinion, be it mine or anyone else's. It is an established scientific fact.

When I started out as a clinical scientist fifteen years ago, focusing on the science of spirituality in health, I encountered enormous skepticism, flat rejections, and doors literally slammed shut during my Grand Rounds presentations at medical schools. When the calendar rolled over to the new millennium, there still existed a quite strong bias in the social and medical sciences against research on spirituality and religion—two distinct concepts in my mind. I quickly came to expect the doubting or sometimes dismissive comments: "Spirituality is not psychology" or "How will your lab ever be funded?" or "Is that the same as prayer in public schools?" (Which of course has nothing to do with the study of spirituality in health.) Every so often, however, came a glimpse of interest, and sometimes burning curiosity. These rare responses came from my heroes, the very top scientists in the field because they are voraciously curious and follow the data.

And while the data on spirituality was initially scant, the few studies available provided a strong signal so bright that it was impossible to ignore as a subject of scientific interest and inquiry. Thus began my scientific journey, which has become my life's work: the study of our inborn natural spirituality as foundational to mental health and wellness, particularly as it develops in the first two decades of our lives. Together with a few labs across the country, my colleagues and I set out to build a new science of spirituality, mental health, and thriving. The resulting extensive and groundbreaking research, advances in our understanding of brain science and the findings of neuro-imaging, lengthy interviews with hundreds of children and parents, case studies, and rich anecdotal material show that:

- Spirituality is an untapped resource in our understanding of human development, resilience and illness, and health and healing. The absence of support for children's spiritual growth has contributed to alarming rates of childhood and adolescent emotional suffering and behaviors that put them at risk. Knowledge of spiritual development rewrites the contemporary account of spiraling rates of depression, substance abuse, addictive behaviors, and other health concerns.

- Awareness of spiritual development creates opportunities to prepare teens for the important inner work required for individuation, identity development, emotional resilience, character, meaningful work, and healthy relationships. Spirituality is the central organizing principle of inner life in the second decade, boosting teens into an adulthood of meaning and purpose, thriving, and awareness.

- Spiritual development through the early years prepares the adolescent to grapple more successfully with the predictably difficult and potentially disorienting existential questions that make adolescence so deeply challenging for teens (and their parents). It also provides a protective health benefit, reducing the risk of depression, substance abuse, aggression, and high-risk behaviors, including physical risk taking and a sexuality devoid of emotional intimacy.

- Biologically, we are hardwired for spiritual connection. Spiritual development is for our species a biological and psychological imperative from birth. The innate spiritual attunement of young children—unlike other lines of development such as language or cognition—begins whole and designed by nature to prepare the child for decades ahead, including the challenging developmental passage of adolescence.

- In the first decade of life, the child advances through a process of integrating his or her spiritual "knowing" with other developing capabilities, including cognitive, physical, social, and emotional development, all of which are shaped by interactions with parents, family, peers, and community. Without support and lacking encouragement to keep developing that part of himself, the child's spiritual attunement erodes and becomes "disaggregated" in the crush of a narrowly material culture.

- The science of spirituality enables us to see adolescence in a new and more helpful, hopeful light: the universal developmental surge in adolescence, previously viewed as a fraught passage toward physical and emotional maturity, is now understood more fully to also be a journey of essential spiritual search and growth. This developmental phenomenon is seen in every culture, and research shows clinical and genetic evidence for this adolescent surge of spiritual awakening.

- Parents and children share a parallel developmental arc in which a child's need and yearning for spiritual exploration coincides with a similar "quest" phase in adult life. For parent and child, meaning and connection often lead to spiritual self-discovery. This mutual impetus means that the adult's quest phase and the child's can be mutually awakening and supportive. Our children can be our impetus for spiritual discovery, our muses or guides, and at times the source of illumination.

With these findings we can see the crisis in the making when spiritual development is neglected or when a child's spiritual curiosity and exploration are denied. Yet a number of factors ranging from cultural to ideological to technological have made many parents reluctant, uncomfortable, or afraid to engage with our children in the spiritual quest. Now more than ever, in a culture where often enormous amounts of money, empty fame, and cynicism have become toxic dominant values, our children need us to support their quest for a spiritually grounded life at every age—and to discover or strengthen our own.

Natural Spirituality Is the Oldest—and Newest—Big Idea for Parents and Children

The history of psychology and parenting in the twentieth and early twenty-first centuries can be seen as a series of "big ideas" that have shaped our culture's understanding of our psychological selves, and that of our children. A new big idea gives parents an *aha!* moment: "Yes, I always sensed that; now I know it's true," or, "I definitely thought something was going on. Now it's clear." Sometimes, it's "I had no idea!" Supported by science, big ideas show parents how to encourage their children in a new way, through an untapped reserve they can access easily.

A big idea for parents is defined by three components. First, a big idea is brought to our awareness by new, cutting-edge science. What we could sense intuitively yet not see definitively before is now confirmed through research. Second, a big idea is shown by science to influence—potentially dramatically enhance—our child's wellness, inner resources, and success. And third, a big idea identifies specific ways that parents can help develop and support their child.

Big ideas of the past two decades include psychologist and author Martin Seligman's *positive psychology*, which revolutionized our popular understanding of happiness and thriving. He demonstrated how these feelings aren't simply a part of our innate temperament, but rather are malleable, and can be taught. Optimism was shown to be teachable, not just inborn, as a big idea that brought positive psychological insights to families, schools, and communities. Other big ideas: Peter Salovey, now the president at Yale University, developed the notion of emotional intelligence (EQ) and captured, with systematic study, our intuitive sense that some of us are more "people smart," an attribute that has benefits for success beyond the previously researched contribution of higher IQ. Dean Hamer, a scientist at the National Institutes of Health, brought attention to the genetic determinants of human behavior; the ensuing discussion of "hardwired" genetic contributions to a child's personality showed parents that something previously considered a choice, like sexual orientation, actually is genetically driven. More recently, Carol Dweck revealed two radically different "mindsets" that come from different types of parental praise: that which encourages children through learning goals, versus that which rewards performance, the latter making children more anxious and prone to "freeze-up." These big ideas help us to see our own children with clear eyes, to understand them more deeply, and to better know our role, as parents, in helping them reach their fullest and brightest potential.

I believe that a new scientifically defined human faculty, which I call natural spirituality, is the next big idea for parents. We can now apply new research and data about spirituality's relationship to human health, happiness, and thriving to our understanding of child development and parenting. Our findings show that natural spirituality exists as a human capacity—just as EQ and IQ are commonly acknowledged human capacities—and is associated clearly with life success and satisfaction.

We know now that an "inner spiritual compass" is an innate, concrete faculty and, like EQ, a part of our biological endowment. It has a biological basis, which can also be cultivated. The evidence is hard, indisputable, and rigorously scientific.

Our children have an inborn spirituality that is the greatest source of resilience they have as human beings, and we, as parents, can support our children's spiritual development. Our parenting choices in the first two decades radically affect our children's spiritual development in ways that last their entire lives. Natural spirituality, in fact, appears to be the single most significant factor in children's health and their ability to thrive.

What I Mean by "Spirituality" in This Book

If we're to understand the importance of spirituality in a child's life, we first need to understand what is meant by "spirituality." The research shows a clear difference between strict adherence to a particular religious denomination and personal spirituality, with the latter focused upon spirituality as "an inner sense of living relationship to a higher power (God,

nature, spirit, universe, the creator, or whatever your word is for the ultimate loving, guiding life-force)." This focus may seem clear and self-
evident, but it took nearly two decades for the scientific community to
embrace it.

For years, scholars sought to concisely define spirituality as conceptu-
ally different from religion, which resulted in many different defini-
tions. For instance, one definition was "that which brings peace, meaning,
and transcendence." Another was "an awareness that I am part of something bigger than myself." Each definition was true in its own right, but
no single one pertained to all people's spirituality, nor could they claim
to be supported in a scientific context. Eventually, the discussion exhausted itself, and the limits of this endeavor were passively or tacitly
acknowledged, while the scientists moved on to the more practical work
of examining the benefits of spirituality. That work suffered, however,
from not being unified in perspective from lab to lab.

Then in 1997, a landmark scientific article published in the *American
Journal of Psychiatry* provided evidence of a hugely beneficial dimension
of spirituality that was empirically rather than theoretically derived: a
personal relationship with the transcendent.

In a twin study on religion and mental health, psychiatric genetic-
epidemiologist Kenneth Kendler and his colleagues looked at "religion"
as compared with "spirituality" in nearly two thousand adult twins. It was
shown statistically that in people's lived experience, personal spirituality
is a different concept from adherence to religion or choice of religious
denomination.

Instead, spirituality was shown to be *a sense of a close personal relationship to God (or nature or the universe or whatever term each person used for
higher power) and a vital source of daily guidance.* The degree to which the
subjects adhered to a religious denomination was shown to be a distinct
set of beliefs and experiences. This isn't to say that spirituality and religion are always unrelated. For many people, it's through the beliefs and
practice of their own religion that they build and foster a relationship
with God. But for others, the two sets of experience are totally unrelated,

and strong spirituality can still exist separately from religion. In the general population, personal spirituality and participating in a specific religion correlate only moderately, which means that some people find spirituality in religion, while other people find it in other ways. In Kendler's study, *spirituality did not meaningfully correlate with one specific religious denomination*; there are highly spiritual people in all denominations, and highly spiritual people who don't adhere to any specific religious denomination. With these distinctions established, science had identified a crucial and valuable dimension of "spirituality," and researchers could get busy exploring spirituality's contributions to good health, mental well-being, fulfillment, and success.

Empirical science, in findings based on adolescence research, also has methodically identified what is *not* meant by personal spirituality. It is unrelated statistically to strict adherence to a religion or creed without a sense of personal choice or ownership. Our own research, published in the Society for Adolescent Health and Medicine's *Journal of Adolescent Health,* shows that rigid adherence to creed without a sacred personal relationship is very different from natural spirituality and is often associated with dangerous risk taking, including unprotected, high-risk, and abusive sexual activity. Furthermore, in the *Journal of the American Academy of Child and Adolescent Psychiatry*, I published evidence that while personal devotion is highly protective against heavy substance use and abuse, rigid adherence to creed without a sense of the sacred relationship does not prevent against substance abuse.

For adolescents who develop a strong spiritual compass outside of a religious tradition, as well as adolescents who develop a strong spiritual compass within a religious tradition, spirituality manifests itself as an inner awareness or a sense of relationship with a higher power. When developed from within a religious tradition, the process is just as personal and takes as much initiative and hard work as when it's developed without a religious tradition. Even when an adolescent benefits from the guidance of a religious tradition, the significance of specific teachings must still be derived at a deep personal level for the benefits to be felt.

Memorizing creed without personal investment is not enough. For some adolescents, questioning spiritual assumptions is crucial to ownership. Finally, other adolescents develop personal spirituality through an intense and often prayerful deepening of faith. In all cases, what makes spirituality meaningful is personal choice and ownership.

So, while organized religions can clearly play a role in spiritual development, the primary engine that drives natural spirituality is innate, biological, and developmental: first an inborn faculty for transcendent connection, then a developmental impetus to make it our own, and the resulting deep personal relationship with the transcendent through nature, God, or the universal force.

How Do We Get There from Here?

But how do we get spiritual in the first place? How does personal spirituality actually happen? Of course we each have our own individual story, but this book looks at that question on a scientific basis. What science has yet to share with our culture is the great story of spirituality's formation that traces back to childhood and adolescence. How does spirituality matter to children and adolescents? What is the developmental path of spirituality? Is there an optimal developmental window of opportunity—a time in which developmental energies converge, primed for progress? How might parents build a strong sense of spirituality in their child that carries into adulthood?

These should be pressing concerns to parents, because the data suggest that it is much easier and more likely for adults to be spiritual if that sense is fostered during childhood and adolescence. This fostering of spirituality used to simply be part of the dominant culture in the United States, so much so that the internal process of spiritual development went largely unnoticed. In the early and middle twentieth century, research showed that most families were religious to some degree. Beyond personal preferences, our broader culture carried some religious assumptions, some woven through our history and others through everyday life in our communities. For generations, this meant that even when parents conveyed no sense of spirituality to their children, some type of spiritual awareness was supported in—ingrained in—the culture.

Surveys today show that to a large extent, an unquestioned assumption of religion in our culture is largely gone. A significant percentage of several generations of current parents—people between twenty-five and fifty years old—were raised without overt spiritual engagement or instruction in the home. This means that a significant number of adults who range from twenty-five to fifty years old were raised with no spiritual structure, no spiritual community, no spiritual conversation or teaching, and often no spiritual practice: in sum, none of the critical pieces for developing a spiritual reality, whether that is a belief in an ultimate creator or an ability to make choices that are informed by spiritual principles. In other words, as commitment to traditional religion declined in the 1960s and 1970s, a generation was raised without an implicit awareness of the relationship between spirituality and well-being. Today, more than one-third of young adults (eighteen to twenty-four years old) report "no religion." Two-thirds of Americans—affiliated and unaffiliated alike—say religion is losing its influence in American lives. Where organized religion was once the backdrop of our culture we now see a rather muted canvas. This creates a great challenge where spirituality is concerned, and an even greater opportunity.

First, the challenge. Some parents assume that their children will develop a relationship to spirituality on their own if they're naturally inclined to. These parents aren't for it or against it. They simply don't see themselves as involved one way or another. For other parents, spirituality may be deemed off-limits as a topic of conversation outside of a house of worship. For them, it's something to discuss only in the context of holidays or rites of passage. Still other parents consider spirituality either nonexistent or unimportant; others are atheists or agnostics who passively or actively pass along their views to their children. There also are committed religious parents, who are focused on raising spiritual children yet who might appreciate some support and backup from science. Finally, there is the majority of parents who care about their child's spirituality but feel unqualified to help. They feel that the lack of spiritual experience in their own upbringing has left them without a blueprint for recognizing and supporting spirituality in their own children. These parents fear that since they've never resolved the big questions themselves, they shouldn't pass on their fuzzy answers to their kids. Parents often are very clear as they tell me the reasons they stop short of joining in a spiritual discussion with their child:

"I don't want to share my views about spiritual things because I'm not so sure myself. I could say something to steer my child in the wrong direction."

"I don't believe in anything, really, other than human goodness. Although I wish I did believe that there was something more. I feel like I am passing on a big fib."

"I don't want to bias my children with my beliefs; I'd rather let them choose when they grow up."

"I am just not sure how to put it. There is almost nothing at all for parents that helps us talk about spirituality, other than religion. But I'm not religious and don't like the way religion was taught to me."

As parents with feelings along these lines, we may hold off on conversations or discourage (actively or tacitly) children from sharing their spiritual questions, reflections, or experiences with us. All of these parental rationales for avoiding the subject are common and understandable. But they're also misguided. In the moment our avoidance may seem like a small redirection, but it actually can derail an important developmental process in our children. The message they get is that their spiritual reality isn't important to you, isn't worthy of pursuit, or perhaps isn't even real. Research shows that a parent's decision about how to approach their child's spiritual life is a high-stakes proposition with lifelong implications. Studies on spiritual development in adolescents who have spiritually minded parents have shown that the right type of parental contribution—the kind that will be outlined in the pages ahead—can make or break the development of adolescent spirituality and can influence the child's lifelong physical health and mental health.

A second cultural shift has brought our attention to our children's need for spiritual grounding. Childhood has become increasingly competitive, from superselective nursery schools and afterschool pursuits to college admission. Parents feel enormous pressure to give their children a competitive edge. As a result, the parenting culture has come to focus almost entirely on accomplishment. The race starts early with the search for just the "right" kind of crib mobiles to propel development; the "right" toys, videos, and computer games and programs that promise to build a better baby and child—smarter, healthier, in every way ahead of the curve. Soon student clubs, travel programs, sports, extra study, and packed schedules take over our children's lives, and ours, too. The original point of it all—to nurture in children the skills, knowledge, and deep inner joy for personal fulfillment and accomplishment—has become a moving target.

Third, a severe economic downturn has financially devastated many families, and we're clear now that the "right" start in life—all the competitive strategies, material accoutrements, and accomplishments—are no guarantee of success, safety, or genuine satisfaction. What's more, we live in a world roiled by natural disasters, fears about global warming, war, and violence, employment insecurity, and bitter political and religious strife. It is no surprise that a 2010 Fetzer Institute survey found that 91 percent of Americans believe that the world is becoming increasingly frightening and violent.

So if material success and stability have become more problematic, what can parents do to reinforce resilience and a positive sense of worth in their children? For some parents, this has become a time to rethink their choices and, in some cases, reembrace the idea that fulfillment in life is found in meaning and purpose, in spiritual bearings, and not in a better computer, a nicer car, the latest cell phone, or more money. The problem is that parents don't know where to start when it comes to communicating these ideas to their kids.

These days I hear many nonreligious people express the feeling that "although I am not religious, I actually am pretty spiritual in my own way." Indeed, as a whole, the United States now seems to be turning more "spiritual" as the population ages. In 2010, the Fetzer Institute found that 60 percent of adults said they are now more spiritual than they were five years before. The institute also found that 75 percent of American adults believe that spirituality can help solve misunderstandings. A Religion and Social Trends Gallup poll showed that more than 90 percent of Americans pray and believe in an ultimate creator. Yet these same adults who understand the need for spirituality in their lives are unaware of the nascent spiritual awareness of their children and are too often in the dark about how to help their children connect with it. What I find in my work is that many adults simply don't have a clue how to talk about spirituality with their children. Nonetheless, I believe, and this book will demonstrate, that parents absolutely need to try. They need to engage in their children's emerging spirituality.

Therein lies the opportunity. In the absence of sound knowledge and credible science, parents have told me they felt stuck. We have books, blogs, online sources, and other media advisers on nearly all sides of parenting, but not for this crucial inner resource of spirituality. I have written *The Spiritual Child* to be that resource, based upon the science published in academic peer-reviewed journals that is not yet readily accessible to parents.

I work from the assumption that good parents can rapidly become spiritually engaged parents on their own terms, drawing from their own knowledge and individual spiritual base. The aim of this book is to guide you to reflect on your child's spiritual expression and awareness and to help you support and encourage your child's spiritual development through active, positive engagement.

In addition to being a scientist and graduate school professor, I am the mother of three fantastic children, aged eleven, thirteen, and fourteen. I live daily in two worlds, that of the university and that of the family. Although my foremost commitment is to spiritual parenting, I do have other, more traditionally ambitious goals for my children, just as most parents do for their children. Yes, I know the academic success game, and I play it well. My husband and I drive three hours a day so that our children can attend a school known for its whole-child curriculm and academic rigor. I'm grooming my children for the A train to success, which will carry them smoothly, I hope, into their early twenties. That said, I'm also acutely aware that the A train goes absolutely nowhere important if the child lacks an inner compass. My greatest fear for my children is not that they'll miss the A train, but that they won't know what to do once the A train arrives at its destination.

But that's me. If you are a parent who is personally skeptical about spirituality, but you are open to trying something new and unfamiliar for the sake of your children, I suggest you don't pass on this book just yet. In every respect, it is written not just for those who want to be spiritually engaged but for the skeptics and outright naysayers, as well.

Again, it's all in the science. I do not proselytize; my intention is to thoroughly inform. I want to offer fellow parents the best information science has to encourage health, thriving, and success for our families. Whenever I discuss these ideas in presentations at schools, in interviews, or in private conversations, parents are absolutely fascinated by the science because it is so relevant to their children's ability to live their best lives. When I give talks around the country to parents and educators, to adults seeking personal growth, and to the scientific and clinical treatment community, people often share from their or their children's experiences. As one parent put it, "I always sensed it was true that children are spiritual, that we have to support their natural spirituality. Now I understand it. Now I have the confidence that there's science behind it."

I have found that the spiritually engaged are equally riveted by science, often taking the new breakthroughs in research as confirmation of what for many years they resolutely knew through their hearts. At the end of a talk in Texas, a priest who leads a large urban congregation approached me with tears in his eyes. "Now it all comes together," he said, "my heart with science, at last it is one."

I often am asked by the media to be the "expert spiritual scientist." In one television interview I was asked what "another opinion" of the existence of spirituality in children might be. While I am always interested to hear from all corners, the fact is that science does not say that children are not spiritual; there are hundreds of rigorous, elegant peer-reviewed scientific articles that show spirituality as the root of wellness in the first two decades of life.

Some of my scientific findings have been covered in leading newspapers and broadcast media and followed by online blogs. In looking over the several thousands of public comments on the blogs, there has been a handful insisting that the science be disregarded because "scientists can make the numbers say anything they want." This really is not the case. Scientific articles go to peer review, through which fellow critical scientists challenge ideas and push hard to see any logical and systematic holes. Science is a community of driving intellectuals, and we work together to be sure our work is sound. Yet there is one way that the blog respondents are right. Science is as revealing as the questions we ask, and until the questions were asked, the answers—or insights—remained out of reach, out of sight.

Parenting at the Intersection of Science and Spirituality

Fifteen years of research in my lab, as well as fellow labs across the scientific field, now make a strong claim that we have a natural spirituality: a biologically based faculty for transcendent knowing, relationship, and experience. You don't have to understand spiritual development completely in order to support it in your child: you can simply welcome the questions and the conversations. In fact, spirituality may not speak to you at all, but it is foundational to your child. Research shows that parents and children do not always share the same degree of spirituality, particularly when parents don't relate to spirituality. The important question for a parent to consider is: Might I offer my child something relevant and beneficial, even if it is not something familiar to me? We enroll our children in music lessons even if we do not play an instrument. We eagerly offer our child a better academic education than we may have received ourselves. For some parents, building spirituality in your child may be the same proposition. Parental generosity extends beyond our own opportunities. Just as we delight in our children's accomplishments beyond our own, skeptical parents just might be moved by the emerging spirituality in their children. As one father said to me, "I have never been spiritual myself. But I look at this data, and would never want to get in the way of my daughter's spirituality."

We catch glimpses of our children's innate spirituality in everyday moments with them, in their wonder and delight in what nature offers up and in the bond of love and trust that they begin life with. I hear from parents who want to take those conversations or experiences further than the moment, to take their children from the window of awakening to a foundational way of living. They ask, *What do I do with this moment of awareness when I see it?* They want to understand their child's experience and where it might lead if given the chance. They sense this is important and want to take this opportunity and run with it, but there aren't a lot of resources and steadying anchors to help them. I've written *The Spiritual Child* to be just that.

My work as a scientist and my life as a woman and a mother have taken me deeply into the spiritual lives of children. In my daily experience as a parent I see a striking and detrimental dearth of information from clinical science. This is especially troubling in light of the recent and very strong body of science on spirituality in child and adolescent development, particularly as a source of resilience and thriving, and as a buffer against the most prevalent forms of suffering and psychopathology. The science is there, but the word has not gotten out.

The growing body of literature in this emerging field at the intersection of science and spirit offers an unprecedented view into the uniquely powerful spiritual potential of childhood and adolescence. My research and that of others explore the protective benefits of healthy spiritual development meeting some of the most serious health challenges of adolescence, such as risk taking, depression, substance abuse, and severe affective disorders. Spirituality is also strongly associated with positive inner assets, such as meaning, purpose, and optimism. As a society we urgently need to see the overwhelming strength of spirituality as a foremost protection against the source of the leading causes of death between the ages of fifteen and twenty-four: accidents due to risk (mostly automotive), suicides, and homicides, as well as the contribution of drug use to these tragedies. This deserves a national conversation to reframe the impact of our institutions and culture on development and the impact of personal spirituality on development, as well.

My intention in writing this book is fourfold:

First, to bring forward the new science that shows conclusively how critical spiritual development is through childhood and adolescence as a basis for overall health and, perhaps most surprising, as a significant factor in reducing the risk of depression, substance abuse, and high-risk behaviors that are of such great concern today.

Second, to bring children's voices forward so we may learn to hear them as they speak in their own terms of their spiritual lives, their curiosity, their connection to all living beings, their fears, their wonder, and their extraordinary spiritual experiences.

Third, to provide parents with encouragement, compassionate coaching, and a language for bringing this vibrant conversation alive in their own families.

Finally, to awaken spiritual curiosity and openness in parents so they may more comfortably accompany their children on this journey and, in doing so, perhaps embark on their own journey of discovery.

How can we as parents recognize and support the natural spiritual capacity in our children? How will our children evolve differently, foundationally thrive, and deeply succeed because we support their natural spirituality? *The Spiritual Child* answers these questions, grounded in science and life. Remember: spirituality is in our nature. As we mature we may learn a specific language and perspective based upon our cultural setting, from Christianity, Judaism, Islam, Hinduism, and a great range of other world religions and beliefs—including the view that spirituality doesn't exist. These are all spiritual languages and views. An understanding of the science of spirituality lets us see what is inherent to our human nature, and then to better resonate with the core spiritual experience of all people around the world. We can be multilingual if we know what we are discussing.

Open Science, Open Doors, Open Hearts and Minds

As I said at the opening of this introduction, the science of spirituality has burgeoned in the past fifteen years, with a rocket takeoff in the past five years. There is a growing fascination with it, and, increasingly, even skeptics and those in the ambivalent middle acknowledge its relevance. When I first entered this field and embarked on this line of research I faced many people's doubts about its viability. I stuck with it because the data was clear, strong, and true. When a few ardently offended people walked out in the middle of my talks, slamming the door, I took it as evidence that such controversial work indeed needed to be pursued. This research, step by step, has been life-energy well spent.

Science is a wondrous journey full of derailments, twists, and turns, and sometimes stunning, awesome surprises. For a decade and a half, I have worked to bear witness to spirituality through the lens of science. Not to prove its existence, but to better know its expressions and ways in our humanity.

Today, the field of spirituality in psychology is growing dramatically. These days, people do not walk out on my talks, but rather, invite me to deliver talks on spiritual psychology around the country and around the world to policy groups, schools, and community organizations. At Columbia University, Teachers College, we have created a concentration of graduate study in spiritual psychology. Opening the door to a spiritual science has enabled a world of clinicians, researchers, educators, youth guidance specialists, and other mental health professionals to expand and deepen their work with children and adolescents—and ultimately people of all ages. The open door has also allowed a new generation of graduate students to study the wholeness of our human journey through the lens of science and spirituality. We have arrived as a culture, ready to learn and to help our children. No longer is work in spirituality a vision for the future; it is now part of mainstream psychology. We are here.

I have written this book as a translation of the cutting-edge science, to reach the broadest possible audience—parents, educators, health professionals, clergy, youth leaders, scientists, policy makers, and others devoted to children's health, education, and well-being. Scientific readers interested in a more extensive presentation of the science will find it in my edited volume, *The Oxford University Press Handbook of Psychology and Spirituality*, and in other resources listed in the notes at the end of this book.

There is no question that the parenting journey wears away our ego, but ultimately we are not made less by the exhaustion, tired eyes, worn short-term memory, and endless laundry. Rather, we are so very much more—from our children's wondrous arrival into our lives to their rounds of questioning and development, when we pay attention and we reflect, we can see great things through their spiritual lens.

What if this parenting journey is actually the ultimate spiritual journey? The equivalent to the deep awakening of the isolated monk, the pilgrimage to Mecca or Jerusalem, or the climb up Mount Everest?

I come to this work as a scientist, a clinician, and a parent. I consider each scientific finding to be a bright dot in an Impressionist painting of my journey. At times in this book I will share specific studies. At other times, I will connect the dots between studies to share the conclusion that comes to me after years of examining this phenomena, and of listening to the voices of children and families. These voices are presented as narratives in order to convey the emotion and life of the picture created by science, told in stories drawn from research, conversations, and interviews. With the exception of the names of my own children, I have changed names and identifying features of those individuals and experiences I have described. In some instances, I combined aspects of several stories to illustrate a larger idea or paradigm. The voices of children, adolescents, and adults sharing from their own experiences and reflections, including transcendent experiences that rarely are shared, have a prominent place in this book. I have also made practicality a priority, weaving in examples and suggestions for parents throughout the book to enable science and theory to serve them in the most direct possible way: in their everyday interactions with their children and one another.

I am hopeful that these narratives bring science to life so that you can feel the presence and power of spirituality and science and explore its place in your journey. A commitment by all of us to foster children's spirituality, grounded in science and in our natural love, can truly change our global culture. We will know our nature, and discover before us an opportunity to live in dialogue with our world.

PART I

CHILDHOOD

BIRTHRIGHT

Built for Spirituality

W e stand chatting by our SUVs and hybrids, a half-dozen moms and dads watching as our fourth-graders finish soccer practice. We're glad to see one another. The parents of my son's teammates are terrific people: kind, dedicated to their children, generous in time and energy as volunteers in the community. Our conversation runs the usual course through everyone's busy schedules, which are primarily organized around our children's packed lives. Even the youngest siblings have preschool and standing playdates or afternoon lessons in foreign languages, dance, violin, or piano. These mothers and fathers are determined to give their children a competitive advantage in school and life. We all want our children to reach their full potential, and we watch to identify their areas of aptitude and natural strength, so that we may actively support their gifts.

We are good parents, loving parents, parents of the highest intention and unyielding commitment. Our conversations tend to focus on how we can prepare our children to be successful in school or on the team, or about their academic or other accomplishments. We care about their social lives, from playdates to prom dates, and we coach them day by day with hopes that they'll make good friends, get along with their peers, and step up to do the right thing when the moment calls for leadership. We want them to be emotionally hardy and resilient, to know happiness and how to take setbacks in stride, to learn how to manage big feelings like anger and disappointment. When they do not get what they want, we hope that they will be able to successfully set a new course, readjust, "hit reset," and move forward to succeed.

There is a bit of anxiety about admissions or placement tests for selective schools or programs, from preschools and child-care programs through high school and college. We're also aware of the psychological toll on kids who are overscheduled and under chronic pressure to perform, and we want to preserve childhood as a joyful, explorative, and carefree time. Our children's development means everything to us. We've read the books and listened to their teachers. We know that this formative age is the epicenter for opportunity, so we push on.

Like all parents, we have hopes and latent expectations, after all. From the moment our children are born, we imagine their future selves. Our hopes for our child—the young adult he or she will grow up to be—inform everything we feel and think and do as parents. If our baby throws a spongy ball, we hope—maybe dream—for the Dallas Cowboys. A clever discovery in the playroom translates into visions of our future inventor or entrepreneur. A love of books brings images of the future scholar or writer. We envision our young children as accomplished, impassioned adults who have achieved school, sports, or stage success and used it as a pathway to opportunity, to love and be loved, to have wonderful friends, and in every way to enjoy a good life and career. We gaze at our gurgling baby or adventurous toddler with love—and a twenty-year trajectory of aspiration.

We don't just talk and dream, we also plan and act on our best intentions. And yet all of those conversations, elaborate schedules of extracurricular activities, and high aspirations often miss the single most crucial ingredient of all, the only thing that science has shown to reliably predict fulfillment, success, and thriving: a child's spiritual development.

It is important to take a moment here to precisely define "spirituality" as I use it in this book, and as it exists as a crucial dimension of spirituality in science:

Spirituality is an inner sense of relationship to a higher power that is loving and guiding. The word we give to this higher power might be God, nature, spirit, the universe, the creator, or other words that represent a divine presence. But the important point is that spirituality encompasses our relationship and dialogue with this higher presence.

Spiritual development, as I define it as a scientist and use the term in this book, is the growth and progression of our inborn spirituality as one of our many perceptual and intellectual faculties, from taste and touch to critical thinking skills. Spiritual development is the changing expression of this natural asset over time as new words, explanatory models, and ideas—whether theological, scientific, or family views—allow us to feel (or not feel) part of something larger, and experience an interactive two-way relationship with a guiding, and ultimately loving, universe.

The precise embodiment of that transcendent universe—the other side of the two-way spiritual conversation—comes in many different forms and has many different names. It can take the form of spirit, the natural world, God, or a sense of oneness with the world, the larger community of which we are a part. This two-way spiritual dialogue may or may not include religion. The connection can occur in meditation or yoga or in something as simple as your child's relationship with family pets, backyard wildlife, or a beloved tree. Natural spirituality is a direct sense of listening to the heartbeat of the living universe, of being one with that seen and unseen world, open and at ease in that connection. A child's spirituality precedes and transcends language, culture, and religion. It comes as naturally to children as their fascination with a butterfly or a twinkling star-filled night sky. However, as parents we play a powerful role in our child's spiritual development, just as we play a powerful role in every other aspect of our child's development.

Science now tells us that this spiritual faculty is inborn, fundamental to the human constitution, central in our physiology and psychology. Spirituality links brain, mind, and body. As we'll see shortly, epidemiological studies on twins show that the capacity for a felt relationship with a transcendent loving presence is part of our inborn nature and heredity: a biologically based, identifiable, measurable, and observable aspect of our development, much like speech or cognitive, physical, social, and emotional development. However, in contrast to these other lines of development, children are born fully fluent in this primal, nonverbal dimension of knowing. They need time to develop the wraparound of cognitive, linguistic, and abstract thinking, but young children don't have to learn the "how" or the "what" of spiritual engagement. Bird and flower, puddle and breeze, snowflake or garden slug: all of nature speaks to them and they respond. A smile, a loving touch, the indescribable bond between child and parent that science has yet to fully explain, all of these speak deeply to them, too. Spirituality is the language of these moments, the transcendent experience of nourishing connection. Spirituality is our child's birthright. We support their development when we read with them, talk with them, sing and play with them, feed and bathe and encourage them. Science now shows that the way in which a parent supports a child's spiritual development has a great deal to do with how a child grows into that rich spiritual potential.

One great thing about our group of soccer parents is that we are diverse, hailing from many countries, many cultures: India, the United Kingdom, Mexico, Argentina, South Korea, China, and across the United States. We are also spiritually diverse: Christian, Hindu, Jewish, Muslim, Buddhist, and spiritual-but-not-religious. When ideas of spirituality or religion arise in our discussions, we have a nice range represented. We hear about one another's much anticipated family observances—such as Christmas, Ramadan, Passover, and Diwali—that bring the generations and extended family together around the dinner table or a special prayer service. Some of us have multiple religious traditions in our families and honor them all; others celebrate in secular ways.

In the midst of this diversity, we are struck by the remarkable commonalities in how our children experience both the wonderful and difficult parts of life. Regardless of religious or spiritual orientations, parents instantly recognize what I would call inherently spiritual qualities in their children—their open, curious, loving ways; their immediate instinct to respond from the heart. These often show up in the way the children interact with babies or older family members, with pets or creatures they find in nature, in their creative sparkle with friends, or perhaps in the way they come up with kind or generous things they can do to help or surprise someone:

> "When I'm exhausted from a hard day, my son will come up and smile and give me what he calls 'an energizer hug.'"

> "My child can tell when our dog is scared, and he'll go sit with her and comfort her—it's so tender to see."

> "My father can be so gruff and irritating—it drives me crazy. But when he's with my kids they don't seem to mind. They've even told me, 'That's just the way Grandpa is; it's okay.'"

The science of the past fifteen years explores these universal spiritual qualities and shows that in children and adolescents, natural spirituality emerges along with other developmental phases according to the same biological timeline. What we hear at the soccer field—and find in the families represented there—is a microcosm of what researchers are finding through studies of spirituality in children and families around the world: spirituality is inborn and emerges in sync with the biological clock of childhood and adolescent growth and development. Just as with other aspects of your child's physical, cognitive, social, and emotional development, the spiritual faculty thrives in the light of your attention and support.

Hardwired for Spirituality: Use It or Lose It

Spirituality is a vast untapped resource in our understanding of human development, illness, health, and healing. Specifically, research in medicine and psychology has found that people with a developed spirituality get sick less, are happier, and feel more connected and less isolated. In the context of illness, people with a developed spirituality show positive effects for resilience and healing. We'll delve fully into those findings in the chapters ahead, but in short, empirical evidence shows that natural spirituality exists within us, independent of religion or culture; it is as foundational to our makeup as emotion, temperament, and physical senses; and the benefits of natural spirituality are significant and measurable. Further, research shows that natural spirituality, if supported in childhood, prepares the adolescent for critical developmental tasks of that age. If supported in adolescence, natural spirituality deepens and can become a significant resource for health and healing through adult life.

How do we know? As scientists, we look for proof in corroborating evidence from many sources. For instance, we have identified a genetic contribution by using a rigorous study designed to pinpoint it. In neuroimaging scans, we have found synchronization of the regions of the brain when in spiritual or contemplative practice. In developmental terms, we look for parallels between spirituality and other developmental pathways (biological, psychological, emotional) that have long been understood.

Using a classic twin-study design to separate out nature from nurture and drawing from nearly two thousand twins in the Virginia Twin Registry, genetic-epidemiologist Kenneth Kendler has shown that there is a meaningful genetic contribution to spirituality. This is a finding replicated multiple times on different samples of twins. Neuroscientists including Andrew Newberg and Mario Beauregard have published numerous scientific peer-reviewed articles on the neural correlates of meaningful spiritual experience, personal prayer, awareness of a higher power, mystical experience, and confrontation with symbols of good and evil as identified through functional MRI (fMRI)—neuroimaging that measures brain activity by blood flow to a region. By tracking blood flow, these scientists have charted a neuroimaging road map of the brain that reveals the neurological design through which humans experience spirituality.

In developmental terms, the timing of change in developmental spirituality coincides, exactly, with that of other forms of development and appears interrelated; it emerges alongside secondary sex characteristics, abstract cognitive development such as meta-cognition and meaning making, and onset of fertility. This has been the focus of groundbreaking research in my lab, studies in which we have tracked the development of natural spirituality and its protective effects from childhood through adolescence into emerging adulthood.

The confluence of evidence is clear. So to recap: biologically, we are hardwired for a spiritual connection. Spiritual development is a biological and psychological imperative from birth. Natural spirituality, the innate spiritual attunement of young children—unlike other lines of development—appears to begin whole and fully expressed. As the child grows, natural spirituality integrates with the capacities of cognitive, social, emotional, and moral development, as well as physical change, to create a more complex set of equipment through which to experience transcendence and spirituality. Ultimately, if maintained and integrated with these other aspects of development, spirituality supports the child through the challenging developmental passage of adolescence.

What does this look like in real life?

Let's step back to the soccer field for a quick comparison. Your child is born with a faculty for physical movement that shows development in the progression of fine and gross motor skills. We see it clearly as our baby advances from pumping her legs and yanking her socks off, to picking up a single raspberry and squashing it between her thumb and forefinger. The next thing we know she's crawling, then toddling, then running and jumping, then suited up for soccer practice (or gymnastics, ballet, or tae kwon do). All along, her musculature, strength, and stamina are growing; she's learning how to move adeptly on the field, learning the skills and the language she needs to play with her teammates, to understand the coach, to respond to the coach's guidance and her team-mates' calls on the field. She develops the confidence to ask questions that occur to her as her own experience deepens the way she thinks and engages on the field and at practice. She hones her skills, including her intuitive skills for discerning the many intangible, unspoken aspects of soccer and her life as a soccer player. Eventually, she is not only cogni-zant of the best form in her field skills but sees an even larger picture of interconnectedness. *Should I stay up late tonight, watching TV with my friends? Not if I want to get enough sleep so I can play my best in tomorrow's game and not let the team down.* This fully integrated "knowing" informs her technically and athletically, but also socially and emotionally, down to how she feels about playing and her contribution to the team, and how she sees this part of herself in the context of her larger life. All of this is shaped by her ongoing inner dialogue and her interactions with all of us: coach, teammates, family, peers, and community.

Our child's spiritual faculty likewise flourishes with support and encouragement to grow strong and to integrate with the rest of her devel-opmental growth. This process of integration is also shaped by her internal dialogue and through interactions with parents, family, peers, and com-munity. The practice field is everywhere, and it happens every time she has conversations with us about life's big and little questions, such as about meaning and purpose, being good people, how to treat others, what it means to be empathetic and compassionate, and why we need to take care of the earth and our environment.

As parents, we can take those ideas into the playing field of daily life and show our children how we live and express spiritual values in every-day interactions with other people, with animals, with nature, with our own inner life, and with the life of the mind and big ideas. We can take our children to explore sacred places and spaces: a house of worship, a sanctuary tucked away in a hospital, a mountain, or a river. We can encourage (and model) acts of expansive love and kindness. This exploration cultivates spiritual knowing and attunement, a sense of the spiritual dimension that is always present and is deeper than superficial attributes and higher than competitive and materialistic priorities. Supported by this exploration, the continuing conversation with us, and by her own internal spiritual dialogue, she continues to define what spirituality is and what the journey is for her.

Without support and encouragement to keep developing that part of themselves, children's spiritual development weakens under pressure from a culture that constantly has them feeling judged and pressured to perform, and that trains them to evaluate others the same way. Our culture has not necessarily been welcoming to spirituality and its questions. Our predominantly materialistic, 24/7 media-infused world is not set up for the introspective thought involved in spiritual reflection. We're pressured to fill downtime with productive activity, and we often feel compelled to fill in any quiet moment with diversions. This is how we live and this is what we're modeling for our children.

Anxiety, Ambivalence, Antipathy: A Generation of Wary Parents

One morning on a school visit, I stepped into the hallway to check for last-minute arrivals before starting my presentation. I had been invited to speak to parents on the subject of the science of spirituality. One mother stood in the hallway at a bit of a distance and I asked if she was looking for this room. She smiled and introduced herself, but she was clearly hesitant to step through the door. She said she had just dropped her children off for school when she had remembered she had seen a flyer for the talk.

"You know, I wasn't planning on coming," she said with a hint of apology. "It's nice to meet you and I don't mean to be rude, but I am just *not* religious. I'm *very* spiritual, but *not* religious."

I hear the same hesitation and explanation from many parents, emblematic of a broad shift in religious and spiritual life in the United States. National surveys have reported the number of Americans who do not identify with any religion has grown in recent years such that about one-fifth of the public overall—and a third of adults under age thirty—were unaffiliated with a religion as of 2012, the lowest in the nearly three generations since researchers started tracking the numbers. At the same time, surveys also report a notable growth in the population of adults who classify themselves as "spiritual but not religious" or who describe their religion as "nothing in particular" but do believe in God or a universal spirit. A Fetzer Institute survey in 2010 found that 60 percent of adults said they are now more spiritual than they were five years before.

A recent Gallup poll shows that more than 90 percent of Americans pray and believe in an ultimate creator. A poll in *Parents* magazine in 2007 conducted by Beliefnet showed that a consistent 90 percent of parents "talk to children about God or higher power," two-thirds say grace at meal times, 60 percent pray during the day, and half pray at bedtime with their child. A poll by Barna Research Group in Ventura, California, showed 85 percent of parents consider it their job to teach their own children about spirituality.

Yet, beyond this clarity on spiritual life, the same *Parents* magazine poll found parents face challenges to spiritual parenting, attributed by 33 percent to "society's general lack of support," by 25 percent to "conflict between practice and everyday life," and by 24 percent to having "busy schedules." When it comes to the fluidity of match between two parents on spiritual development in their children, 50 percent feel "in sync," another 25 percent say they are "in sync but it's a struggle," and a quarter of parents feel at cross purposes, so they punt, argue, or quit the topic. The Barna poll also reported that through the week prior to the poll, the majority of parents did not open or direct a discussion of spirituality with their child (under the age of thirteen years).

I read these polls to suggest that there is often a strong spiritual life in parents themselves, and a loving intention to raise spiritual children. Yet, there is not a clear and certain understanding in our culture about the place of spirituality in child and adolescent development.

In my nearly two decades of conversations with parents about spiritual development—their children's or their own—I have found that whether parents identify as religious, spiritual but not religious, undecided, or really anywhere on the spiritual continuum, they are unaware of research on their child's inborn spirituality. Many are at a loss about how to help their children develop spiritually. Ambivalence runs deep. Challenges commonly arise for several sometimes overlapping reasons: when parents aren't certain about their own feelings regarding spirituality, when one or the other had negative experiences associated with religion when they were young and don't want to subject their children to something similar, or when complications about religious affiliation create tension in the couple or the extended family.

"It depends on how you define spirituality, and what exactly it means," says Marcie, mother of Aiden, three years old. "It seems like 'everything goes'—spirituality is anything that is different from the physical, more concrete realm." Marcie's spiritual ponderings have included whether her son "is just a happenstance based on the particular sperm and the particular egg that met and all the cells they created, or is there a sort of life, a soul, a spirit that would have come into his body regardless? I haven't resolved that, but it's that kind of existential question that I have thought about."

Parenthood doesn't settle existential questions for most parents—it only deepens them. The mother of a five-year-old daughter shared with me, "I'm not quite sure how I understand spirituality in my own life but I do wish that there was a God and that there was a heaven because I hate the idea that my daughter would ever suffer or hurt. So parenthood hasn't given me faith where I had none, but it has made me more aware and philosophical about some of the existential questions and realities."

Other parents describe a range of experiences and feelings: their faith, doubts, wonderings, and wishes for their children, whom they may or may not want to sway toward a particular spiritual path. Struggles also arise around differences with a partner or others involved in a child's upbringing. A 2009 report by Pew Research Center's Forum on Religion & Public Life reported that more than one in four (27 percent) American adults who are married or living with a partner are in religiously mixed relationships. If people from different Protestant denominational families are included—for example, a marriage between a Methodist and a Lutheran—nearly four in ten (37 percent) couples are religiously mixed. This survey found that people who are unaffiliated with a particular religion are the most likely (65 percent) to have a spouse or partner with a different religious background. Parents often are coming from families in which religious faith traditions were different or absent. According to a 2010 YouGov survey, commissioned by author Naomi Schaefer Riley, 45 percent of marriages between 2000 and 2010 were between members of differing faiths and denominations. This is more than double since the 1960s, when only 20 percent of marriages were interfaith.

So the ambivalence and the tension are greater than ever, and parents are struggling. The questions I hear show deep caring for their children's spiritual development but also their own conflict or confusion about how to handle it honestly, responsibly, and lovingly.

"It feels wrong to choose one for her or to give one top billing. How do we figure out which of our religions to choose for Sunday school and which beliefs we instill in her?"

"He went to church with his friend and now that's what he wants to do—he wants to keep going! But we have a very different belief system."

"I didn't have a good experience with organized religion when

I was a kid and I don't want that for my child. But I don't want
my child to have nothing."

"I don't believe in God but my son asks about it."

Even parents who feel spiritual with certainty aren't sure how best
to pass that along to their children. "I want them to have not only good
morals, but I want them to know that there's a higher power that they
have to answer to, not just me," said the mother of three children, ages
seven, ten, and fourteen. "I want them to know that somebody else
knows even if I don't."

The mother of two children, ages one year and four years, struggled
to reconcile her religious ideal of unconditional love with the everyday
challenge of tending to a young child.

"Christ just loves us unconditionally and forgives us for our sins
and so, certainly, if he can do that, can't I help my son to see
the same aspects of life? And if I can do that—love
unconditionally—then holding a grudge because he spilled
milk on the tabletop just seems unimportant. Being a parent
does make your spirituality a little more in your face, as far as,
do you really walk the walk and talk the talk—or are those just
words? So, you know, it's a struggle."

Even if fathers or mothers aren't clear on their own stance, they know
that becoming a parent has affected their relationship to spirituality; it
has made them think, yearn, love more deeply. "I'm not as spiritual as I
would like to be, but it definitely feels like it's there," an expectant mother
told me. "And I guess I can't verbalize it that well because I'm not *that*
spiritual—maybe if I were I would be able to explain it better. But it
definitely feels bigger than myself, and that's all I can really say."

The practicalities of acting on good intentions regarding spirituality
or religion can feel impossibly complicated, especially when Mom and

Dad hold different religious views. "It was really important for me and my family to have her baptized," says Daphne, mother of Julia. "My husband is atheist. He does not believe in God or religious structures so there was a little tension there. I think that motherhood has made me a little more spiritual, maybe less religious, but more spiritual," she says, adding that since she became a parent it seems more likely now to her that a divine presence exists "out there."

The difference between her and her husband's views of religion also makes Daphne particularly sensitive to the need to respect each person's own spiritual path—especially her child's. "How do you do that? How do you guide a child and how do you not completely overwhelm them with your own beliefs about the world?"

Parents aren't alone with their questions or in not knowing what to do. We all want our children to be free, to follow their hearts in all areas. Parenting is hard and spirituality is a tough topic to tackle with fewer resources if you don't have a handle on it yourself. This is the question so many parents feel with such great urgency: *What should I do and how should I do it?* As Aiden's mom, above, said, after sharing her own status as spiritually "undecided," whatever she may have felt about it before she had children, motherhood has only intensified that. "Before, I had questions that I thought about here and there," she said, "but now they have become more real."

Spirituality Is Bedrock for Thriving

Let's return for a moment to that image you have of your baby grown up to be all that he or she can be, a shining star on a passionate path. The biotech entrepreneur, doctor, lawyer, CEO, or activist, the sports or film star, the leader. In this envisioned life of success your child probably does not struggle with anxiety or substance abuse. When you envision your grown child, there is not a dark and painful private depression. No tragic losses or insurmountable setbacks. We parents want deep inner peace and happiness so strongly for our children that we assume it when we envi-

sion our hopes and aspirations for their future. We assume a life of accomplishment that has a joyful and purposeful core. We assume that some
grounding sense of themselves provides a strong anchor in a world that
is for them primarily happy and fulfilling, with inevitable bumps, but
overall full of love and connection to other people.

Looking more deeply into the image of your child's future, what is
that joyful and satisfying core made up of? Deep love and support from
family. Good morals. Curiosity. Being healthy and comfortable in the
world, and excited to learn. Now, nearly twenty years of scientific research
shows that there is something more: a close, sustained awareness of a
two-way relationship with a loving and guiding higher power that opens
into a sense of a vivid spiritual world. Whether you call that higher
power spirit, or the universe, or nature, or something else, it is through
this relationship that children and young adults seek clarity or guidance
during life's challenging passages or openings of opportunity. In the
course of child development, this dynamic two-way relationship constitutes the bedrock of spiritual life.

Whatever future we envision for our child, without spiritual development a full dimension goes missing from the picture. This is true
not only at what we might consider the most abstract level of belief
but also at a biological, even the cellular, level. And this is where
science has grown increasingly exciting in recent years, shedding light
on aspects of spiritual connection that have been beyond our ken since
time began.

Today we have evidence-based research and imaging technology that
show the effects of spiritual engagement on the brain, mind, and body.
In scans and data we can now see the difference in brain structure and
function in people for whom spirituality is the lead foot in life versus those
for whom spirituality is not a strong presence. For example, in the spiritually attuned person we see flourishing, healthy, thick portions of the
brain right where, in the case of depression, for instance, we would have
expected to see the thinner brain. Also, in the face of stressful events, a
strong personal spirituality regulates our levels of cortisol, a stress

hormone, which if disregulated or at sustained high levels wears on brain and body and slows growth in children.

This interconnectivity is precisely what we see in studies that show that spirituality has a clear impact on our mental health and thriving. From the perspective of mental health and wellness, spirituality is associated with significantly lower rates of depression, substance use and abuse, and risk taking. This includes sexual risk taking in young adults and exposure to STDs, along with thrill seeking, driving fast, and physical endangerment, especially in boys. No other preventive factor known to science and medicine has such a broad-reaching and powerful influence on the daily decisions that make or break health and wellness.

Other studies comparing the brain-wave patterns of monks in meditation with those of self-described spiritual people found that the energy given off by the brains of spiritually engaged people when simply resting with closed eyes is the same wavelength as that of a monk during meditation. It appears that their set point, or inner resting state of the brain, becomes a bright and peaceful state of transcendence.

Related research from the field of positive psychology shows that spiritual development is associated with positive emotions and qualities of thriving that include a sense of belonging, optimism, elevation, and a connection to "something larger" that gives purpose and meaning to life. There is nothing known to science as profoundly associated with thriving and success in our children.

Science Charts the Course Across Two Decades

Science from many labs and researchers demonstrates that spirituality is innate, that it is a faculty that grows with attention and can be stunted by neglect, and that there is no substitute for it. Reading about riding a bicycle is no substitute for riding one. No level of skill on the soccer field will help your child pass a math test. There is no substitute for spiritual development, but there are many different ways to support and encourage it. And without it a child's robust developmental potential is diminished.

Emerging research has also mapped the developmental arc for personal spirituality, and it clearly shows differences between the first and second decades of life, as well as points along the way that have special relevance to the child or adolescent. We'll explore these stages fully in the chapters ahead, but in brief, we see that the formative first decade of life is a period of natural spiritual awareness when a spiritual road map begins to develop—neurologically, psychologically, and embodied in everyday life.

Adolescence represents a crescendo, a developmental "surge" period for spiritual development, just as puberty creates a surge in every other aspect of your teen's physical, cognitive, social, and emotional development. This primed inner environment creates a crucible for spiritual growth and understanding, and the experience of oneself as a spiritual being. As adolescence brings your teen a newfound motivation to become his own person, he may revisit spiritual paths from childhood now open to new, more meaningful explorations. For instance, a childhood experience of closeness to nature or animals may draw the adolescent into a more deliberate engagement with nature as a way to connect with his inner life of spiritual dialogue, and, perhaps, to explore nature as a calling for his life's work.

In broad strokes, we see a journey from innate and foundational spiritual knowing (the first decade) through a journey of engagement outward into the world of others in family, community, and culture (the second decade). With this journey comes the challenge to integrate new levels of experience, information, and understanding with the innate sense of connection to "something larger." All of this happens simultaneously as language, cognition, emotional range, physical capabilities, and auditory and sensory development continually change a child's capacity to interact with that external world, engage with it, and be shaped by it. Spirituality is in fact a strong organizing principle for all other aspects of your child's development.

We all lean in to support our children as they grow into their capacities for reading, writing, math, sports, and critical thinking—the skills that ground them in the world of everyday ideas and activities. But do we do the same thing for their spirituality? Too often we step back or actively discourage them from cultivating their spiritual selves, in essence train them away from the inquiry. Among the most common ways we turn off our children's spiritual development are what I call the "seven avoidances." We turn our kids off when we:

1. Ignore their spiritual awakening, questions, and experiences. Your voice makes an experience real for your child; if a child doesn't hear a parent discussing a topic, then the child assumes that topic is not important.

2. Disavow their spiritual reality. A definitive, negative statement by you about your child's spiritual experience can shut down your child's exploration because it signals to your child that her spiritual experiences aren't part of the parent-child connection.

3. Discourage spiritual discovery. A negative response to your child's spiritual exploration is a lost opportunity, a moment when you could have, but didn't, support your child's tender, vulnerable, and emerging spirituality. You don't have to agree with your child—you simply need to be interested, curious, and open to his exploration.

4. Quash questions. A child's questioning propels growth. Responding with an "I don't know," or "I don't know and nobody else does, either," often ends the discussion. Your child hears that spirituality isn't worthy of pursuit, nor is it central to daily life.

5. Base affection or discipline on performance-based values that don't align with spiritual values of unconditional, noncontingent love, acceptance, and loving guidance.

6. Overlook the need for a spiritually supportive community in which children can discover their own identity and be accepted and appreciated for their spiritual selves.

7. Ignore signs that a community has punitive or other outdated values of conformity that twist spiritual values to serve dogma.

Shutting down spiritual development creates a developmental gap, much as we might see in a child who is three grade levels above his age peers in math and science but woefully behind the curve in basic social and emotional skills. Typically when we see a child struggling in the developmental gap we try to help: get him a tutor for reading or math, or work on social-emotional skills and how to see the cues in a classmate's expression, body language, or tone of voice. We may help him learn to read his own cues so he can become better at managing his responses to people or situations that stress him out. There is no such broad understanding and enthusiastic support established in school or society to encourage spiritual development in childhood and adolescence. We tend to see a child's struggles or missteps as flaws or errors to be fixed, whereas if we looked at them as challenges of a spiritual nature, our responses would be completely different and perhaps much more effective. Let me share two examples:

Drugs and Alcohol: Shortcuts to Transcendence Are Dead Ends

When a child reaches adolescence there is important work of individuation to be done, deciding what is "me or not me" in a way that provides a deep sense of self that is whole, is meaningful, and gives the teen direction. Erik Erikson, the grandfather within psychology of the notion of adolescent individuation, emphasized that a teen seeks to find an internal sense of consistency that drives purpose.

Individuation is crucial to the setup of our adult ways, particularly concerning our internal habits of thought and feelings. The habits we start in adolescence often persist into adulthood—this goes for habits of exercise, drug and alcohol use, and spirituality. In this brief window of development our inner blueprint, our core spiritual map of and approach to the world, takes shape.

Most questions of me-or-not-me return to a core sense of meaning and purpose, the nature of our deepest self, how we approach our work and relationships, and even our understanding of ultimate reality. These are profound and important questions, upon which the teen begins to build his personal spirituality: ideas of right and wrong, his place in the world, the meaning and purpose of his life. Because this work is so important, and so central to the individual, spiritual individuation is at the core of all other forms of individuation.

Spiritual individuation has a paradox. It is grueling, yet eminently satisfying, uplifting, and mind-opening. Because the road is sometimes so hard, and can be very dark, the teen often gravitates toward spirituality "shortcuts." Drug and alcohol use can bring fleeting exposure to a counterfeit of the same kind of experiences that teens are working for in their biologically primed spiritual individuation: clarity, a sense of calm, a feeling of bonding with fellow teens, and love for the bigger world.

These shortcuts can cause big problems if they become the path of habit. The hunger for spiritual knowing, connection to others and to the bigger universe, the quest for transcendence—all of these can be found momentarily from the quick (and illusory) fix of drug or alcohol use.

Having been caught drinking, a teen might argue, "It was harmless; it felt as if we were all just one big happy group." Or, "I could release all of my pressures and worries about college, I could just be."

Without the lens of spiritual development, a parent's logical comeback might be, "Can't you find other ways of doing this—like playing sports?" Or, "What are you thinking? You could lose your shot at college if you're arrested!"

But listening with the ear trained to spiritual development, we can hear something different. Go back to the teen's words, and this time listen for the spiritual need that is falsely served by alcohol use. Feeling like "one big happy group" sounds like the desire to connect and escape isolation. Releasing "pressures and worries" to "just be" sounds like the state of peace that comes with mindfulness, meditation, or experience of sacred presence.

In a study of spiritual individuation published in the *Journal of the American Academy of Child and Adolescent Psychiatry*, we found that a developed personal relationship with God (expressed in comments such as, "I turn to God for guidance in times of difficulty," or "When I have a decision to make, I ask God what I should do") was highly protective against slipping from experimenting with to addiction to alcohol and drugs.

Our published findings showed that an adolescent with a strong personal relationship with the higher power, compared to an adolescent without this inner source of spirituality, is 70 to 80 percent less likely to engage in heavy substance use or substance abuse. There was no protectiveness at all related to the intensity of adherence to the family religious tradition. In fact, religion helped only when the adolescent had independently, working within their own faith, developed a personal transcendent relationship.

We know that many adults get into rehabilitation programs only after years of substance abuse. Substance abuse beginning in adolescence can be the onset of decades of suffering; adolescence is the window of risk for a lifetime course of disorder with alcohol and drug abuse, often set in motion by unmet spiritual needs.

The escape and connection described by teens needs to be understood as a spiritual quest, inherently good and important. We as parents need to help the adolescent see that spiritual hunger is not met by alcohol or drugs. The illusory jolt from drugs does not last; it only jump-starts the physiology. There is nothing sustaining in it. Authentic spirituality requires reflection and the development of a road back to transcendence through the cultivation of our inner life, through prayer, meditation, or perhaps good works, intertwined with our general capacities of cognition, morality, and emotion.

We can say, "I appreciate the warm feeling of being connected. I know how good it feels to sense that you are part of everything. These sound like spiritual feelings. But now that the warm glow of alcohol has passed, can you get back there without the drink? If not, then it is not real, it is an empty jolt of the brain. Let's talk about other ways to get to that sense of moving beyond daily struggle and finding connection."

Girls: Impressive Development for Emotional Depth and Discernment, Not Drama

Adolescents, particularly girls, are often described as being "helplessly emotional" or "histrionic." One exasperated mother described her adolescent daughter as "totally emotionally wrought, way over the top, gushing with emotion. And when she gets her period, she is like a ball of oversensitivity and tears."

However, research on spiritual development shows that with the burgeoning of fertility in girls, specifically getting their period, comes the start-up of an augmented spiritual capacity. Many ancient traditions have built into female puberty ceremonies the interwoven expressions of fertility and expanded female spirituality. Now science has recognized a unified path of sexual development and spiritual development in girls.

In the *Journal of the American Academy of Child and Adolescent Psychiatry,* I published with my colleague Merav Gur the results of an investigation of the benefit of personal spirituality in warding off depression in girls, before and after the onset of menstruation. We drew from a large sample of 3,356 adolescent girls in the Adolescent Health Survey, generously provided by the University of North Carolina.

Along with other forms of physical maturation, such as body curves and mature breasts, we found that the onset of menstruation was associated with an increased sense of a personal relationship with God, and the two together showed an increasingly significant degree of protection against depression. As compared to when she was prepubertal, once a girl has begun menstruating, a personal relationship with a higher power was even 50 percent more helpful in protecting against depression. Meanwhile, no such increase in protective benefits was associated with any specific family tradition or religion over another. This coinciding surge of spirituality and fertility comes from within the girl and is associated with physical and emotional puberty. Research shows this increased reaching for spiritual connection goes hand in hand with an augmented openness to experience, sensitivity, and perceptiveness. This means that with the arrival of menstruation, the full range of emotions appear bright and strong, and tears are part of this arrival.

Instead of saying "I think this is an overreaction," or "this is not the end of the world," or even "control yourself," consider this emotionality part of an extraordinary increase in perceptual faculties, including the spiritual perceptual capacity. A response that honors this would be:

> "You have the gift of a great heart, and the sensitivity to pick up on what is going on."

> "It can hurt at times, but ultimately, you are fortunate—when girls become teens, they become more spiritual, which means that you can feel all things more."

> "Because you can feel so intensely, you are able to know the full register of living, and to pick up on the deeper meaning in it all."

Whatever the source of a misstep or confusion, you are never mistaken to support a child's spiritual self. There is nothing to lose and everything to gain. I speak with children of all ages in my school talks—from preschool to high school and college. To varying degrees of complexity, I share with them the new science that helps us "see" spiritual engagement. I explain to them the multiple levels of analysis in which our human engagement with spirituality is observable scientifically, including through MRI and EEG scans that show brain function and brain development. They understand. Typically what ensues is lively conversation and questions that range from goldfish to God to gluons. If, as French Jesuit priest and philosopher Pierre Teilhard de Chardin wrote, "the difficulty lies not in solving problems but expressing them," then children are our born leaders in the spiritual realm. Children converge immediately on the big questions. They are not hesitant to challenge entrenched assumptions. They are endlessly eager to explore, experience, and express.

In an impromptu discussion session following my talk at a high school in the West, Morgan, a senior, described a moment in a hiking trip she had taken with classmates and a school counselor the year before. The semester had been a particularly tough one, academically and emotionally. The group made a physically grueling hike up a glacial mountain. As she hiked down, her feet aching and blisters burning, at one point the trail turned toward a lake cradled in the ice floe. Morgan described what was for her clearly a transformative moment:

> I saw the light on the water of the glacier and the brightness and the beauty—it was like I could *feel* the beauty and I was part of it—and it's really hard to describe, but it was like a real feeling. It felt sacred. And ever since then, when I'm stressed out or feeling really down, in my mind I go back to the mountain. I can take myself back to the mountain and that feeling is always there for me.

That is the language of transcendence, of an experience of spiritual awakening, a direct awareness at the deepest level of our inner wisdom. That moment was transformative, and she has carried it with her since. Her experience is now foundational—not just a place she saw or a feeling or a beautiful memory, but a transcendent experience to which she returns and which informs her view of a vital world. This is the kind of experience and knowledge we want to help our children seek and find.

"Let's Go In!": Children Summon Us for a Sacred Journey

Our children's innate spiritual faculty is ever-present, accessible, and inviting us into the conversation of the most ordinary of everyday trials and triumphs. They will ask, "May I be in the choir?" or "May I sing with the rabbi?" They may ask to light a candle in the cathedral, to make Shabbat challah, or to visit a sacred site. The young child may ask if Grandma's spirit will come back in a different person or if she is here now. "Is Grandma watching me, taking care of me even though she has died?" They will ask if God punishes people who are bad or forgives all bad people, even Adolf Hitler. The older child or adolescent may question, "Before the big bang, what was there?" Or, "How can we justify war—ever?" The questions evolve with age, and as with every other developmental passage with our children, we adapt our responses to meet them where they are. Whatever they may ask, they are not looking to us for specific answers; they are looking to be met for the journey of inquiry and discovery. No matter how well or poorly prepared we may feel, we have exactly what we need to meet our child on their journey.

Over coffee one morning, Fran, a colleague, told me that she and her husband, Nick, made a conscious choice when their daughter Maya was born not to affiliate with a particular religion. Fran's parents had come from very religious backgrounds and were critical of what they experienced as limiting, dogmatic thinking. They had raised Fran and her sisters with great love and a zest for life and learning that emphasized a critical mind and included a cautious view of "organized religion." Her father in particular had been explicit about his disdain for religion, citing the brutality that some religious people had inflicted on others through their institutions historically and currently and the religious teachings that many use to justify prejudice and wrongful acts.

"They saw the hypocrisy in it, but they didn't necessarily give us a spiritual replacement," Fran said.

My father said, "When you come of age you can choose, make your own decisions," but he'd already made some decisions for us by saying "this isn't for me . . . I'm not interested in it . . . I think it's stupid. I think it's a crutch." I didn't realize for a long time that when my child asks a question and I say, "I don't know," and just leave it at that, I'm actually stopping the conversation. That's what my father did, and not by bad intention. They taught us morals, certainly. They taught us ethics. They loved us. But there was not a sense of what you can call God, or a larger "presence," or even being part of a larger spiritual community. That sense of "something larger" was the baby that was thrown out with the religious bathwater.

Nick came from a similar background and, like Fran, didn't want to expose their daughter to religious influences. Fran thought at times about what a "spiritual replacement" might be for Maya, but she simply had no answer. So there had never been any religious training or context at home for Maya. The family celebrated holidays—many kinds of holidays—in a nonreligious way, so Maya looked forward to family gatherings at Christmas, Hanukkah, Easter, and Passover with a special sense of significance and excitement.

"We just didn't talk about God in our household," Fran said of Maya's first four years.

By age five, Maya was a sparkling child: loving, adventuresome, curious, and delighted by life. One morning they passed by the towering church a few blocks from their house and across the street from the coffee shop that Fran often stopped in during their busy days of errands and activities. They had passed the church many times before and never entered. This morning was different.

"Mama, let's go in! Let's go in!" Maya said excitedly.

Fran and I had talked about the crucial need for parents to support children's developing natural spirituality, and since then she had been mulling this over. She had found the science fascinating and the evidence convincing. But what had struck her most of all was this new awareness of spiritual development as a foundational aspect of child development—Maya's development—and all she had to do to support her daughter was to pay attention, welcome Maya's spontaneous expressions of wonder or curiosity, respect her observations and questions, and share in exploring the ideas. There was no need to have "right" answers or detailed how-to instructions. All she had to do was join her child in the moment, let her child be her guide, welcome conversation, and leave the conversation open, rather than avoid it or shut it down.

"So when she said 'Let's go in! Let's go in!' what I really wanted to do was go get the grocery shopping done so I could get home and make lunch and do all the things we needed to do," Fran told me. "But instead, I sort of gritted my teeth and took a deep breath and said 'Okay, sweetheart,' because if she wanted to go in then I should encourage it."

Once inside, Maya led the way with her observations and questions and Fran discovered a new experience in viewing the moment purely through her daughter's eyes. She was able to welcome Maya's questions without feeling pressured to provide definitive answers. She was free to wonder aloud and ask Maya what she thought. It was, Fran said later, an exquisite experience.

Parents often hear spiritual questions as requests for answers or knowledge that they aren't prepared to provide. But that's a misunderstanding, or perhaps a reflection of our own natural anxiety to do everything right. We worry that we don't know the right answer or that we're dealing with something so big that we don't want to ruin it or say the wrong thing. Or it may be that spirituality has not been something important in our own lives, or it isn't a space in which we've spent recent time exploring, developing, and wondering. So it may be tempting to repeat what you heard as a child: *Oh, we don't do that.* But the precious opportunity before you is that your child is giving you an opening and saying, *Hey, come with me.* You don't need to know where you're going or how you're going to get there—you are simply being asked to go with her. Our children look to us, but not really for the answers. We're being asked to show up. We need to show up, but we don't need to have all the answers.

Like every other aspect of human potential, spiritual development and growth is part of our birthright. As the Buddhist monk Pema Chödrön wrote, "It's as if everyone who has ever been born has the same birthright, which is enormous potential of warm heart and clear mind." This is true not only for children but for parents, too. The moment we are "born" into parenthood, our child's spiritual development—that cultivation of a warm heart, a clear mind, and the capacity for transcendence— becomes part of our shared journey and our birthright as parents.

Following your child's spiritual journey may transform your entire family.

You have the opportunity to hop aboard this journey with your child, and through your child's journey, to travel on your own journey, as well. Say yes and see where you go.

2

THE SCIENCE OF
THE SPIRITUAL BRAIN

For most of the twentieth century, the conversation about spiritual life was a conversation about the scientifically untested: about faith or belief, about the ineffable, impenetrable, unknowable dimension of spirit or soul. If you were strongly spiritual or religious, your inner certainty might not require scientific evidence for validation. But for many others who did have questions, a lack of scientific evidence foreclosed their involvement. *If there's no evidence, why should I "believe"—and what should I believe in? Every religion has a different story and everyone believes their God is the right one. People have done terrible things in the name of religion—I know I don't believe in that!* The scientific community itself also largely ignored the subject because spirituality appeared to be outside the domain of data-driven study. All that changed about fifteen years ago, and today, thanks to determined researchers and advances in the science and research technology available to them, we can at last see, study, and talk about the spiritual brain.

On the strength of empirical research, we now know that spirituality is indeed part of our natural endowment, just like our abilities to see, smell, and think. Spirituality is experienced through a biologically based faculty and we are born ready to use it; we enter the world prepared to have a spiritual life. Science also shows that while we are born inherently spiritual, this faculty can be sustained and cultivated by parents or dulled by neglect. In the past two decades our lab and those of colleagues around the country have conducted pioneering scientific research to define the pathway of spiritual development, how it can be supported by parents, and the related benefits to children's wellness and thriving into adulthood.

We'll explore the science fully in the chapters ahead, but in short, what we've learned is this:

1. We are inherently, genetically spiritual. This is our *natural spirituality*.
2. Genetic expression of spirituality surges in adolescence along with other innate faculties—for example, maturing sexual and cognitive development—and personal spirituality is the most potent form of protection against suffering in adolescence.
3. Our natural spirituality is closely allied with human bonding, creating *relational spirituality*, or the experience of transcendence through relationships with one another, with a higher power, and within ourselves.
4. Clinical insight picks up where research has yet to expand, highlighting the significance of spiritual awakening and intuitive *heart knowing*, or perception of the sacred through deep inner wisdom, transcendent sense, and often the body.

All told, science now offers strong evidence that biologically, neurologically, and psychologically, spirituality is part of our nature and is foundational to thriving. This growing body of scientific literature represents a breakthrough for scientists, surely, but also for parents, educators, clergy, and counselors. Further, and most important to the purpose of this book, the evidence is unequivocal in showing that parents or loving relationships with spiritual direction really matter. How we parent our children for spirituality from birth through adolescence can open this developmental pathway for them—or shut it down.

When it comes to raising our children, science and spirit are part of the same conversation. Both inform how we perceive and understand our world. As parents, we eagerly share with one another our best discoveries, to support each other and all of our children. So as a parent-scientist, I share by far the best thing I have seen as a scientist that will help all of our children: the cutting-edge research showing a foundationally new view of the psyche as inherently spiritual, and how parenting can help our children lead an optimal spiritual life.

Today, the awareness that spirituality is helpful to our health is a familiar message in our popular culture and media, and science journals offer a steady stream of new findings linking spiritual practices to less drinking and smoking, recovery from some systemic immune disorders, and even helping to prevent against relapse from diseases such as cancer. These well-publicized findings often leave people wondering, *Well, how do we get spiritual in the first place?*

The fascinating answer to that question has been percolating through the annals of science for more than a decade, but has only recently begun to be more broadly understood and recognized for the breakthrough that it is. Equally important, sound, scientifically grounded knowledge about the human capacity for spirituality and its development has also been established, as well as how we can apply it in our daily lives to benefit our families and communities. This science has not made its way into mainstream culture yet, but is presented throughout the top peer-reviewed scientific journals.

Let's start at the heart of the matter with a simple definition: What is the human capacity for spirituality?

At the core of spirituality is the *transcendent relationship*, a dynamic sense of connection with a higher power or sacred presence. To feel transcendent is to know our selves beyond the limits of the physical or ordinary self, as part of the greater universe. The name or identity of the higher power may differ in the way it is understood across people and traditions, but regardless of those variations, the transcendent relationship opens us into a sense of a sacred world with direction and connection that gives us meaning and purpose. The transcendent relationship may be perceived as a personal dialogue with God, or sense of oneness with the universe (as it often is in Eastern traditions), or a sense of relationship with a universal spirit through the many living beings and natural forms around us, from majestic mountains to soaring eagles. The transcendent presence can be felt as a guide in our relationship to other people or nature. What makes us spiritual? Beyond our natural, biological wiring for it, what makes us spiritual is our awareness that our lives, our relationships, and the natural world both seen and unseen are filled with an ultimate presence. It is our awareness of transcendence, in us, around us, through us, and beyond us, that is spiritual.

Children's spiritual development from birth through adolescence, the lifelong implications of their spiritual development, and our parallel developmental journey with them, as parents, is the focus of this book. Science is the foundation. When we reach the edge of this rapidly progressing field of science, I draw on clinical insight, my own and that of colleagues. The following four major findings, well grounded in science, represent a synthesis of the research we'll be exploring, the essential stepping-stones into the new science of the spiritual brain and the transcendent child.

FINDING 1

WE ARE INHERENTLY, GENETICALLY SPIRITUAL

We are born with an innate capacity for transcendence, a natural spirituality. Spirituality is foundational to our biological nature and is different from religion. It is an inherent part of us from birth and is integrated with our biological capacities for perception and detection—our senses, our intellect, our emotions, our consciousness. Religion is an embrace of this

innate spiritual faculty. Spirituality and religion exist together
for some people, and separately for others.

We take for granted that our skin lets us feel the tactile world around
us, and that our other senses for discerning the world—sight, hearing,
taste—are part of our biological endowment. So, too, are we each born
with an innate biological faculty through which to experience transcendence. Because this capacity for transcendence is biological, it is to some
degree carried and coded in our genetic makeup. Just as our genes give
us taste buds so we can engage the world through taste, our genes give
us brains and minds primed to engage with the world on a spiritual level.

How do we know it's genetic? A common way to establish whether
or not a human tendency is genetic is to conduct a twin study. Researchers tend to swoop down on identical twins throughout their lives, with
invitations to share information about their physical and mental health,
as well as their habits, personal choices, beliefs, and tastes. Because the
amount of genetic material twins share is well defined, the extent to which
twins give similar answers to research questions can be analyzed to understand how much genes and/or environment contribute to the attribute in question.

Twin studies have even been used to understand the degrees to which
personality traits such as conscientiousness, adaptability, and reactivity
are inborn. Yet only in 1997 was there a landmark twin study that focused
on inner personal spirituality as a transcendent relationship (earlier twin-
study researchers had looked at religious observance and attitudes, without separating out a look at spirituality). Kenneth Kendler, a genetic
epidemiologist from Virginia Commonwealth University, investigated
the distinction between inner personal spirituality, religious denomination, and style of religious observance from a twin study research
perspective. Kendler and his team looked at 1,902 female twins, listed
in the Virginia Twin Registry, who were about thirty years old at the
time of the study. His research found that in terms of genetic contribution and environmental shaping, spirituality and religion may overlap

for many people, but they are not the same. Someone who finds deep spiritual connection in nature might never set foot in a church or temple.

Kendler's research showed that a transcendent relationship is not just one part of personality or temperament, but its own important, separate part of our inborn human nature. This was the first of two major findings in his work. The second had to do with the relationship between the transcendent relationship and a person's decision how or if to experience this within a religious tradition.

Kendler determined that a person's particular style of religious adherence, or the way in which they approach religion, was learned through the environment. Parents and community teach, or individuals choose, a style of religious adherence, which includes concepts such as whether or not someone endorses a literal view of the Bible or believes that God rewards and punishes. Kendler defined adherence to views of religious interpretation as "personal conservatism," to represent the level of observance of faith tradition, a notion that I call *personal religion*.

In Kendler's sample from a predominantly Judeo-Christian background, he called the part of spirituality that focused solely on the transcendent relationship "personal devotion." In the study, personal devotion was empirically defined by aspects of inner engagement with the higher power, including the frequency of seeking spiritual comfort, strong satisfaction with spiritual life, importance of religion or spirituality, consciousness of religious purpose, and frequency of private prayer. Subsequent research has shown that the experience of the transcendent relationship exists while varying across people, cultures, and traditions. For some people, it is a two-way conversation felt in the heart, for others a bodily awareness of union or oneness, or a sacred relationship with nature.

The distinction between personal devotion (as the transcendent relationship) and personal religion (which involves religious interpretation) is an important one that is sometimes overlooked. This distinction also deals with an essential part of our lives and of human development. Our human capacity for a transcendent relationship is inborn. Whether or not we decide to cultivate or strengthen this capacity, it is ours; whether we cultivate it through religious or nonreligious practice is a separate matter. Religious orientation is not inborn; it is a matter of choice or the result of socialization from our family or community. That said, personal devotion and personal religion, while separate concepts, still are related for many people. The natural capacity for a transcendent relationship is cultivated through religious faith traditions. For other people, it is cultivated through reflection, meditation, nature, beauty, or acts of service:

"Meditation is how I feel oneness with the universe."

"Service to humanity, what I actually do, is prayer in motion. It makes me part of the goodness in all of us, I feel 'the love,' and a sense of connection to something more."

"When I walk through nature, I feel part of all life. That life energy is the same in all of us."

"I talk to God all day, and I feel the guidance from beyond myself. Sometimes it comes with a wink—in God's love there is humor and joy."

The difference between the two human tendencies of personal devotion and personal religion is extremely relevant to parents raising children, as well as to our collective social, political, and ethical culture. Far too often they are lumped together and confuse important issues of human development and potential. Individuals or cultures may judge one another harshly over religious affiliation, when their fundamental spirituality has more in common than they recognize.

The stunning discovery in Kendler's studies is that if spirituality is heritable, then personal devotion is most likely foundational to all humanity. Spirituality is not built from the outside-in by this religion or that culture; innate spirituality is not something into which we must be socialized any more than we must be socialized to breathe or to digest a meal. While the contours, methods, and language develop around our natural spirituality through socialization, our natural faculty is inborn, ours already, and part of our endowment.

Along with Kendler, other scientists have measured the biological basis of transcendence. One meaningful body of work on the biological correlates of transcendence often is derived from the earlier work of C. Robert Cloninger, who developed a "self transcendence scale."

Transcendence, particularly as measured by the Cloninger transcendence scale, has been shown by multiple research teams to have biological markers, such as structural differences in the occipital and parietal regions of the brain, increased levels of the neurotransmitters dopamine and serotonin, and genetic markers in the human genome that are associated with production of these neurotransmitters and their regulation. These markers include DRD4 for dopamine receptor, and 5-HTTLPR for serotonin regulation. These are some of the biological building blocks of transcendence.

Kendler's landmark contribution was this: Whereas religious denomination and style of adherence to religion are shared by our culture and socialized, the capacity for a deep personal sense of spiritual connection, the transcendent relationship, is very much driven by genes, or heritability. Specifically, by comparing monozygotic and dizygotic twins, Kendler showed that the variance, or difference, in our tendencies around personal devotion are due 29 percent to broad heritability, 24 percent to family environment, and 47 percent to our own personal unique environment. By contrast, there is no genetic contribution in how we approach religion: About half is due to family environment, about half to personal unique environment—our approach or adherence to religious creed is not part of our genetic makeup.

In a subsequent article two years later, in which Kendler responded to critics and elaborated on the work, strong personal devotion was associated with higher levels of optimism, education, and income and with less neuroticism. We will discuss later its protective effects against a broad range of problems, but for now it is relevant to know that Kendler showed that heritable personal devotion was associated with a 20 percent decreased likelihood for depression or substance use and abuse. To be extra clear, Kendler is not at all saying that people have big or little souls. The data suggests that the biological substrate through which we experience and seek the transcendent relationship varies. The strength of our wiring, or "antennae," is about 30 percent due to our genetic endowment.

Kendler's sample of twins from the Virginia Twin Registry were primarily of Judeo-Christian origin, such that personal devotion—*a transcendent dialogue*—might be seen more broadly as the transcendent relationship. Among Eastern traditions and religions, the transcendent relationship may be a sense of being one with the universe, which in this book I call the *transcendent oneness*. Within indigenous traditions, the transcendent relationship can also be experienced or known through other people, through nature, animals, forces of nature, and the universe, all expressions of the sacred universe: *the transcendent other*.

These three forms of the transcendent relationship—transcendent dialogue, transcendent oneness, and the transcendent other—as first described by spiritual philosopher Ken Wilber, represent different conceptualizations of the universal transcendent relationship. This idea is borne out in the research and opens the work to the world's great religious traditions. For instance, through Taoism or Buddhism we may experience ourselves as part of everything or as the universe (*transcendent oneness*), as well as offer utmost respect to sacred consciousness and sacredness in all "sentient beings," including birds, dragonflies, palm trees, willows, and all of nature, and other people (*the transcendent other*). Christianity or Judaism tend to emphasize direct relationship with God (*transcendent dialogue*) and the sacredness in our relationships with other people (once again, *the transcendent other*). In some Native American traditions, the transcendent other includes "all our relations," a reference that encompasses animals, earth, and elements.

But are these forms of the transcendent relationship across cultures calling on the same genetically based human faculty as found among Judeo-Christians by Kendler? Is there a core universal transcendent faculty, one that allows us to engage in relationships and experience a unitive world? For this, we also need to explore transcendence at the level of human psychological composition, experience, and functioning.

The Psychology of Natural Spirituality

If it is universal, natural spirituality then should be much more similar than different across religions or cultures. In my view, the deep message to be drawn from Kendler's work is the possibility of a universal innate spirituality. There is indeed a core sameness to our transcendent relationships despite the names we give to it or the wraparound structure of our conceptualization (as oneness, otherness, or dialogue). By analogy, throughout the world basically all sports that involve balls and sticks are far more similar than different: baseball, cricket, polo, croquet, even lacrosse and hurling; we just bend and swing in different forms. Essentially, around the world we all are balanced and built with the same legs and arms, and nature has it that sticks and balls move the same way. So, too, with natural spirituality and the core transcendent faculty: the way in which we connect in the transcendent relationship really does not differ much; it is foundationally essential to how we all are built.

The question then is, can we see the expression of a universal core transcendent faculty, expressed by people around the world of many ethnicities, cultures, and religious faiths, inside and outside of religion?

Around the time of the breakthrough news of Kenneth Kendler's twin study, I met my colleague Ralph Piedmont, from Loyola University (who since went on to take a term as president of the Society for Spirituality and Psychology and is editor of an APA journal), at an American Psychological Association convention in Toronto. In his research, he, too, had been searching for a natural human faculty that he also calls spiritual transcendence.

For his research, Piedmont first had gathered women and men of the world religions together to discuss the core components of spirituality they understand and experience through their own faith and lives. He also spoke to just as many people outside of faith traditions. He then systematically used questionnaires to investigate personal experiences of transcendence with thousands of people of various faiths. Through rounds of empirical winnowing away, Piedmont identified three core components to transcendence, which could be translated into just about any other culture. They may sound familiar to you. First, universality, our sense of the unitive nature of life, that we are all one and part of one whole ("there is a higher plane of consciousness or spirituality that binds all people"). Second, that we can have a profound and fulfilling ongoing relationship with the transcendent through any form of dialogue or prayer ("I have experienced deep fulfillment and bliss through my prayers or meditation"), as well as a connectedness with other people now and through time ("although dead, images of some of my relatives continue to influence my life"). Third, he found through this broad data collection that the transcendent relationship was indeed the core of spirituality.

Piedmont anticipated the next scientific question to prove that a spiritual transcendent faculty is core to our human nature: Does it exist irrespective of someone's personality? That is, spirituality is not just another way of saying that someone is a nice guy or a happy type of person. In psychology, the current gold standard for personality conceptualization and assessment is known as the "five factor model of personality," which includes the dimensions of extraversion, conscientiousness, agreeableness, neuroticism, and openness. Research shows that how much we can be described by each of these five traits is determined to a meaningful extent by our genes. Twin studies show that these traits are 30 to 50 percent heritable—notably in the same range of magnitude as Kendler showed the genetic contribution to the personal transcendent relationship to be.

If spiritual transcendence could be shown to exist in us as separate and irrespective of these other established five core personality traits, it could be empirically argued to be an independent faculty separate from personality. So Piedmont conducted a personality assessment using the five factor model on a sample of 735 college students, who then also shared their views of spiritual transcendence. Just to be sure that people did not represent themselves as more spiritual or less spiritual out of a cultural motive, Piedmont asked 279 of these students to ask a friend to describe them using the same personality and transcendence assessments. It turned out that spiritual transcendence had no more overlap with the five factor model than the model had within itself. Actually, it had less overlap—spirituality and personality were separate entities. His findings were published in 1999 as a landmark study in the *Journal of Personality*.

Is it the case that good guys tend to be spiritual? Yes, but it appears that "spiritual" leads to "good"—but "good" and "spiritual" are not the same inborn trait. While still far from being one and the same, there was a mild relationship between spiritual transcendence and the personality traits of being agreeable (think back to good guy), as well as open to experience (think creative artist or musician). So, our hunch was right that good guys and open people tend to also be spiritual, but they are not one and the same. Transcendence calls on additional capacities.

Although we all have the transcendent capacity within us, the natural intensity of it, the way we experience it, and the ways we express it vary for each of us.

Finally, Piedmont showed that while transcendence is in all of us, it is expressed differently. Some people pray and others meditate and others do both. Some people practice in collective company, others alone, and many both. There are hundreds of world religions and indigenous cultures, all of which have a different form of expression. Research again confirmed that transcendence was found through religion for many people, that religion is a pathway, roadmap, or way of being into transcendence. Religion does not make people transcendent, but rather, it engages our natural transcendence. Irrespective of which faith tradition (or none at all), people with greater hunger and pursuit of spiritual transcendence were viewed by other people as more self-actualized, emotionally balanced, and delighted in living. They led lives that were driven by purpose, did much for other people, were less materialistic (irrespective of wealth), and felt fulfilled.

Now, let's combine Kendler's twin study showing a heritable contribution to transcendence with Piedmont's research showing that spirituality is independent from personality and is associated with, but not the same as, engagement in religion, to make a prediction. Since our human capacity for the transcendent relationship is innate, it should likely be universal, as well. Is the transcendent relationship experienced all around the earth?

Together with Mark Leach in 2002, Piedmont published in the *American Behavioral Scientist* a repeat of his original transcendence study on U.S. college students, this time done with 369 students in India, representing a broad range of Christians, Muslims, and Hindus. Once again, among Indians—as among U.S. participants—transcendence predicted engagement in religion across denominations, but was not the same. It was separate from personality, and predicted prosocial behavior, thriving, and fulfillment. The last critique to remain was that the study was conducted in English, so Piedmont then translated the assessments into Tagalog, the indigenous language of the Philippines that emanates from a lexical system culturally and historically different from English. Again, among the Filipinos, inner spiritual transcendence was found to be associated with seeking religious life, but it was not the same, and again it predicted positive attributes and relationships.

Transcendence is not taught or socialized or made by humans. It can be deliberately cultivated, harnessed, and supported to evolve. It is not 99 percent cultural fact, not stamped upon us like learning the names of the presidents or the multiplication tables. The capacity for transcendence is inborn and universal to all human beings. Through this capacity we experience the transcendent relationship. This is our birthright named and shaped by the varied cultural and religious languages on the earth.

Research measures in recent years have been developed to explore universal spirituality, as an innate capacity to be engaged by parenting, religion, and community. However, despite a formidable body of work, this strong evidence for the developmental significance of natural spirituality has yet to be shared with parents through conventional channels for parent education. This collective silence on the matter is perhaps as important for you to know as the research findings. Because as you'll see when we talk about the data that shows how vitally important spiritual development is to your child, and what a critical role you play in supporting it, it matters that this data is only now being provided to you. You have most likely never heard it in conversations with your child's physicians, nurses, teachers, counselors, or perhaps even your religious or spiritual advisers. You've been left to wonder perhaps at times whether spirituality is real, whether it matters, and what your child needs, when in fact, there has been clear evidence for at least fifteen years that it is real, it does matter, and we know what a child needs—and when. Spirituality is part of each and every child's birthright, accompanied by an inborn biological capacity.

FINDING 2

PUBERTY AND ADOLESCENCE BRING A SURGE IN THE SPIRITUAL CAPACITY

With physical puberty comes a biologically primed surge in natural spirituality. Teens are propelled like clockwork into an accentuated hunger for transcendence, a search for ultimate meaning and purpose, and the desire for unitive connection. Puberty is a unified developmental path for both fertility and spirituality. The development of spirituality occurs in tandem with other forms of maturation, including sexual, cognitive, social, and emotional development.

It seemed to me that behind the Kendler portrait of adult spirituality, there was a developmental story of personal devotion and personal religion that could be told in the same constructs, back-ended into childhood and adolescence. Given that they have two different origins, personal devotion being largely heritable and personal religion being socializable, one would assume they would exist as separate entities in

youth. But youth may differ from adults in not perceiving a distinction—
early adolescents in particular may not express the difference between
religious adherence and a natural spirituality. I decided to find out through
science if this was indeed the case.

Adolescent *individuation* is the process of testing and questioning the
world as handed to us by parents (and school and community) against
our own inner felt sense. It is the ongoing moment-by-moment litmus
test of lived reality over borrowed reality, and Western psychology lo-
cates it as central to adolescent development. Given the adult findings
about spirituality and the data that shows spirituality as a distinct human capacity, I reasoned that natural spirituality may well have its own
individuation process, just as there are individuation processes for social,
moral, and physical development.

My senior colleague Ron Kessler generously shared his nationally representative sample of 676 adolescences, ages thirteen to nineteen, in which
we looked for empirical evidence of a spiritual individuation process as
represented by personal devotion and personal religion. What we found
was the first evidence of spiritual adolescent development in a nationally
representative sample of which I am aware. Whereas Kendler had shown
that personal devotion and personal religion were barely related in adults,
we found that in early adolescence they were more closely related. This
means that for some adolescents the two were almost perceived as the
same thing. As we move from early adolescence to late adolescence, personal devotion and personal religion become 50 percent less correlated,
and that correlation again decreases by 50 percent from late adolescence
to adulthood. So by adulthood, we are far less likely to perceive spirituality and religion as necessarily overlapping compared with childhood.

In other words, for the child, inner spirituality and what they learn
in religion classes are often thought to be the same thing (even if all the
while the child has spiritual experience that may or may not be discussed
in the family religion). They do not cognitively reflect upon their own internal spiritual life as separate from what others teach them about religion
or God or spirituality as the road to spiritual growth. As the child enters

adolescence, what she thinks of spirituality—like what she thinks of music, politics, and curfews!—starts to separate from the opinions and teachings of the adults and society around her. She starts to individuate spiritually. By the time she is an adult, she recognizes her personal devotion and her personal religion as distinct things, with perhaps an interweaving or relationship between the two that she now brings into resolution.

What does this sound like and feel like for adolescents? In a five-year qualitative study, my lab found the voices of individuation in comments like these from the adolescent participants in our research:

I used to wake up and do the early morning prayer—my mom was very strict about it. But as I got older I realized that I wasn't praying for God or myself, I was praying for my mom. My mom is making me. So I realized that wasn't right. You should be doing it for yourself, not for someone else. So I talked to my mom, and she had a tough time dealing with it. She didn't talk to me for a really long time. (Josef, fifteen)

Now that I am getting older, I am getting more into it. Before when I was younger it really didn't matter to me. Now when I go to church I feel the spirit. I feel the spirit of God in me. (Thomas, sixteen)

Individuation takes emotional investment and a great deal of intellectual work. Why would adolescents put so much effort and focus into individuation? As parents, we know that we cannot force adolescents to mentally invest in things that do not interest them. So what makes teens do this work? The answer, we found, is a push from within. All forms of development have windows of growth and acceleration: linguistic cognition surges when your first-grader learns to read, and physical maturation is surging in the body of your adolescent. These show the time-sensitive developmental clock unlocking genetic potential. A biological surge likewise unlocks the capacity for spiritual development in your child during adolescence.

In adolescence, the awakening of transcendence surges like a tidal wave and brings with it a hunger and an ability to experience the transcendent relationship, the desire to feel a transcendent connection with other people, and a sense of being part of the universe. The push from within—the surprising, wondrous, and sometimes without guidance, upending experience of transcendence—mobilizes the teen. The heritable contribution to adult inner spirituality identified by Kendler and others arrives via a steep increase of heritable contribution in adolescence. The biology that seemingly overnight gives your child breasts or facial hair also brings them an increasing capacity for awareness and a desire to understand their inner spiritual life.

Here is another way of understanding the biology. At the University of Colorado at Boulder, Tanya Button studied 2,478 adolescent twins to assess the heritability of inner spirituality over time. The research team asked adolescents about their inner spiritual experience, focusing on the transcendent relationship, with questions such as, "Do you believe in God?" or "Do you rely on your religious beliefs as a guide for day-to-day living?" or "Are you able to turn to prayer when you are feeling a personal problem?"

The Colorado team found in this sample of twins that at around fourteen years old, human variability in inner spirituality (in other words, how much the degree of spirituality varied from person to person) was 29 percent due to genetics, 44 percent due to shared family environment, and 27 percent due to individual personal environment. By late adolescence—just five years later at about age nineteen—the heritable contribution had increased to 41 percent, while the shared family environment and unique personal environment had receded to 37 percent and 22 percent respectively. In other words, at fourteen years old, the largest impact to a teen's spirituality comes from her family but by nineteen, it is shaped primarily by her biology.

The Colorado team looked deeper. To learn more about the surge, they looked at it in terms of the change in intensity of inner spirituality and related practice over the course of adolescence. How much does the capacity for the transcendent relationship come from the biological clock versus the environment? In this study, none of the surge in intensity of the transcendent relationship was due to family environment. Rather, the spiritual surge was due 52 percent to the force of genetic expression, the unlocking of the window, and 48 percent to the selection of a unique personal environment that teens created based upon their emerging experience (for example, taking themselves to youth group or picking their own house of worship, or beginning to meditate with friends).

The thrust of spirituality from within is on par with other emerging faculties in adolescence. A sense of transcendence and spirituality is not the only faculty to burgeon from the inside out, but occurs alongside social attitudes, personality IQ, and risk for depression and anxiety.

When does the spiritual surge associated with adolescence stop? Laura Koenig and colleagues at the University of Minnesota examined this with a large sample of twins from the Minnesota Twin Family Study. To trace a developmental path, over a period of four to five years across adolescence, the team looked at the change in genetic and environmental contribution to personal engagement with religion and religious experience. The team wanted to follow the developmental process of adolescence and then see how it might change or stop in emerging adulthood. During the period of the study, one twin cohort of 641 adolescents grew from being fourteen to eighteen years old, the other twin cohort of 573 traveled into emerging adulthood, from twenty to twenty-five years old. Koenig's findings even more dramatically showed a biological surge in capacity for spirituality across adolescence, well over that of environment. The Minnesota team showed variability in spirituality among young adolescence (mean age of fourteen years) to be only 2 percent heritable, then it rapidly surges across the course of adolescence to 21 percent at age eighteen, 27 percent at age twenty, and 46 percent at age twenty-five, showing that the surge continues past adolescence into emerging adulthood. At the same time, the impact of family environment rapidly falls off from 74 percent at age fourteen, to 55 percent at age eighteen, 49 percent at age twenty, and 30 percent at age twenty-five.

From these and many other studies we can say with surety that it is primarily across this decade that the surge happens, from the inside out. From early adolescence to emerging adulthood, we live through the most intense surge into spiritual arrival, the bright awakening, the lion's share of the individuation work. Now individuation becomes about building a life that makes sense. We hear this in the research interviews with adolescents:

> I'm just always thanking God—on holidays, and we always do grace and thank God for our food and for everything. The other night, me and my two friends had a scary situation happen to us, and we were just like sitting in the car, and we were like "thank God," that sort of thing. But we're not going around, like, preaching. I recognize that He is looking over me, and just recognize that I'm being watched over, and that I always have someone above me. (Bethany, seventeen)

> I think the very young ages of your development are when these things [spiritual experiences and values] become part of you, but I think that over time, they *develop* . . . as far as really beginning to be conscious about it all [spirituality], maybe eleven, twelve years old, you really start to have thoughts about more complex areas of it. When you're younger, you more just listen to what people tell you and you believe . . . you don't have as much individualism, so I think that probably around eleven or twelve is when I began to think about it [spirituality], and you know, really contemplate what, whatever it is. . . . (Christopher, eighteen)

A genetic contribution to the surge of natural spirituality predicts a universal surge along with puberty in every country. Just as Piedmont investigated universal transcendence across cultures in adults, Peter Benson and his colleagues at the Search Institute in Minnesota conducted an international study based on interviews with 6,725 adolescents and young adults in eight countries. Benson and his colleagues set out to investigate the possibility of universal spiritual development in adolescents. Adolescents across Thailand, Cameroon, the United Kingdom, Canada, the United States, India, Australia, and Ukraine were asked about their own personal spiritual and religious life. The international team discovered there was a tendency for spiritual engagement to surge in adolescence, no matter what country or religion, or without religion. Moreover, they found a universal core to spiritual development that included foremost a relationship with a higher power, spiritual practice, profound transcendent experience, and the goal of putting spirituality into action. Even more striking, when asked to reflect on the meaning of spirituality, in all of these countries the most frequently endorsed notions were a relationship with God (by whatever name their deity was known) and believing that there is purpose in life, while consistently less than 10 percent of adolescents in any country thought that spirituality was synonymous with religious attendance. Adolescents in all countries are well aware of spiritual feelings they experience.

We know that the transcendent faculty surges in adolescence, and that this surge is part of a universal spirituality in teens around the earth. My lab, together with labs around the world, were identifying an innate capacity for spiritual development. I wanted to know how teens experience this from the inside so that I could find useful and practical insights to the question, *How can we help support and encourage natural spirituality?* I was curious to know up close the feelings, fears, and anxieties of spiritual development and to figure out how to help support a successful developmental path of natural spirituality.

So for nearly a decade, together with my lab, I listened to the voices of hundreds of adolescents across the United States. We asked teens the open-ended question, "What is the surge like on the inside?" We sat with youth groups to hear the teens talk to one another, and also conducted individual interviews. We visited youth groups of diverse religious and nonreligious spiritual orientations from coast to coast, from YMCAs and Waldorf schools in San Francisco and the beach near Big Sur, to Christian summer camps in Illinois and Florida, to Jewish youth groups outside of Chicago and New York City, to the Hip Hop Church in Harlem and Baha'i Temple in Manhattan. My lab interviewed youth of "nondenominational Christianity," of observant West Asian Muslims, and of Thai and Tibetan Buddhists. What we found was clear: Adolescents are profoundly spiritual, they are experiencing spiritual stirrings as the momentous and wondrous, and they are surprised that for the most part, *nobody has talked to them about this experience.* Nobody, even people they love dearly, have asked, or commented, or said something to make spiritual development part of a conversation, shared words that would make their inner life a spoken reality.

This human impetus for spirituality at adolescence has been expressed through history in the rites of passage of many cultures. In the Native American culture, the Lakota sun dance for adolescents, for example, and the Cherokee tradition of lacrosse, honor adolescent boys' emergent physicality and spirituality, one and the same, interwoven. The Christian confirmation and the Jewish bar and bat mitzvah herald the adolescent's coming of age in the spiritual and religious sense with puberty. In many communities, even the ritual huddle by a high school football team on the playing field includes prayers for strength, service, and protection. Whether the meaning is lived or legacy, these ritual passages recognize that spiritual awakening is perfectly synchronized with physical maturation and the adolescent's passage to adult life.

Without supported and guided spiritual awakening in adolescence, our teens are left to fend for themselves. The cost is high. As we saw in Kendler's study, spirituality measured as personal devotion in adults was associated with a 15 to 20 percent reduced risk for depression and substance use and abuse. In our investigation of the nationally representative sample of adolescents, spirituality was associated with a 30 to 40 percent reduced risk for substance abuse and depression, two times greater benefits than for adults. The protective benefits of spirituality for teens against episodes of depression and substance abuse have since been corroborated by fellow research teams many times.

The period of time that clinical scientists know as the window of onset for potentially lifelong illnesses, such as substance abuse and depression, is smack during the period of adolescent spiritual awakening. While we will get to an in-depth description of this process in later chapters focused on adolescence, the point is that spiritual development is foundational to adolescent development, and if it is not supported, we often see other failed attempts to achieve direction, connection, and a sense of transcendence and inner peace, through substance abuse, risk taking, and casual sex.

FINDING 3

RELATIONAL SPIRITUALITY IS THE EXPERIENCE OF THE TRANSCENDENT CONNECTION AND PRESENCE IN OUR RELATIONSHIPS

Transcendence and the transcendent relationship (our relationship with a higher presence) bring love to our human relationships. In other words, the love created in the transcendent relationship is brought to bear in the love of human relationships. This is particularly present and crucial in the love between parent and child, but here we discuss a general focus.

George Vaillant, a physician and researcher of life span at Harvard Medical School, is well known for his study of adaptation and thriving over decades of our lives. In his book *Spiritual Evolution*, he firmly asserts that the natural outcome of transcendence is human love, care, and service. Vaillant writes, "Human spirituality is deeply rooted in relationship."

A strongly felt relational spirituality is the natural expression of transcendence. Vaillant shows that religious figures, sacred mystics, and spiritual leaders from many religious traditions consistently value the presence of spirit as the most important part of human relationships and service. Speaking of St. John of the Cross, Buddha, Gandhi, and Mother Teresa, Vaillant urges us to "pay attention to the loving behaviors engendered by their mystical meditations." He sees transcendence as most apparent, and for him even most real, in the positive emotions we bring to one another: compassion, forgiveness, hope, and joy. He highlights compassion as a spiritual emotion, and feels that our evolving civilization increasingly engages this interpersonal form of spirituality.

Vaillant quotes Buddha, who says to his first sixty disciples, "Go forth, Oh Monks, and travel for the welfare and the happiness of the multitude, out of compassion for the world, for the good welfare and happiness of gods and men," and Gandhi, who says, "Such power as I possess in the political field has derived from my experiences in the spiritual field."

Research from Bruce Greyson, professor of psychiatric medicine at the University of Virginia, looks at events following surges of transcendent awakening, such as in near-death experiences and sudden illuminations. His studies show that after these kinds of events people often experience emotions that open them to deeper relationships and lives of service. Transcendence naturally leads us to feel the sacredness and wonder in the people around us, the awesomeness of their creation. Our possibility for human love becomes greater, infused with this great surge of transcendent love. Our natural spirituality is closely allied with human bonding, and creates relational spirituality—the experience of transcendence through relationships with one another, with a higher power, and within ourselves. As we'll see, transcendent love is especially present in the parent-child relationship.

FINDING 4

HEALING AND GROWTH COME THROUGH SPIRITUAL INSIGHT AND SPIRITUAL RELATIONSHIP

Spirituality draws on some or all of three relationships: (1) the transcendent relationship with God or a higher power, (2) spiritual relationships with other people based upon unconditional love, forgiveness, joy, and compassion, and (3) the awareness and perspective of our transcendent self, or our higher self. Underlying all of these relationships is what I call *heart knowing,* or the spiritual perception of the sacred through inner wisdom, intuition, and often the body.

Throughout this book, just as in my academic teaching and clinical work, I draw on the great importance of spiritual perception and its cultivation through three relationships: the transcendent relationship, relationships with other people, and the higher self. In all of these forms, there is a type of perception that includes felt awareness of love, transcendent love. Spiritual perception is not abstract knowledge, it is intuitive knowledge plus felt love, which I call *knowing of the heart* or *heart knowing.* Clinically speaking, here is what I see: among mentally ill teens and adults, heart knowing is missing. It has been annihilated by an outer voice that said, *This is not real, your inner wisdom is "not scientific."* But that is wrong. Science says conclusively that we are inherently spiritual. Heart knowing is our spiritual perception. This is a clinical observation that also has been discussed alongside emerging treatment outcome evidence by the psychotherapy research team led by Scott Richards at Brigham Young University. There is also emerging science that points to the heart as a neurophysiological organ of perception, particularly in relation to intuition.

In the past decade a growing number of psychotherapists have adapted practices to awaken knowing of the heart, or spiritual perception, such as prayer, contemplation, visualization, yoga, or meditation. There is now an official academic journal of the American Psychological Association called *Spirituality in Clinical Practice,* as well as over a dozen books on the subject published by the APA and related professional practice publications. To date, thirty-eight clinical trials have been conducted that directly compare the outcomes of treatment with a core explicit spiritual element added to the same treatment without a spiritual element. A meta-analysis published in *Psychotherapy Research* by clinical researcher Tim Smith and his colleagues found that, indeed, there is a 20 percent added benefit to symptom relief, such as improvement in depression and anxiety, and an enormously greater benefit—three times (300 percent) greater—to spiritual well-being (all provided that the patient is interested in spiritual work).

In the real world beyond a clinical study, spirituality comes up on a patient-by-patient basis in psychotherapy. Patients who want to do spiritual work integrated with treatment usually benefit enormously, particularly when it comes to moving beyond symptoms and into growth-based spiritual awakening. With spiritual growth also come the positive psychology assets shown to accompany spirituality: thriving, optimism, grit, and the relational assets of forgiveness, intimacy, and commitment.

Within the mainstream practice of psychotherapy, a felt clarity, wisdom, or guidance from the transcendent experience redirects the client's struggles. It is a fresh view on reality, the client then sees the once-plaguing situations with a new perspective—from the view of the higher self or with guidance from the transcendent relationship—and this can provide opportunities, new insights, meaning and purpose, and even a deep re-orientation.

This kind of growth draws on some or all of the three forms of transcendence. First, a direct transcendent relationship, whether understood as the higher power, the surrounding universe, spirit through fellow living beings, or a sense of oneness. Second, human spiritual relationships, as in Vaillant's view of relationships based upon values of unconditional love, forgiveness, joy, and compassion. And third, seeing from our higher self, the view of what I call our *observing eye*, which carries great perspective, wisdom, natural humility, and often a sense of peace or humor.

These three epic transcendent forms are echoed through faith traditions: honor of the ultimate higher power, respect for spirit in others, and a renewed awareness of the view by the higher self. In many indigenous and some Eastern traditions, the "other" applies to all living beings. We already have explored the first two transcendent forms from the view of science so I focus here on the higher self, which naturally is given different names by various faith traditions, cultures, and clinical science perspectives.

The body of science on contemplative practice, most often on mindfulness meditation, tends to focus on an inner cognitive stance, a way of relating to our thoughts and experience. Cognitive and clinical science describe the perspective as one of "decentering" from the nagging thought, or an "objectification" of the thoughts that once tossed us about emotionally. Another way to conceptualize this idea is to imagine a view high above ourselves and our situation, looking down and through and in; this view from the mountaintop is the view by the higher self, or observing eye.

Research using MRI on people in active meditation shows activity of the middle prefrontal cortex, a central structure that links to and regulates other brain regions such as the limbic system, such that our emotions, governed by the amygdala, are eased; when we meditate we feel less revved up for fight or flight. The middle prefrontal cortex is a grand regulator, a source of equanimity and brain synchronization. In his lovely book *Mindsight*, psychiatrist Daniel Siegel encourages cultivation of a "lens," which is an autonomous view of the mind upon the inner landscape of the self, and in turn the outer world. Siegel writes of mindsight—what I call in this book the vantage point or GPS position of the observing eye—as an open and objectifying perspective, one we choose and practice, and in which Siegel suggests "mind shapes brain and brain shapes mind."

Here is the illusive rub for neuroscience: neither the centrality of the prefrontal cortex to regulation, nor the ensuing harmonizing of the brain explains the observing eye, or the higher self, or the knower, that invokes the entire shift in awareness. Neuroscience recognizes that there has yet to be a single study that identifies the neural correlates of the higher knower in the brain. We cannot point to an MRI scan and say this region or this pathway of interconnectivity is used in awareness of the higher self. Yet while this is unanswered by MRI studies, its beneficial clinical effects are well shown through an extensive body of research on mindfulness meditation in cultivating attention and reducing symptoms of stress and suffering. We can see the broad and pervasive positive effects of seeing life from the seat of the higher self, which is filled with the clarity, perspective, and wisdom of the knower.

Science is a whirlwind work in progress. Today, as advances in science, medicine, and technology have given us access to unprecedented views into the brain and body, we are right up to the edge of knowledge and still searching when it comes to forms of transcendence and the brain. Just as no research team has found the circuitry for the higher self, no research team has found the neural correlates for engagement with the higher power. Much of what neuroscience shows is that the usual busy regions of the brain "pipe down" or "get out of the way"—they defer to the higher task during these transcendent states. We also seem to be discovering regions of the brain associated with spiritual perception.

My lab, in a collaboration with an MRI team at Yale Medical School led by Marc Potenza, is currently conducting an experimental fMRI study that compares the brain during engagement with the transcendent relationship versus a state of stress. Our MRI findings so far are showing that in a state of stress, activity in the brain is in the regions associated with craving (the insula and striatum). For centuries, the world religions have said much about craving and attachment as underlying suffering, that a state of craving in our inner life means we never feel satisfied. No matter how much money, alcohol or drugs, success or recognition we may have, craving makes us run an emotional treadmill. In our fMRI study, when participants next shift their mind to the transcendent relationship, there is a cessation of blood flow in the region of the brain associated with craving. Neurologically speaking, we are set free. At the same time, blood flow increases to areas of the brain that appear to be associated with spiritual perception (occipital and parietal regions), which is essential to our heart knowing.

Due to socialization in our current society, heart knowing is often blocked, denied, or disintegrated. This leads to enormous suffering, as we can become cut off from other people, our higher selves, and even our transcendent relationship. Treatment, then, is about reawakening heart knowing and then reintegrating it with our other faculties to make us whole again. Once heart knowing is restored, the patient gets better. All of this adolescent and adult struggle to replace what is lost seems like a great deal of unnecessary suffering when the child, as we'll see shortly, was born with heart knowing.

Spiritual Parenting Translates into Stronger, Fuller Personal Spirituality for Children

So here is the picture: We are foundationally spiritual. It is in our very constitution to have the structure through which to experience spirituality, and if we do, it is the most powerful form of resilience, protectiveness, and thriving known to medicine and the social sciences. We also are increasingly aware that some of the most pervasive forms of suffering actually are the other side of spiritual struggle or foreclosure, and supporting spiritual development is probably the most important thing we can do as parents. Spiritual parenting indeed does pay off and translates into a stronger, fuller personal spirituality for our child that usually lasts throughout life. Parents naturally want to know what they can do, and in the chapters ahead we will talk about the first and second decades, and the unique opportunities open to parents as they support their child's journey.

3

THE NOD

The Intergenerational Transmission of Spiritual Attunement

The role we have as parents in this sacred journey is extraordinary, and our children's need for spiritual parenting is great, but that doesn't make it complicated. You may have been doing some spiritual parenting all along without necessarily thinking of it that way or thinking of your role as uniquely profound. Perhaps you've taken the time to walk in the park and just marvel together at what you see—the sky, the flowers, or an ant hauling a crumb across the dirt. Maybe you've asked your child to help you gather food or clothes to take to the homeless shelter or encouraged him to befriend the new kid at school, share the last piece of cake, or watch for opportunities to step up and to lend a hand. You've likely shared your family's history and kept alive the memory of those who've passed on. Perhaps when your child fails or makes a mistake, you share what you know about growing through those experiences. Maybe you go to church or temple or send your children to Sunday school. Maybe you say grace before meals or share a bedtime prayer to bring the day to a peaceful close. Or, you say "I love you," and mean that your love is for always and unconditional.

You may have thought that all of these things are just everyday ways to be a loving parent and teach your child how to go about living a good, compassionate life, and you would be right. However, research also tells us that a parent's impact goes much deeper. Studies designed to learn how children's earliest relationship with God or a universal spirit develops show that a child's first and formative experience of the transcendent relationship very often is through their parents' love. The spiritual brain is wired for this sacred connection that includes parents as essential partners. We also see that a child's transcendent faculty, the biologically based capacity for spiritual connection, is allied with the bonding and attachment faculty, designed to actively seek out the parent as partner in the transcendent relationship—so much so that, absent the mother or father, a single loving, caring "parent figure" can also be this spiritually grounding presence for a child. Children by nature seek out vibrant, luminous, healthy spirituality—they are naturally attracted to the "brightest light"—and through something we call *selective spiritual socialization* they may find it through another family member; for instance, a second parent or stepparent, grandparent, aunt, or uncle.

Very often a grandparent becomes this special spiritual partner even when the parents are healthy and functional and spiritually supportive. In our busy lives, so often it is a grandparent who sits and listens to a child's questions, welcomes a child's feelings, and has the long deep talks at the kitchen table. In fact, it was a grandmother and granddaughter on the subway one sweltering morning in Manhattan nearly two decades ago who showed me the answer that was buried out of sight in the data I was studying. What I witnessed that morning on the No. 1 train was a signal breakthrough that opened the way to a new understanding of how children "get spiritual" and how spiritual parenting is an unparalleled source of resilience for children.

A Study of Suffering and the Mystery
of Spiritual Transmission

The scientific data that confirms a natural spirituality and its benefits for youth simply did not exist in 1997, as I was starting my research career at Columbia University as an NIMH postdoctoral fellow. Science had well established the positive role of spirituality in adult life. We knew from a decade of research that spirituality in adulthood was linked to less suffering in life, less depression and substance abuse, higher rates of recovery from physical illness, and even a longer life span. Despite how hopeful the research was for adults, there was very little science on whether the great benefits found in adults might apply to children growing up, or even if childhood spirituality mattered to a child's health and development at all.

It seemed to me that an investigation into spirituality as a source of resilience in children might begin with the most common form of suffering. Depression is the most common form of mental suffering and damage to well-being and relationships known to medical science, and some of the foremost research in depression at that time was under way at Columbia University by a research team headed by the eminent psychiatric epidemiologist Myrna Weissman. I turned to data from her ongoing three-generational study of depression to search for answers.

Starting in the late 1970s, Weissman had studied a group of severely depressed women, their children, and eventually the third generation—the depressed women's grandchildren—as they moved through childhood and adolescence. In these families at high risk for depression (from both genes and family environment), Weissman and her team were studying how lifestyle, relationships, socioeconomic factors, and a host of other factors influenced wellness or suffering over time.

Weissman's core findings were these: mothers with severe, and particularly those with recurrent, depression have offspring at high risk for depression, who, as they reach puberty, are two to three times more likely to face depression than other young adults. The data showed the biologically inherited sensitivity to developing depression. Yet, science also shows that while we may come into the world genetically predisposed to depression, those genetic factors are not immutable.

A large body of research on depression by Weissman and others says that a key factor in thriving has to do with the habits of living, particularly around relationships, that we establish in childhood. These are daily patterns of thought and relationship that become a stance toward life. Often transmitted from parents, they continue to surface as latent habits as we grow older. *When we were children, did our parents take missteps or failures in stride and perhaps even as opportunities, or did they catastrophize or criticize us about them? Did the family celebrate each member of the family—accept and enjoy one another—or were members judgmental or critical? Was love and affection unconditional, or was it contingent upon measuring up to expectations or outward success?* Some of these daily ways of living are so much a part of our family culture and conversation that we absorb them like a sponge. Then down the road as adults we may discover that some of these practices in living help us thrive and offer resilience, while others actually dig us into depression.

Even though children of depressed mothers are two to three times more likely to face depression, the severity and even more importantly the number of bouts with depression many of them experience is not fixed in stone at all. Depression after the first experience, usually with a first episode in puberty or adolescence, is to a meaningful extent based upon how we deliberately manage our innate natural sensitivity. How we manage early moments of feeling low, deriving the needed support or joy from family, may too come from early family socialization patterns absorbed in childhood. Weissman's cohort of depressed women, their sons and daughters, and then in time their grandchildren, sheds light on how mothers can cultivate less suffering and more thriving in themselves and in their families, even as those families have a vulnerability to depression.

It seemed to me, however, there was a huge missing dimension in the field-wide research portrait showing that depression travels in families, yet its expression is not locked in and instead is based upon life practices.

Growing up in Missouri I had shared in the family life of my friends, sat in cars and kitchens, and rubber necked into adult discussions about the ups and downs of life, including painful disappointments. I listened as a friend's mother responded to the news that her husband (my friend's father) had lost his job in a contracting economy, saying, "God has a way of making things work. We'll use this as a chance to bring our family closer. Stan had been traveling nearly every week." I remembered the community rallying around the deaths of a classmate in an automobile accident and of a lovely field hockey player from a rival team, who was killed crossing a highway. Our community dealt with these shocks as tragic losses, adolescent impetuousness, difficult times, and also, ultimately, spiritual events. I watched as the midlife struggles of some parents who questioned their purpose and faced depression and anxiety were handled with participation in right action: giving food to the homeless, running school fund-raisers, helping those in need. This right action in quiet and appropriate ways illuminated the spiritual path through life's challenges.

The people who raised me in Missouri had a bedrock spirituality that was not discussed in the hallways of academic psychiatry at the time, but I knew it was a possibility for us all. It was clear to me that spirituality was a source of great resilience and power and was life-sustaining for my parents and family, my friends' families, and our close-knit community.

Years later, as a researcher at Columbia, I scoured the medical literature day after day, searching for even a trace of research on spirituality in families that struggle with depression. I could never quite shake the notion that the field of psychology just didn't make sense without spirituality; it seemed almost inconceivable that nobody had ever investigated the question relative to depression. I grew increasingly certain that there was work to do in scientifically identifying any potential contribution of spirituality as a way out of depression in families. The genetic factor was, after all, only a sensitivity, and not the condition itself. The family habits of socialization were what plucked the strings of the sensitivity. Might spirituality play a role in impacting the family habits of socialization?

The data in Weissman's study traced twenty years in the lives of the brave women who lived with depression, and their daughters and sons, who during the duration of the study had grown up. There in the data, might spirituality point to a way out of the intergenerational trap of depression? Might spirituality fit into the well-hemmed equations often used in research to test factors of resilience and reservoirs of strength? My first question was this: *Are spiritually engaged offspring of depressed mothers less likely to get depressed?* The answer, statistically speaking, was a rather mild yes, but not much more than that. Then I checked for a different pattern: *Are spiritual mothers less likely to transmit depression?* Again, the answer was a statistically very mild yes. I sensed that there was more to this picture, something deeper in the data. One morning I found my answer in the most unlikely place: the New York City subway.

Subway Spirituality: A Grandmother and Granddaughter Light the Way

Every day, along with thousands of other New Yorkers, I descended into the roar of the underground transit system and took the No. 1 train up Broadway to my office in the clinical psychology department at Columbia University. The subway is a city's arterial system of humanity, presenting a rich cross section of psychological and behavioral elements. Naturally, my research question—*What protects some people from depression even when they are genetically loaded for it?*—was never far from my mind, and eventually the question presented itself in the faces of the people I saw on the subway. Regardless of race, ethnicity, or apparent material wealth, some people shone with a brightness of warmth and kindness, with radiant eyes and expressions, while others were visibly downcast and burdened. I came to think of this brightness as a sign that, spiritually, "the light is on."

Each day on my ride in, I mulled over the decades of formal research data that awaited me at the office like a giant jigsaw puzzle, and each day I casually witnessed this brightness of being in some people in the commuter subculture. On one particular day, a sweltering August Sunday morning, I was going into the lab for a few hours, and joined the throng of workaholics, weekenders, and churchgoers waiting at the 86th Street subway platform for the No. 1 train. When the train stopped and the doors slid open, the car was jam-packed, so I was surprised as I stepped in to see the back half of the car almost empty. Then I saw why: a dirty, disheveled man was at the very far end yelling and fuming, his fast-food lunch sack open and balanced precariously on his lap. His hands and chin smeared with grease, he brandished a piece of chicken at each passenger who boarded and yelled, "Hey! Do you want to sit with me? You want some of this lunch?" Everyone studiously ignored the man and hurried to join the other riders standing as far from him as they could get. They pressed together, hot and uncomfortable at the far end of the car. I stepped through the crowd and went to an empty seat across the aisle from the man and sat down.

The awkward scene continued for a few stops more, until the doors opened at the 125th Street station, where an eye-stopping couple boarded: an elegant older woman accompanied by a young girl about eight years old. They appeared to be a grandmother and her granddaughter. They wore fresh pastel dresses—the grandmother in green, the little girl in pink. Both wore gloves with lace trim, and the grandmother wore a pill-box hat with a small decorative veil. They stepped aboard, heads held high with a dignified bearing. They looked elegant in their Sunday finest— and shockingly out of place.

The commuters cringed as this lovely couple boarded, everyone anticipating the crazed man's inevitable "offer" of chicken. And sure enough, he erupted right on cue, instantly accosting them as they crossed the door with his roar, "Hey! Do you want to sit with me?"

Without even pausing, the grandmother and granddaughter looked at each other and nodded, then looked squarely at the man, and without hesitation walked over to sit down right next to him. "Thank you," they said in unison to him. He was shocked. The other riders in the car were, too. Everyone stared with surprise and concern at the regal twosome.

The man then resumed waving his chicken in the air and bellowed at the two again, "Do you want some?" The grandmother and granddaughter looked squarely at him again and replied politely and in unison, "No, thank you," and then nodded again to each other. The man, as if he couldn't believe someone had responded to him, said again, this time loudly but somehow more contained, and without roaring, "Do you want some of my lunch?" Again, with a resolute nod to one another of shared purpose and understanding, the two answered kindly, "No, thank you." This continued for several rounds until the man seemed calmed, and relaxed quietly into his bright orange plastic seat.

When a few stops later the train reached their destination and the couple departed, I realized that the grandmother and granddaughter had in their own way shown me the answer to my research question. *What protects some people from depression even when they are genetically loaded for it?* I had just seen it, literally, in front of me: *it was the nod.* The nod, or what the nod represented, was the missing piece to the research puzzle. Greater than the spirituality of one *or* the other, the nod represented a shared sensibility, a shared spirituality.

There was more resilience, health, and strength in that nod between grandmother and grandchild than in any theory I'd studied in academic psychology. That grandmother was spiritual and she was making sure that spiritual sensibility reached her granddaughter. The nod was spirituality shared between child and beloved elder: spiritual direction, values, taught and received in the loving relationship. I felt I was watching the passing of a sacred torch, the intergenerational transmission of spiritual connection, a flame passing through generations of family and humanity. This was the very heart of spirituality: in the nod was recognition of a shared understanding of this ordinary moment, right there in our subway car, as sacred ground. I could almost hear the voice: *What you do to the least of me, you do to me. You shall treat the stranger as your own, as you were a stranger once in the land of Israel.* The words taught from generation to generation over centuries were loud in my ears.

I got to the lab twenty minutes later and ran an equation testing the effect of the nod—shared spirituality taught and received between parent and child—on the depression data. Now I asked: *Does spirituality shared between a depressed mother and her child counteract, at all, in any measure, the generational slide of depression?* I searched the data for mother-child pairs in which both the mother and her adolescent child had reported a connection with the same religion, no matter what that denomination might be. I also included those pairs who reported feeling personal spirituality without religion. I looked statistically for the nod, the passing of spiritual or religious sensibility, intergenerational concordance between mothers and their teenage children.

There are few moments in science when the results are astonishing. These findings were the most amazing science I had ever seen. They were statistically robust beyond any previously examined protective factor published in scientific literature. If the mother and her son or daughter both reported the same personal relationship with a religion, then there was a dramatic positive effect—shared spirituality was over 80 percent protective in a sample of families otherwise at very high risk for depression. I reran the analysis, over and over. Statistically, a spiritually oriented mother alone or a spiritually oriented child alone showed only marginal protection against depression, but if the two shared being spiritually oriented, and the spirituality was something that had been shared during the child's formative years, then there was a protective effect that dramatically lowered the incidence of depression *by 80 percent.*

The spiritual nod was far more powerful than all of the family risk factors for depression combined—genes and socialization. To put the force and magnitude of the nod into perspective, in offspring of depressed mothers, a shared spirituality was between three to seven times more protective than any other sources of resilience against depression known to the medical or social sciences: four times more protective than demographics like privileged social class or education and twice more protective than favorable family functioning or parenting style. Neither biology nor relationships, education, socioeconomic situations, pills, or supplements could compare with this. Nothing radically low-ered the risk for depression like a shared spirituality.

As we would learn later, this shared spirituality typically comes first through a spiritually engaged parent, but it might also arrive through a grandparent—just as we saw on the No. 1 train—or through another family member, youth group leader, or any other steady and loving rela-tional source of spiritual connection.

The Joint Effect of Parenting and Spirituality

The data was clear, the science solid. Our study of sixty mothers and their 151 offspring, "Religiosity and Depression: Ten-Year Follow-Up of De-pressed Mothers and Offspring" was published in October 1997 in the *Journal of the American Academy of Child and Adolescent Psychiatry*. Subse-quent research has confirmed and expanded on it: spirituality—as it most benefits youth, in the long term—is not found in the mother or the youth alone but in the nod: the passage from parent to child or grandparent to grandchild. In science, we now call this the *joint effect* of spirituality and parenting, or the *intergenerational transmission* of spirituality.

Our lab recently repeated this study, as scientists are patient and more than another decade had passed! I went back to the place I started at the medical school, to collaborate once more with Myrna Weissman, and now brought my doctoral student, Molly Jacobs. This time we fo-cused on the third generation of the sample, the grandchildren. The joint effect was found again to be true and significant. This time, we studied the daughters who had grown up to be moms and were now rais-ing their own children. The data showed that if the new generation of mothers and their children shared spirituality, then the protective effect in the grandchildren was even greater than in the previous generation: now it was 90 percent. When I saw the data, I thought of that grand-daughter in pink on the No. 1 train more than fifteen years ago. She was possibly a mother herself now; if so, I had a sense that her children were doing well.

The joint effect of parenting and spirituality was the most profoundly protective factor in relation to depression ever to be found in the clinical sciences, and that breakthrough study in 1997 opened a new frontier of inquiry and discovery. We'll explore this more fully in the chapters ahead, but in brief we can draw these insights from the growing body of literature:

- A parent, grandparent, or other spiritually engaged, loving adult is equally capable of transmitting spirituality and religion to a child. The transmission comes through the child's sense of parental love and transcendent love (some call it God's love) mixed together as one felt experience.

- The nod, or the intergenerational transmission of spirituality, is passed through its practice, whether in personal prayer, religious observance, or other spiritual practice: an ongoing shared awareness of spiritual presence in the world. The child sees the parent's experience of spirituality, and then follows suit, while being immersed in the love of the parent.

- The parent living out spiritual values and morality together with the child guides the intergenerational transmission of lived spirituality and spiritual values. This is spirituality put into action, with care, respect, moral courage, and compassion—as exemplified by the grandmother and granddaughter on the No. 1 train.

- Components of the nod or intergenerational transmission of spirituality are often held in religion—through family prayer, attending services or holidays together, and other religious practices, for instance. However, the nod can exist and does exist outside of religion, when the spiritual value or spiritual presence in living is clear and spiritual life is made apparent by parents.

- The spiritual value of the nod is held in that it is (1) explicit, (2) jointly acted on by the parent and child, and (3) supported by the love in their relationship.
- The intergenerational transmission of spirituality is more protective than anything else against alcohol, depression, and risk taking for children.
- The nod or intergenerational transmission of spirituality has since been examined cross-culturally, and appears to be a universal phenomenon, validated by research across cultures and religious traditions in Asia and the Middle East and in a broad range of faith traditions including Hinduism, Islam, Judaism, and Christianity.

The common thread through all of these is a child's experience of a parent's unconditional love and spiritual values together embodied in everyday interactions. This means the parent represents or acknowledges the transcendent relationship and provides a spiritual road map for living, along with a spiritual compass for doing the right thing. Intergenerational transmission of spirituality works because the child's experience and guidebook to spirituality is taught through the parent-child relationship. A child's innate natural spirituality becomes a powerful lifelong capacity through the unconditional love of the parent-child relationship.

Parent as Spiritual Ambassador

After considering all the research, literature, and my own experience as a therapist and a mother, I have come to think of the parent as an ambassador. The parent is an ambassador of transcendence, the guide on the ground who introduces a child to the spiritually attuned life. The parent does this with love: it is through the great similarity—or perhaps even sameness—of unconditional parental love to the universal love of transcendence that a child's relationship with a loving, guiding universe is formed.

Each parenting relationship (or parent figure relationship) is unique and carries spiritual impact. This was first noted in psychology in the late 1970s and 1980s by a perceptive psychoanalyst, Ana-Maria Rizzuto, in her book *The Birth of the Living God: A Psychoanalytic Study*, describing her work with children. She found that children spoke and drew pictures of God that resembled the way that they experienced their own parents and important adults in their lives.

More recently, in a series of studies spanning two decades, research psychologists such as Pehr Granqvist and Lee Kirkpatrick at the College of William and Mary explored the power of the parent to shape the transcendent relationship—their child's relationship with God or a universal spirit. They found that children literally take the attributes of their parents and stamp them on the face of their higher power. In a child's brain, parental love and God's love speak the same language. In their studies, Granqvist and Kirkpatrick asked people of all ages—children, adolescents, and adults—to describe their childhood experience of being parented. Participants reported the extent to which they found each of their parents to be unconditionally loving, warm, affectionate, or, on the other hand, unreliable yet strict, unavailable, harsh, and punitive.

The team then asked the same people to describe their felt sense of a higher power, their own transcendent relationship with their higher power, and the way—when and how—they turn to the transcendent relationship in difficult times to cope in the world.

The connection was clear and strong. An unconditionally loving and reliable parent—mother or father—was associated with a strongly felt sense of an always present, accepting, and loving God. The nature of an individual's daily lived relationship with their higher power, particularly the way they understand, struggle with, and resolve suffering, was strongly affected by the parenting they had received.

A parent's unconditional love supported their child's sense of a higher power that "I can turn to in times of difficulty" and "who is by my side," one who gives direction and offers guidance. From youth through adulthood, this body of research showed that these transcendent relationships remain a guide during loss, death, divorce, or relationship crisis, as well as a felt presence throughout daily life.

By marked contrast, a mother who is emotionally unreliable, whose love is not constant but conditional, "strings attached," or erratic, or a father who is overly harsh, unpredictable, and punitive was directly associated with a felt sense of the higher power as negative, harsh, and punishing. This powerful negative experience of a parent creates a deep source of suffering for the child, and a view of a higher power as punitive often comes with the strong sense that a child's inner suffering is punishment for wrongdoings.

Granqvist and Kirkpatrick called the child's experience of sameness between a parent and God a form of "correspondence" of parent to higher power—in the child's mind the parent acts as a surrogate or stand-in for God. I call it same-sameness. Psychologists filled in the developmental process to show that the social-emotional bonding faculties of attachment, a sense of presence, and feeling safe and secure extend from the parental relationship to the child's perception of the relationship with a higher power. As parents, the ripple effect of our behavior, and the same-sameness that conflates our way with God's way, has a profound impact on our children.

Do we see our children anew each day, as full of possibility for love and goodness?

Do we delight in discoveries, insights, or new relationships found by our children?

Are we forgiving with our children when they say, "Sorry"?

Are we patient with our children, most determinedly in the moments when we feel the impulse to hurry or snap at them?

Do we express spiritual gratitude for the joys of a day at the beach, fun birthday parties, and being together on a nature hike?

Do we meet adversity or challenges as opportunities, with an expressed intention to learn and grow from them?

Do we show deep respect by refraining from gossip about others and instead talk with our children about the kindness, strengths, and goodness in others?

Do we teach the importance of relationships with fellow living beings?

How we speak and act shapes our child's sense of relationship with his higher power. In the most basic sense it trains his emotional sensors to perceive a spiritual presence in the world. The felt love of a mother, as the child sits next to her in prayer during religious services, extends to the love felt for the higher power in prayer itself.

Walking in the park, when we explicitly say, "The mama duck loves her baby as I love you," the child taps a deeply sensed feeling of kinship with all fellow living beings, all babies and mamas. It becomes clear to a child that we live in a naturally loving universe. Love is all around and is a common denominator for all.

Hello, God, It's Me: Spiritual Bonding Can Be Direct and Potent

Parent bonding and transcendent relationships are intertwined. But the usual same-sameness correspondence between parent and higher power is not the only way. For some youth, faced with no loving parents or not even a loving parent figure, there is an opportunity to fill the empty bucket of parenting affection and constancy instead through a direct relationship with God or the universe.

Granqvist and Kirkpatrick also found that in the relatively more rare cases of absence of parental love, such as a dead parent or a severely mentally disturbed, hostile parent, a child may cut directly to the higher power and literally seek and fulfill much of the needs of parenting. This pathway to transcendence the researchers called *compensation*. The child can fill the empty bucket of parental love with transcendent love. When there is no human to provide that constancy, he can get that rock-solid sense of security and safety from his higher power.

Often transcendent compensation occurs through a specific religious or spiritual figure, like Mary or Jesus in the Christian faith, or, as in many religions, God as a father figure, or the ultimate creator. This *spiritual bonding* appears across diverse faith traditions and even outside of religious denominations. Antoine Vergote and Alvaro Tamayo, two Italian researchers, have chronicled internal images of religious figures across cultural and faith traditions. Very often the relationship with the higher power combines elements of both an embracing mother and a safe, authoritative (not authoritarian) father as an inner image of the transcendent relationship.

Sometimes the companionship and guidance of the transcendent relationship can counteract the negative mental health impact of relatively poor or absent parenting. In our study on a diverse sample of more than six hundred adolescents, those teens whose parents were harsh rather than loving often turned instead to the transcendent relationship. This relationship compensated for about 60 to 70 percent of the negative impact posed by the erratic or insensitive parent. In other studies on youth with harsh parents, a transcendent relationship is associated with a 40 to 70 percent reduction in severity of depression.

The intertwined nature of the transcendent relationship and the parent highlights the spiritual presence—the presence of the higher power—in attachment and close relational love. Parenting alone does not fully create the transcendent relationship, but it profoundly hones, shapes, and cultivates the transcendent relationship. It may be that the spiritual direction contained in parenting, in the nod, helps cultivate the transcendent relationship even at the level of our brain.

The role of spiritual parenting and the nod in the transmission of spiritual direction harkens back to the work of Harvard psychiatrist George

Vaillant, for whom transcendence is primarily relational—existing fore-most in our human relationships. He goes further to focus on parenting as the ultimate source of this formation, and the ultimate opportunity for human spiritual love. Vaillant focuses on maternal bonding—specifically the impact of hormones (such as oxytocin) and the neurophysiology of bonding that include the mirror neurons in the anterior insula and ante-rior cingulate cortex (parts of the brain found deep within the cerebral cortex) and other specialized cells—as the developmental bedrock for the highly spiritual emotions of compassion and empathy. For Vaillant, pa-rental attachment is the honing of our natural capacity for compassion, which is to him the central source of spirituality. He proposes that the practice of compassion "yields intimations of transcendence."

It is worth noting that similar brain wiring for empathy and com-passion, wiring that includes mirror neurons and other specialized cells, is found in dolphins and whales, who even have more of these cells than humans! (We all have heard remarkable dolphin stories of care for and saving of human lives.) Wiring for empathy is also found in fellow primates, such as orangutans and apes, as well as in cows, sheep, and dogs. All this neuroanatomical sameness further suggests that compassion is present beyond humans. The classic mama-baby picture across species speaks to us for a very deep reason. When we teach children about mama-baby love in animals, it isn't just a sweet metaphor: evidence sug-gests strongly that animals share real love.

The Nod Passes the Torch of Spiritual Values in Everyday Life

As we know now, everyone is born with an inherent spirituality, a nat-ural sense of transcendence. It is the child's endowed nature to feel tran-scendence in and through daily life: her bright love for people and animals, her sense of life as sparkling and numinous. Life is spiritually infused for the child.

But a child usually stays aware of the spiritual infusion through the direction and engagement of a parent (or parent figure). Spiritual parenting, through the nod, integrates natural spirituality with the embodied practice of daily living. The integration of natural spirituality means that the child learns how to access the transcendent relationship deliberately, by watching the parent for support and guidance.

Whether through prayer, meditation, nature, or spontaneous opening of the heart, a parent opens the door for the child to experience the spiritual significance in daily life. The parent is the ambassador showing awareness of spiritual presence. We can give them a language for spiritual expression in whatever way we find comfortable:

"I don't have all the answers, but I know that there is a great loving energy to this world, to our lives, something beyond anything we alone could invent. We are partners with a higher presence. And we are here for a higher purpose."

"As I meditate I can feel my heart opening up and the flow of love around us, and in our family. Do you want to join me?"

"Our hikes are so special. From up here on the hilltop, I can see that the world is beautiful, and is actually built to be peaceful and abundant."

"I feel the great love of creation, of God, alive right here in our family!"

Integration also includes a spiritual sense of who we all are, really. Is the man bellowing on the subway a "crazy bum" or a soul on earth? Is the awkward child at school "a joke" or "a loser" or a soul on earth? Who is inside the outer shell of the body, perhaps trapped by physical or mental challenges? Who we are, what other people are, and how to behave toward each other: these all link to natural spirituality through the nod, through a parent's inspired guidance. The nod of spiritual parenting is how we put our own inherent transcendence into play here on earth, and it lasts forever for the child. Once there, that connection is always available to your child, and, as we will see later in the book, it is crucial for spiritual development in the second decade.

The nod sends a daily and consistent message that the transcendent is in us, through us, and around us. The nod points the way toward how to live as an embodied spirit on inspired ground—to sit next to the man on the subway and treat him like a soul. The nod, as I explain to children, is parental love and the higher power love all mixed together. As one of my graduate students said to me, "My grandma loved me so much and taught me. So God and my grandmother are all rolled up into one."

Selective Spiritual Socialization: A Child's Reach for Spiritual Connection

The power of the nod—the passing of the spiritual torch from elder to younger—was illuminated for me by the compassionate "grandmother-and-granddaughter royal couple" on the subway that Sunday twenty years ago. But in a broader sense, the transmission of spirituality through the joint effect tells us that the child is wired for shared spirituality. The child looks among available parent figures for the nod, the spiritual guidance through a loving relationship.

Adolescents generally are out and about in the world and have greater access to these spiritually significant others. Young children can only draw from what is available, so we need to make spirituality available, either through a religious community or by making ourselves available and sharing with them our own authentic spirituality, whatever that may be. If we do, as steady, loving, trustworthy spiritual parent-figures, the child connects with and grows into the bright *feeling* of her own spiritual faculty arousing. I have seen children, tweens, and teens from homes with addicts for parents or absent parents, once given the chance, immediately connect to a youth minister or youth worker—someone who offers a clear spiritual message.

One thirteen-year-old girl at a church youth group told me, "*This* is my family! Right here. You see, my mother is addicted, so I found Reverend Juan, and then I started coming. Then I started bringing my little brother, the two of us together. We live here according to God. This here is our family."

In my clinical practice, in conversations with children for my research, and as a mother immersed in the world of young children and teens, I have heard similar stories from boys and girls as young as eight or so, who have a parent who is an alcoholic, or severely and chronically depressed, or for other reasons is emotionally unavailable to them. They often find their spiritual "parent" in the extended family or community. Some find that soulful connection in nature.

A Lakota woman told me that her parents were drug users and that from the time she was a very young girl, it was her grandmother who was her connection to spirit. Then when she was fourteen years old, her grandmother died and she had no one. But she was Lakota and, having been raised with the Lakota reverence for nature, with the foundational awareness of "all my relations" in nature, she felt a special closeness with a towering old oak near their home. When she yearned for her grandmother, or simply felt the need for comfort of a spiritual kind, she said, "I would climb up, up high in the oak and talk to the tree. That tree raised me."

She found spiritual parenting through that tree. As I've mentioned, a single loving, caring parent figure can positively inform selective spiritual socialization. That is, we tend to internalize the healthy spirituality—we intuitively know the truth and the good—and then derive the benefits of spirituality from that healthy parenting figure. For fourteen years the Lakota woman's healthy "parent" had been her grandmother, and when her grandmother died it was a tree who raised her.

Our ongoing research on thousands of emerging adults—more than four thousand college students—confirms that a direct relationship like the Lakota woman's with nature or a higher power, protects like a parent's love against the perils and sufferings in the first two decades. It also supports formation of the positive traits that have been associated with life success and satisfaction, like optimism and grit.

Selective spiritual socialization shows us that children naturally seek a healthy spiritual connection. Some children find direct spiritual access to a higher power—they talk to God or feel a transcendent guiding presence through nature. Our research on both depression and thriving has shown that any and all of these nods, these spiritually infused relationships—with a loving parent or other parental figure, with nature as a transcendent guiding presence, or with God—can be protective in adolescence and beyond.

When I think about selective spiritual socialization, I often think of my son, Isaiah, who spent the initial ten months of his life in an orphanage. The morning we arrived to bring Isaiah home from "Babies House" orphanage north of St. Petersburg, he was full of delight and affection. The caretakers, who were loving and proud of their work, explained, "He knew that today was special, he got up early and was excited." Isaiah was in touch with the birthright of natural spirituality, and already within his first year had forged the sacred relationship—without a parent. The nod came at times from his loving caregivers. Perhaps there were also times during this parental absence when he went directly to God. Once home, the nod was the context of our family, and Isaiah's direct relationship with his higher power flourished. Sometimes at bedtime I would stand outside his door listening. Rather than cry, Isaiah would talk to himself about the beauty of the day, musing at night, "Blue, Water-Moon." By sixteen months old, he would open the porch door at night, look up to the stars, and yell, "Thank you, God!"

Unconditional Love *Is* Spiritual Parenting

So many parents tell me that they aren't spiritual, or don't think of themselves as spiritual, or that they're not spiritual *enough*. But ask them if they love their child and the answer is a passionate *yes!* Worry not, because pure selfless and unconditional love goes a long way. In fact, strong and healthy parental love can fill much of the spiritual developmental need. Unconditional love *is* spiritual parenting.

Several years ago I had a graduate research assistant who was helping to interpret our data on the transmission of spirituality from parents to adolescents. Ora, a young woman in her early twenties, explained to me that she and her parents had escaped Soviet Russia as refusenik Jews and immigrated to Canada. She said that throughout her childhood in the USSR, her parents had never mentioned their religion in public, rarely in private, and that her father had vehemently denied his Judaism to colleagues, and even to his closest friends and family. Ora sensed that she was Jewish, and naturally adopted the idea that something about her religion was dangerous and forbidden, both inside and outside of her home. Though her father's motivation was to protect his daughter from the persecution that may have resulted had she been known to be Jewish, he didn't realize that when he expelled religion from their home, he also put an end to any discussion about transcendence with his daughter and unwittingly encouraged her to put an end to her own spiritual awakening. But there was a hitch.

"I am very spiritual nonetheless," Ora eagerly explained to me. "Why? Because my father just really, really loved me. I mean he absolutely adored me. The way that his love felt, I now feel a similar feeling, it's that feeling, from God."

Ora's story beautifully illustrates what my research on the link between parental affection and their offspring's spirituality has shown. In predicting the degree of personal spirituality in the young adult, two factors contribute equally: (1) the parents' own spirituality and (2) unconditional parental love and affection.

In Ora's case, her father's denial of religion and spirituality was much compensated for by his unconditional love, which gave Ora a foundation for exploring her spirituality later. Ora's story is consistent with research findings: when parents show children deep love, this, too, supports them on their spiritual path.

The essential developmental support that parents are uniquely positioned to provide includes early exposure, awareness, and cultivation of our spiritual assets, time and space, nature, a vocabulary, and a spiritual social context. As parents, we are biologically equipped to assume the role of spiritual ambassador, by introducing our child to the spiritual dimension and joining in the conversation as a loving, open guide.

You can do this—just loving your child openly and honestly helps develop their natural spirituality. Because they experience transcendence through the same apparatus through which they experience your love, your unconditional affection is a big step in the right direction. And maybe you'll want to try to take another step.

As we'll see in the chapters ahead, spiritual parenting comes in many forms. It is in the many moments that you thoughtfully embody spiritual values, awaken your family to spiritual presence, and meet life's challenges and opportunities to deepen your child's spirituality. Science says that this is the most powerful connection you have to your child's well-being now and throughout life.

4

A SOUL ARRIVES

From the moment of birth, an infant is nature's most potent catalyst for love. "It takes a village to raise a child," the saying goes, but in the most profound sense we could say that it is the child who raises a village. An infant galvanizes all forces for good, from the devotion of parents and family, to the generosity of friends and neighbors, to the spontaneous acts of strangers who happily step forward. *Here, let me help you.*

New parents are awestruck, changed forever as a soul arrives in a small bundle of humanity no longer than your forearm. A new mother described to me "a love so bright it is blinding." A great force of love comes forth from the child.

The infant upends the world and opens our heart in ways we never imagined possible. Loving relationships deepen, opportunities for family reconciliation arise, new people come into our lives, people we know reconnect with us in new and thoughtful ways.

A child is born and so, too, a parent is born. One mom told me, "I used to barely want to get up, day after day. Now I look at her and everything is different. I have something bigger to live for. Now I have a purpose to my life." Ron, father of twenty-month-old Daniel, has moved past a decade-long struggle with alcoholism during which he faced family arguments and constant scrutiny. Now sober for six years, he says, "I still see that in their eyes, but I look at Daniel and he sees something different from everyone else. He sees me for who I really am." In addition, grandmothers and grandfathers are born with the baby's arrival, and our relationships with our own parents open into a new chapter.

A young child draws us in at the deepest level, psychologically and even neurologically, and recalibrates our orientation with one another and with life itself. "The deepness of love and joy—the gifts they brought into this world were humbling," says Jan, vividly recalling the births of her son and daughter, now in their twenties.

That is the universal truth about babies: they come bearing precious, unparalleled gifts—and the power to illuminate our lives in ways we never imagined possible. "His eyes," says Linda, as she turns so she can look straight into the beaming gaze of her four-month-old son, Gabriel. "Just the way a baby looks at you, and especially your own baby—they look at you with this sense of *you are my everything*, and that is amazing."

That look, that gaze, is innate, abundant love and it awakens the innate love in us as parents. Despite the long nights, the frustration, and the exhaustion, it is your instinct to be loving. You also know without being told that this intangible factor, your love for your child, has great power and meaning for your child now and in life to come. Your connection is your baby's first experience of relationship with a loving universe. Through you, your love is the universe, the *everything*, as Linda put it, and your relationship becomes the template for understanding of a loving universe—the first nod.

Science has yet to fully explain the phenomenon of love or even find the scientific language to hold the concept. We can with some scientific certainty talk about mirror neurons and limbic resonance, the brain's specialized capacity for processing emotional cues, and the inner states of those around us. In addition to whatever neurological explanation may eventually evolve, the loving responses that infants arouse in us can be understood in spiritual terms. That is, the power of an infant to orient us to love is a reflection of the innate, biologically based spiritual faculty we have discussed in the previous chapters. As she draws us into this deep loving connection, we can, perhaps for the first time, reach beyond what we know, and reflect.

This is the love that opens your heart as a parent. In this shared field of love many parents feel there is a hosting of something greater—a "third piece"—which they sense as a spiritual oneness between them and their child. The transcendent presence *through* the infant awakens us to our higher self and that in other people around us: to a sense of transcendence itself.

Parents often tell me that becoming a parent was the first time they ever felt anything spiritual. "I never had believed in anything, really," confesses David, a Manhattan banker, "that is, until my first child was born. Then I knew there had to be something more." Annette Mahoney and Kenneth Pargament from Bowling Green University have conducted nearly a decade of studies on what psychologists call the "sanctification" of family, the natural regard of family as sacred. Their studies have found that even among people who do not connect with a religion and who have a mild to moderate sense of spirituality, a sense of sanctification arises in marriage and, even earlier, around pregnancy. More than 80 percent of respondents said they perceived becoming a parent as inherently sacred.

Babies bring out the best in us. We don't need science to tell us that. But now that we know that natural spirituality is a biologically based faculty, we can reexamine existing research and see spiritual cognition in infants and young children—an implicitly spiritual view of reality. We can also see clearly how the spiritual faculty shapes and infuses the parent-child relationship, and why spiritual parenting is so essential to a child's earliest development.

The Science of Children's Spiritual Cognition

Like any culture, science as a human culture has inherent biases and, as we know now, these biases effectively kept researchers for most of the past century from pursuing a full scientific investigation of spiritual development in children. Today a new generation of empirically based postmaterial scientific research supports the biological basis for spirituality, upending long-held assumptions about the mental life and spiritual nature of the young child. The new science also gives us a way to reexamine existing data that is related but was not originally conducted directly on spirituality, now with a fresh interpretive eye to find insights into a child's innate spiritual faculty.

For example, in a series of elegant studies conducted over a decade at Yale, chronicled in *Just Babies: The Origins of Good and Evil*, psychologist and author Paul Bloom describes the moral development of infants. Bloom's studies found that even before they can speak or walk, babies show that they discern between what we commonly consider good (sharing, friendly) and bad (greedy, unfriendly) actions of others.

Bloom's Yale team investigated babies' capacity for moral evaluation around sharing. The researchers had five-month-old infants watch a puppet show featuring three puppets: a center puppet who played ball with two other puppets, rolling a ball to the other puppets; a puppet to the right who shared the ball by returning it, and a puppet on the left who did not share the ball and hogged it. The babies' responses to the puppets were measured by the duration of the baby's gaze at each puppet, assumed to reflect awareness of moral infraction. Then the babies were given candy to share freely with the puppets.

Bloom found that at five months old, infants both held a gaze of awareness on a nonsharing moral infraction by the puppet, yet also still shared candy equally. I consider this to be a nonpunitive regard for all puppets, irrespective of the puppet's hindering or helping behaviors.

While Bloom's studies were focused on moral development, and did not address spiritual development, we can do that now. Through a science-based spiritual lens, the babies' nonpunitive stance looks like a basic unconditional love and acceptance to me. The infants' feelings toward the puppets, so many years prior to building elaborate cognition, are noncontingent, irrespective of merit. Their hearts are generous and complete, without retribution or withholding.

Bloom, writing in *The New York Times*, notes that, "Human babies cry more to the cries of other babies than to the tape recordings of their own cry. Babies also want to assuage the pain of others. Once they have enough physical competence they soothe others in distress by stroking and touching, or by handing over a bottle or toy."

Bloom's and others' research shows that infants feel empathy and compassion and will act to soothe other infants in distress, which I call natural empathy and compassion. I am reminded of the famous story reported by Liz Townsend, of the premature twins Brielle and Kyrie Jackson, born each at about two pounds, in 1995 in central Massachusettes. When tiny Brielle's breathing and heart rate became irregular, to the point of danger, a wise nurse, Gayle Kasparian, lifted her out of her incubator to rejoin her healthy sister. Kyrie, the healthy neonate, tossed an arm over her twin, a "rescuing hug," and reportedly "instantly" Brielle's normal vital signs were restored.

I also am reminded of my son, Isaiah, who you recall had spent his infancy in the Babies House orphanage in Russia. There, the kind, loving women who cared for dozens of babies would arrange them in a circle—faces toward the center—with toys in the middle. When we arrived, we saw that the tendency to share and comfort fellow infants was evident in him and others. If a fellow baby cried, Isaiah quickly handed them the toy he had been using. The move—a quick twist of his wrist outward—was almost reflexive, except that he would at the same time look up into the other baby's face. He naturally recognized suffering and offered comfort. Others did the same.

Now we have strong data from many labs that indicates that spirituality of young children presents as a natural set of social-cognitive assumptions—cognitive dispositions, inborn perceptual tendencies, and styles of reasoning—that are foundationally spiritual. That is, a deep implicit view of who we are, what we are doing here, and our human capabilities all have the qualities of natural spirituality in a spiritual world. The data show three distinct features of natural spiritual cognition in young children.

1. An intentional, intelligent universe

The child perceives the agency in all living beings. To the child, the dog is a friend in the truest sense, feels happy or sad, and listens with understanding. A tree wants to be watered and welcomes a hug. An ant hurries home to its children. The child perceives an intentional universe, a universe that is alive and intelligent, with a guiding sense of justice and the understanding that we can become part of that to make the world safe and loving for all.

2. Parents as all-knowing with God-like omniscience

Children assume that parents are knowers, by which we mean they assume parents know everything: what's for dinner, where is Daddy, why is it raining, why is that man crying, why is the train going so slow, what did your great-grandma have for breakfast when she was a little girl? But in the child's mind, the parents not only know concrete things, the child assumes his parents are *all* knowing, all seeing. As we've seen in the same-sameness of spiritual parenting and the higher power, parents are perceived as generally carrying divine qualities. In experimental studies of young children, through age five years they have responded in ways that indicate they assume a parent will "just know" where something hidden or missing will be. The sense that our child feels we are omnipresent or omnipotent is something most parents have encountered.

3. An afterlife or nonmaterial realm

Children assume an afterlife or nonmaterial realm. Only later are they socialized out of it. In fact, in families where the culture does not teach them otherwise, children's initial assumptions of intergenerational and transcendent connection remain intact and deepen. In our own culture, I have encountered many, many children who maintain this kind of close connection with a deceased loved one—perhaps a relative or friend with whom they were close—whether they have been brought up to believe in an afterlife or not. They say a little prayer to Granddad or Grandmother when they're facing a tough moment. They feel the spirit of a deceased friend in a place that they used to spend time together. They'll sit at the grave of a pet and talk to their old companion.

Harvard neuroscientist Rudolph Tanzi and Deepak Chopra in their book, *Super Brain*, convincingly argue that the natural long-term developmental trajectory of the brain is toward enlightenment. This path is only disrupted, they posit, by our contemporary culture putting spirituality "on the back shelf." Chopra and Tanzi list in order the steps that make up the natural path to enlightenment: feeling connected, empathy, clarity, truth, and bliss. By this spiritual map, it would seem that the newborn starts at the top as she floats in a state of bliss. The core qualities of the developed adult "super brain" in fact may be much like the young child, but with the added layer of adult control, and a sort of deliberate cognitive inner reflection, choice of cultivation, over the integrated brain that only forms through adolescence and into adulthood. The deeply soulful presence of a newborn or youngster grabs our attention, shows us the realm of human possibility, and perhaps jolts us into remembering a bigger reality from our own childhood. They show us our true spiritual nature.

The young child's spiritual reality may be one that most contemplative and religious traditions help us to understand through years of practice, reflection, and faith: a perception of intention in the fabric of reality that humans know beyond what we see, and that consciousness continues beyond and outside the body. Consider the qualities we associate with the most deeply meditative state or spiritual way of being: love and compassion, mindfulness, acceptance, a sense of oneness with all, and innate connection to nature. The child starts there, in a sacred transcendent realtionship. The infant arrives with the transcendent faculty intact and completely engaged. By many adult conceptualizations of enlightenment, the young child arrives fully enlightened. Let's look at what the child's soul does—how it demonstrates enlightenment.

The Smallest Sages: Open Hearts, Open Minds, and Fully Aware

Let's start where your child does, with the open heart and open mind that distinguish the very young child from birth through about age four. Research on children entering elementary school shows that internally driven prosocial behavior and emotional sensitivity to other human beings are interrelated with awareness of transcendence and the transcendent relationship. They all seem to naturally come packaged together in young children, before socialization gets to them. In a study of 479 five-year-olds, researchers Anat Shoshani and Ilanit Aviv, at the Interdisciplinary Center in Israel, found that the degree of the child's "transcendent strengths," based upon spirituality, hope, humor, and gratitude, was more predictive of teacher's ratings on school adjustment than the child's other inborn capacities of intellect or temperament.

These prosocial traits and emotional skills have been identified as important to long-term thriving. Research also has shown they can be deliberately cultivated by parents and community and are associated with thriving and fulfillment, mental health, and better school performance starting with middle school GPAs. These are surely the values we hope our children will embrace and develop. And now research suggests that if we look anew at the central role of spirituality we may see where these values and traits come from most fundamentally. When we follow the developmental thread of these prosocial values to their origin, we discover that for many children the foundations are found in the natural spirituality of the child, which is present from birth. It's up to us to give them the nod.

As parents we can listen for our children's spiritual expression to help them embrace this part of themselves. *Does she dream vivid or emotional dreams and want to talk about them? Does he sense "vibes" in a place or in the presence of someone new? Is she curious and engaged in questions or conversations about spiritual ideas?* We can watch to see if our child is exceptionally spiritually oriented or in what way our child is spiritually perceptive so that we know who they are as spiritual beings. To disconnect a highly spiritual child from this expression is like silencing a child who naturally loves to sing or keeping a child who loves to run from going outside. To neglect this aspect of development in any child is the very opposite of our intentions as loving parents to equip them for a good life.

How do we recognize our child's natural spirituality? What are its qualities and characteristics? Children's natural spiritual qualities are remarkably similar across widely varying cultures, socioeconomic conditions, religions, communities, and families. In my research and years of experience with children and my conversations with parents, teachers, clergy, and children themselves, five strong commonalities emerge with great clarity and consistency. Think of them as five core spiritual assets. Every child begins life with these assets, through which they spontaneously experience daily life through a capacity for spiritual perception and live out natural spiritual values. When they do, we have the chance as parents to mirror with our words and attention, as we would all other dimensions of our child's discovery, the significance of what they share.

We'll see these assets interwoven as an integral part of your child's natural spiritual expression in the pages ahead, but in brief they are:

1. A natural love of spiritual ritual and prayer
2. Capacity for spiritual perception, or "heart knowing": intuitive guidance, love, and *unitive empathy*, a sense of oneness with others
3. Right action and the desire to be helpful, giving, contributing, sharing
4. An innate sense of the specialness of family

5. An affinity with nature and fascination with the life cycle: birth, growth, next generation

Children Love Ritual and Prayer

Young children naturally sense the immediacy and brightness of life and they love to pray in all ways and forms, to connect though this bright awareness. To sing, to dance and sway, to honor and make ceremony: children delight in prayer and ritual.

Children thrill at the opportunity to join in a first communion, swaying with Sufi chanting, following the Torah around the synagogue. Children naturally form their own prayers, in dance and song, and feel a transcendent dialogue with their bodies. With all of their healthy integrated being—body, mind, and soul—the child connects and relates to transcendence. If we encourage this natural relationship with transcendence—this innate ability to enjoy and share prayer, chanting, or meditation—the connection sticks.

Children naturally recognize sacred moments and build organic spiritual ceremony. A squirrel found dead on the school playground will receive a respectful burial; in winter a frozen bird is placed in a shoe box, shrouded with leaves, and carried down to the river. This shows a natural sense of sacred transition, awe for creation and its departure from the physical earth. Children's inherent respect for life shows in their actions, their own practice, ceremony, and ritual. Praying gives natural practice to what they already are experiencing. Prayer guides their natural spiritual connection and gives voice to their natural spiritual attunement with the world around them.

Children are born happy and able to pray in any faith tradition, or through a form of prayer that is shared through family outside a religious faith tradition. They unselfconsciously step right into spiritual practice, prayer, and ritual. They immediately connect, not only with ritual and songs, but from deep within.

Kathleen tells the story of her four-year-old son Dan on a family trip to a Buddhist monastery in a remote valley in California. Members of the community were painstakingly erecting a statue of the Buddha in front of the temple. Finely crafted in wood, covered in gold leaf and maroon, green, and yellow paint, the figure towered perhaps twenty-five feet tall, a powerful presence visible from nearly a mile away. In a quiet pause as they neared the work site, Kathleen says, "Dan walked straight up to the statue and stared up into its face for nearly a minute. Then he turned and sat down on the ground directly in front of it with his legs crossed, hands lying flat in his lap, palms-up, head erect and stretched toward the heavens, in exactly the posture of the Great Buddha. Everyone fell silent as we watched this four-year-old child imitating the great Teacher." Dan had never been taught to pray this way. He held the posture for more than a minute, Kathleen said, "then popped up and turned back into a kid, running and playing again." He just knew. This is natural spiritual perception at work in young children.

"Children experience the presence of God," says Shahine Travakoli, a Sufi family and marriage counselor in Houston. "They haven't lost the touch of the presence being in the moment, of God welling up in you, creating energy, beautiful energy." She describes a three-year-old Sufi girl when she came to a prayer service for the first time: in just moments she had picked up the Farsi chants and prayer movements. "How quickly the spirit came over her—her ability to catch up so quickly just blew my mind," Travakoli says. In such moments, "children never say, 'who is God?' or 'where is God?' because they do not question that. They feel the situation, they have no need to ask or search for it. They feel it within them and the presence is there with them, and then they gradually begin to move and sway with it."

The rabbi of a Jewish congregation in a community full of young families describes the joyful ritual of the Shabbat service Torah processional, in which the congregation sings a lively chant as the sacred scrolls are carried high, welcoming anyone who wants to join in to do so. Children are ever eager to join the procession, dancing and singing. "I just see them happy, their joyousness, how they sing along when they're young," Rabbi

Shaul Marshall Praver says. "Something happens after fourth grade and it's not cool anymore. Before that, they dance, sing, they're very free and uninhibited with their feelings, still in the garden, innocent babies."

Many parents who aren't religiously active but once were so as children remember how they were moved or delighted by the music and singing and sense of joyful activity of religious rituals and practices, and they want to provide that for their children. Regardless of religious engagement, traditions and rituals that celebrate the sanctity of family, friendship, and community cultivate a child's spiritual sense, as well. Thanksgiving and New Year's observances, birthdays, anniversaries, or a family walk in the woods—even a nightly ritual of a bedtime story and a good night hug and kiss—all of these strengthen the spiritual connection when grounded in love and appreciation.

JUMPING INTO PRAYER

When your child asks to pray, say, "Oh yes!" This is a very big moment that is of deep value to him. He is eager to connect with the ultimate source of all life, to be appreciative or to talk to the larger world, or the loving world, or a bright God—however you feel comfortable envisioning the association.

- The young child naturally knows how to pray, but is also eager to learn how you do it. When you sense his hunger to learn about prayer, ask if you might say a prayer together, if this feels comfortable.
- Show an interest in their experience and freely share your own, by saying, *What did you feel?* or *Did you feel the loving brightness?* or *It feels so good to say thank you!* or *I love connecting!*
- Some prayers are in words, others in song. Some prayers are prayers of action, such as volunteering in the community or

collecting towels to donate to the animal shelter. You can suggest to your child that this is sacred, too: we can feel it in our hearts. Even when they already know it, it still feels good to hear it confirmed.

Young Children Are Mindful

Awareness of our world is sacred. A well-known Sabbath prayer calls us to pay attention: "*Days pass and the years vanish and we walk sightless among miracles . . .*" It ends with asking for God (or spirit, by any other name) to illuminate the path upon which we walk.

Infants and young children are inherently mindful: present and totally alert to life. While the rest of us struggle to practice mindfulness, radical unconditional acceptance, mind-body-spirit integration, and unconditional love, young children are already there.

Once your newborn opens her eyes at just a few weeks old to take in the world with singular intention, make eye contact and her gaze can stop you in your tracks. Your infant finishes exploring your car keys, opens his hands and *plop!* they hit the ground. He opens his hand and releases the previous concern, moving unfettered into the next moment of life. Once the keys are gone, they are out of mind. Now, if you pick the keys up and place them within reach again, he is likely to grab them and drop them again—throughout it all, mindful, totally "in the moment." A few years older, at three or four years old, when they are fixed on us—or on anything else—they are focused with 100 percent attention—*right now, right now, right now, Mama!*

Well-established research into mindfulness training and meditation among school-aged and adolescent youth shows that practices to improve mindfulness are effective in calming emotions, focusing attention, and relieving anxiety. Mindfulness also is the gateway to the form of engagement—integrating mind, body, and spirit—that increases spiritual awareness and can lead to a spiritual path.

My doctoral student, Sarah Zoogman, together with our colleagues at the University of Wisconsin, conducted a research study in which we pooled all of the research on mindfulness with youth to date, to summarize the helpful effects of mindfulness practices. (This is called a meta-analysis or quantitative study of studies.) The body of findings showed that mindfulness meditation programs delivered in schools and community settings indeed increase awareness and attention for children and teens. They also increase prosocial behaviors, improve school performance, and ameliorate symptoms of anxiety and depression. When it comes to alleviating symptoms of depression, mindfulness appears to be especially helpful to those most in need: more than twice as helpful for those adolescents who are in clinical settings with more severe symptoms of depression.

The good news is that mindfulness can readily be cultivated in children in large part because they are born with the skill. The bad news: the youth in the study, and most kids by elementary school age, have already been socialized out of a naturally mindful way of being. Focus and attention in children are cultivated in long silences and introspective moments. The frenzied pace and fractured attention of days spent rushing to multiple afterschool classes, and too much time on screens, crowds out the space for the natural formation of this gateway to spiritual awareness. Children and teens need time to watch the bee and sit with the tree, let their minds wander and wonder, and engage what neuroscientists call the "default mode," essentially a time of reflective reverie and a mental housecleaning. Kids need time to declutter their inner space to make room for discovery.

But younger children start fresh, without any interference, and if supported, the intense temporal presence of the young child allows for an open field of spiritual perception in which far more can be seen, felt, and understood. The young child needs no training in mindfulness. Rather, she needs protection from the disruption of focus, from exposure to spinning or running thoughts, from rushing, and from lack of peaceful moments. By allowing and cultivating peaceful moments, we encourage mindfulness.

MINDFULNESS OPENS THE DOOR FOR SPIRITUAL AWARENESS

Science shows that mindfulness can be the gateway to spiritual discovery. We can encourage mindfulness in the many ways we communicate through ideas and actions:

- "Being" is worthy and it counts. We do not need to be always "doing" to have value in life. Say so and show it by your actions.
- Hold open space for your child to fill. Allow your child to sit or enjoy imaginative play and exploration in the backyard and "just be" in that natural environment. Create similar opportunities in your home and family time.
- Slow down the family pace. Allow life to come forward. Your child learns to attend, builds awareness, and sees more when there's time to look around.
- Ease up on directives to "rush" and "hurry" (when not crucial) to get into the car for an organized class at the gym or art studio. This teaches that it is the journey, not the pace, that is most valuable.
- Encourage exploration and awe. Touch the tree, stroke the flower's stalk, note the smell of the air. Appreciate when your child observes the lamppost or yellow line in the parking lot, wants to touch the dead leaf, or sees the flower sprouting from the crack in the pavement. Pause to note the wonder.

Let your child walk in circles or patterns of their own making as they so often wish to do. Think of the labyrinth, the time-honored spiritual tool of cloister gardens. Your child was born to walk her own spiritual path. This is natural mindfulness at work, strengthening the spiritual faculty.

As parents, we may even start to notice more going on in the parking lot, too!

Helpers, Healers, and Little Beings of Service

Stone Soup is a popular folktale with young children around the world. In its many iterations in different cultures, it is essentially the story of two hungry travelers who are completely penniless and have nothing they can trade or use to buy a meal in the village where they stop. After their earnest requests for food are turned down, they take a different tack, borrow a pot, fill it with water and a stone, and place it over a cook fire. As curious passers-by stop to ask what's in the pot, the two fellows describe a magical soup in the making that needs only one more ingredient to be perfect. One by one the villagers run home and return with an ingredient to contribute. The story ends happily with all the villagers joining the travelers to share the soup, which is indeed magical in how it transforms a community of closed hearts into open ones. On a recent visit to a preschool, I heard this story shared with the children. For my visit, I had also brought along potatoes, carrots, peas, corn, green beans, and an onion.

Each child sat eagerly as the teacher started a soup pot, and an older student volunteer began to read. At each turn in the story, as a villager contributed an ingredient to the soup, one of the children would step up with his or her contribution from home and into the pot it went.

Throughout the story, the teacher paused and invited discussion. How would you respond to someone coming to your door to ask for food? The children were a bit wary about the notion of strangers at the door, but when it came to the question of feeding the hungry they were unanimous.

"I would give them food."

"I have enough to share."

At different intervals the teacher also asked whether a particular action by a character could be considered mean or kind, and the children sorted those out, debating a bit about tone of voice and what constitutes good manners. Said one little girl: "I would just tell them if you have a nice voice you can have what you want, but please don't say it in a mean voice." Ultimately they were very clear on what constitutes meanness and kindness. When the teacher asked, "If you fed them because they were hungry, would that be an act of meanness or kindness?" they sang out in unanimous chorus: "Kindness! Kindness! Kindness!"

Young children delight in meaningful work and contribution. They are naturally motivated by and have enthusiasm for right action. They naturally want to help and love doing for others. This is spiritual "right action" and we are as a species designed not only for "fight or flight" but also to "tend and befriend."

At another preschool, Earthplace in Connecticut, the teachers talk to the students about acts of kindness or generosity as "filling your bucket with love." Teacher Kerry shared with me the story of Tagen, three years old, who watched one day as his classmate Tina struggled to get into her winter coat to go play outside. He watched another friend go up to Tina and help her zip her jacket. "And then he comes over to me just in his nonchalant way as we are getting ready to go outside and he goes, 'Mrs. Peterson, Tina is getting her bucket filled over there.'"

Our children are born with the unitive empathy of love and connection, hardwired for loving connection. This does not mean that not wanting to share is outside of our nature. We are mixed bags. Unitive empathy can go side by side with selfishness and greed. There is playroom squabbling over sharing Thomas the Train. One moment your four-year-old is grabbing the biggest slice of a cake at a birthday party, the next he is giving another child his last cherished apple slice or bestowing upon his new infant sibling his most treasured toy. It is essential to see that inherently we have both sides, and if we build our positive assets, we have a far-enhanced inner landscape through which to relate and ultimately thrive in the world.

Nursery children happily pick up on the classroom culture of love; it is their natural way, too. As one teacher said, "They throw the same kindness that you give to them back to you." And they pass it along, as young Poppy showed one morning at school.

At two and a half years old, Poppy was quite proud that she was becoming adept at using the toilet independently at nursery school. One day during a bathroom break her teacher left Poppy sitting on the toilet for a moment and asked her to stay put—the door open—while the teacher briefly helped another child nearby. When the teacher turned back she saw that Poppy had finished and was now instructing a younger boy to come have his diaper changed. She was pulling the step stool from the sink into position for him at the changing table and was coaching him for the climb up. All the while Poppy was directing she had yet to pull up her own underwear and tights. The teacher continues:

> I ran into the bathroom and I said, "Poppy, let me help you," and she goes, "No, no, no, I am helping you!" So she is pulling the stool over and assisting him to climb up and he is doing it—he is listening to her and he is getting ready to get changed! And then I looked at her—tights and everything were down as she's walking. I said to her, "Poppy, that is kind of dangerous." She said, "But I was helping!" Little tears started coming down my eyes and I said, "Let me give you a hug, a really good hug. Thanks for helping me, but that's a teacher's job, not one of your jobs." She said, "Okay, okay," and I said, "Now, can I help you with your underwear and everything?" She said, "No thanks. I am a big girl. I am almost going to be three and I know how to do this myself."

These are the contributions of goodness of heart by your young child. They eagerly create right action, a universal expression of spirituality. Buddhism calls right conduct or right action *samyak-karmanta*. Christian faiths call it "mercy and charity." Jews call it *tikkun olam*, fixing the world. We can acknowledge our children's natural expression of right action, appreciate their generous spirits, and "use our words" to tell them so.

ENCOURAGE YOUR YOUNG CHILD'S GENEROUS SPIRIT

- Let your young child take the lead on meaningful work. Your toddler can be the first into the homeless shelter door presenting the pie.
- Let your child plan and cook special holiday meals for the family, arrange decorations or preparations of family traditions and religious holidays.
- Help your child in serving or supporting others in ordinary ways: catching the door, allowing others with fewer groceries to go first in line at the checkout.
- The eighteen-month-old child can visit the nursing home and enjoy being together with the residents, her presence and contribution lighting up smiles.

Beyond Words: Heart Knowing Bonds Us Parent to Child

The circle of nursery school parents sits wide-eyed, eager to talk, holding coffees just after morning drop-off. I have been invited to the school to share the science of the spiritual brain with parents of young children, but I'm delighted to find that these parents are eager to make it personal; they want to discuss their own preschoolers' spirituality, or what they describe as an ultimately loving and connected, seemingly enlightened or bigger "otherworldly" quality about them.

Stories pour forth, as parents lean over the table. "My son Adam, he just knows what I am thinking," one mom says. "We'll be driving along, Adam in the car seat, and I just look into the rearview mirror, and our eyes connect, and we are right in the same place. You can almost feel a physical connection between us." Another mom, Carrie, jumps in: "If I'm sad, then Ella, she knows it, she comes right up to me and puts her hands on my head, and says, 'What's wrong, Mommy? That's all right, Mommy.'" We all nod in the shared understanding that mother and child—or father and child—are connected so very deeply that we sense one another's feelings, whether we are physically touching, in the same room, or at a distance. The bond is powerful and real, felt well beyond physical space and time.

"You know, it just feels like there's this psychic spiritual connection between us that flows very naturally back and forth," says Melissa of her four-year-old daughter, Clara. Every morning over breakfast, Clara likes to tell her mother about her dreams of the night before. One night after Clara was tucked into bed, Melissa sat up late reading a haunting essay by the New England poet Mary Oliver, who on a walk on a Cape beach had discovered the remains of a dolphin. She had carefully studied the remains and in the essay had reflected on the creature's life and death. In the morning, when Clara bounded down for breakfast. Melissa greeted her as usual. "I said, 'So, Clara, what were your dreams last night?' And she said, 'Oh, Momma, I had a dream about dolphins last night.'"

When my older daughter, Leah, was an infant and routinely sleeping through the night, sometimes I would suddenly awaken at 2:30 A.M. or 4:30 A.M., with a sense of rising anxiety. Thirty seconds later, from her room across the house, would come her cry. Parents of older children have told me similar stories of feeling this sudden wave of inexplicable awareness of their child sometimes very far away, followed shortly by a phone call or contact from them.

We see this so-called *sympathetic harmonic resonance* in other realms—strike a C note on one stringed instrument and the note will resonate in another stringed instrument across the room. Child and parent are attuned to one another, both as senders and receivers, well beyond physical sight, sound, or touch. This phenomenon is the unitive state, a shared experience between child and parent.

Sometimes the child enacts the role of helper and healer. Beth shared in a discussion following our group of nursery school parents how "Kaly just knows me. She wants to protect me. I had the worst round ever in the divorce with Kaly's father. I was sacked. I put her to bed and went to bed myself, and just quietly cried and cried, silently into the pillow so that there was no way Kaly could hear. I fell asleep and when I woke up a few hours later, I looked toward the door and there was Kaly sleeping at the threshold. As if she were a lion or a dog protecting me."

Findings have shown that mirror neurons help us feel what those we love are feeling, sometimes even the same physical sensations. Now some novel science shows this to be true even at a distance. The pioneering physician, researcher, and author Larry Dossey has been at the fore of bringing this one-mind unitive knowing into the realm of healing and the medical profession. As the former head of the Medical City Dallas Hospital, it was Dossey who more than twenty years ago coined the term "nonlocal mind" in the context of medicine and healing. Dossey explains the nonlocal mind as an aspect of spiritual experience that is part of "a larger, encompassing mode of consciousness" within direct knowing.

Dossey's claims on the reach of loving and healing intention gain support from meta-anlaysis on the positive effects of loving, healing prayer on behalf of others, as well as MRI studies on mirror neurons, most strikingly one on traditional healers and patients. A research team in Hawaii led by Jeanne Achterberg and colleagues ran fMRI on traditional healers at work and simultaneously on the patient located in a different room. As the healer started to work, a distinct pattern emerged in the fMRI that moments later appeared identical in the fMRI of the patient down the hall.

These studies showing shared fMRI readings between bonded people, even at a distance, have yet to be conducted specifically on the ultimate bond of mother and child, but the body of literature suggests that we'll find a similar pattern. We are very connected with people we love. Heart knowing by parent and child is not a conventional cognitive knowing, but a knowing in and through relationship and love. When we validate our child's heart knowing, we encourage the child's awareness of the higher self, the part of us that sees wisdom and clarity unencumbered by limitations of a situation in the moment.

HEART KNOWING FORMS A NATURAL BOND WITH OUR CHILDREN

How can we encourage our children's heart knowing in their earliest years? Simple ways are best:

- Share your intuitive feelings with your child and encourage her to share hers openly, as well.

    When you were just a baby, I would always wake up just before you woke up and cried, so I was already on my way.
- Acknowledge that you have a special bond.

    Even when you're away at school we're always connected heart to heart—that's forever!

    Our family bonds are so strong that we sense each other's needs, sometimes even before anybody asks!
- Let your child know that you value his or her intuitive sense and heart knowing.

    You have a wonderful feeling of knowing—you just sense what is going on, when it is important!

A Child's Close Personal Relationship with Nature and "All Relations"

Children are entranced by nature. They love the smallest caterpillar and the giant oak. All things in nature are assumed part of the family. This natural curiosity is human, and the sense of a caring relationship with all living beings is spiritual. Children have a natural spiritual attunement with the world around them: they relate to animals, trees, and the life that happens when adults are distracted by the demands of the day. We see their connection to nature in how they respond to the core elements of nature: the seasons, the cycle of renewal in the face of death, the urge for healing and rejuvenation. Engage them. Children meet nature as they find it.

The year after Hurricane Sandy struck the East Coast, Madeleine, the mother of two young sons, shared just such a story. The graceful stand of trees in Madeleine's backyard had been no match for Hurricane Sandy. Where Patrick, five, and John, three, had played in the shade the summer before, now was a muddy gash of earth, the more than half-dozen trees gone and nothing yet growing in the tracks of the storm's destruction. Mother and sons sat together one afternoon snacking on apples as they surveyed the ruined yard from the kitchen table. Suddenly Patrick took a seed from his apple and said to his three-year-old brother John, "Can I have your seed?" Then he asked his mom for a seed from her apple, too. Madeleine continues:

So he takes these three seeds in his little palm and he goes into the backyard and starts digging, and John and I are looking at him, and John says, "What is he doing?" I didn't know. We go over to see and Patrick had put these seeds in the ground and he says, "I'm going to plant an apple tree since we don't have any trees left back here." Then John ran back in the house, found four more apples and . . . you know, I wasn't going to stop them. I wasn't going to tell them, "Oh, by the way, it's going to take a little more than that

to grow an apple tree." (*She laughs.*) But I thought it was so wonderful. I think they felt a sense that they wanted to see some sort
of growth back there. And every morning since then, they look
out the window and say, "I think I see some sprouts," and I just
answer, "Do you? Keep an eye on it."

The young child is born with this assumed relationship with all of
nature, from goslings to galaxies. Buddhist thought holds that "at the
most fundamental level of life itself, there is no separation between ourselves and the environment." Children look to any living being and wonder, "What is she like?" and envision starting a relationship. I remember
a day in the park when I was walking with Isaiah, then sixteen months
old. He was enthusiastically trotting toward a gaggle of yellow baby geese
as an invitation to play. Suddenly the protective angry mother goose hissed
and charged, not at little Isaiah, but she turned ninety degrees to face me
with her scolding. She knew I was the mom and that I was being negli-
gent toward the security of her children. Yet, for Isaiah, it was as natural for him to greet the goslings as it would have been for him to engage
with any child in the park.

Chief Luther Standing Bear of the Lakota Sioux wrote of his people's
deep reverence for nature as the source of life, growth, and wisdom—
"a mothering power"—and of their sacred duty to bring their children
into the same relationship with it. The Lakota speak of "all my relations" to include the family of every living being. It is my view that all
children intuitively approach the world filled by "all my relations," turning to animals and plants in relationship unless or until we teach them
otherwise with comments such as, "Yuck, a bug!" or "Don't go near the
duck—it's dirty!" Instead, consider focusing on the natural capacity
children have for relationship with animals: "Look, this beautiful insect
wants to be your friend," or "Duck is interested—he wonders, what are
you doing?"

Children show us this oneness with nature and animals in so many
ways. They talk to animals, not "as if" the animals can understand them,

but rather in direct communication with them. Maggie's son Jason talks to animals and tells them what he thinks they need to know. "I'm driving the car and he's leaning his head out the window, warning the birds, 'Be careful of the telephone wire!'" she says.

At Earthplace one morning during the daily class walk, four or five children follow a woolly caterpillar on their path. They all go down on their hands and knees and examine it closely but nobody hurts it. They move aside as it makes its way down the path, and when the children think it might be in search of leaves, they bring it some. They want to see if the caterpillar will eat them, and when it doesn't, they continue to back out of the way for it to continue its crawl to the nearby garden.

A mother tells me of her five-year-old son who loves to sit on the back porch and watch the ants, and how one day he admonished her to slow down and watch out so she wouldn't step on them. "They have families," he explained. "Think what it must be like to be an ant!"

In their book, Chopra and Tanzi tell of Chopra meeting a noted neuroscientist who told him that she was more comfortable in the world of birds than in the world of people. Like others we've come to know for their remarkable empathic way with animals, this neuroscientist's nervous system was attuned to birds, they explained.

A decade ago the claim would have seemed flaky. How can someone think like a dog, the way Cesar Millan does, or like a horse, the way Monty Roberts, the original horse whisperer, does? The answer is sensitivity and empathy. Being self-aware, we can already extend ourselves to how other people feel. . . . You can train a dog or a horse almost effortlessly if you whisper in their language, without using whips, muzzle, or mistreatment.

Children identify deeply with animals, not only as their protectors but as kindred spirits. Animals have traits that we also have—ferociousness, fear, tenderness, vulnerability—and children naturally find in them an embodied vocabulary for their own emotions and energies that might otherwise be remote or perhaps overwhelm them. These are spiritual concerns: understanding ourselves, understanding our place in the world, understanding our emotions and ways of being. By encouraging and keeping these outlets of expression open, we encourage the spiritual interface and the possibility for future growth.

When your child licks your arm and says, "I am a cat!" she is not just mimicking, she is trying to experience being a cat. Your daughter is discovering her cat-likeness, much as she dresses up like Mommy to discover you. Your toddler delights in making animal noises: "A sheep says *baaa!*" or "The little chick says *peep peep peep!*" This is not vocalizing sounds as a spectator but as a participant in the animal kingdom. The kindredness of humans and animals is natural and fluid to children. In that alchemy of spirit they are able to safely explore a full range of emotions that animals hold; animals are their teachers. As the tiger, the young child can build courage and confidence.

The summer Isaiah was four, he spent every day splashing and playing in the river by our home. He didn't need toy boats or floaties; he loved to touch the waves and dig in the earth, and talk to frogs, connecting with, as the Lakota say, "all our relations." Then one July day, while running near the river, a bee stung Isaiah on the foot. The pain was new, shocking, and unexpected from a relation!

Isaiah went inside distressed and became even more befuddled, departing the river in the middle of the day, the only time he did so all summer. After about an hour of contemplation, Isaiah came back outside. "Mommy," he said, staring right in my eyes, "if a bee stings Buddha, what does Buddha do?" I did not have an answer. So I went with the child as the source. "Tell *me*, Isaiah, if a bee stings Buddha, what does Buddha do?" With a twinkle of delight in his eye and a little grin, he explained, "Nothing! Buddha does nothing!" and then skipped back to the river.

The child seeks and finds spiritual teachings in nature, watching and listening for its nod. As parents, we do not need answers; we simply need to stay genuinely fascinated and say, "Yes!" to the child's knowing. Nature (as many spiritual traditions note) answers the child's questions. As Rabbi Praver said, nature "puts us in spiritual alignment." Isaiah had the answer to the bee sting—he figured out the natural order. The bee only knows to sting. The sting was not an action of aggression, only the bee's nature. We do not need to meet a sting with violence, merely know its nature. Nature does this for all of us. It helps us see the larger picture, our place in it, and our place in relation to other living things.

Where a child's human family or community have fallen short of love, animals can be a loving and healing force. Seen with the perspective of the concepts of the nod and selective spiritual selection, nature can be a child's direct link with a universal spirit. As parents, teachers, and mental health providers, we can encourage these loving relationships as real and healing. For example, a respected residential treatment center in New York State for angry and acting-out boys, some of whom are survivors of mistreatment, requires upon admission that each and every boy become the primary caretaker for a wild animal. When they meet their animal for the first time, the boys are surprised to discover that each animal has been wounded by something made by humans. A wing torn in a power line or hit by a car; damage that the majestic wild being did not incur in the natural order. The boy's job is to clean the cage, offer food and water, and care for the physical needs of the animal. However, time and time again, most of the boys start to talk with the animal, checking in several times a day with what seems to be a deep identification. Not by projecting their own woundedness but by feeling a shared woundedness, they develop a connection of the heart. Animals are teachers, healers, and true friends to children.

Marta's four-year-old daughter becomes "tiger girl" when she is feeling drawn to that fierce energy. For that moment she finds her spirit match in the tiger and sees the world through her tiger eyes and senses. From children's literature to the living room, we see children's vibrant sense of oneness with their animal mentors. Even the parents can feel the wake of the animal nature surging in the child and have the opportunity to support this connection: *Yes, you are tiger! What does tiger feel? What does tiger say?*

ENCOURAGE YOUR CHILD TO HONOR NATURE AND ANIMALS AS TEACHERS

Savor and celebrate with your child the many different animal personalities, voices, and ways of being. Build the authentic relationship with living beings.

See the mama bird feed her baby the way I fed you?

This little frog leaping reminds me of the way that you run and jump when you play!

Look, it's a loving seagull! Thank you for joining us here at the beach!

At apple picking, let's say "thank you" to the kind generous tree for the apple!

Nothing is wasted in nature: the little earthworm eats old dead things, and then makes fresh new soil for baby plants.

The Young Child Opens the Door for the Family

Is everyone coming on the car ride? Who will be at dinner tonight? When is Grandma coming back? These are questions that young children ask, with a natural love and excitement for family. My young friend Daniel literally jumped up and down in anticipation of "all the aunts and uncles and cousins coming for Easter dinner." With everyone assembled, he walked from relative to relative around the table to say hello and to share a hug. "I love you, Nanna. I love you, Paul. I love you, Grace." Then he looked up and sprinted to the playroom, energized and invigorated. The child's pure happiness for the assembled relatives may reawaken us to the joyousness of having a family beyond the petty concerns or unfortunate wrinkles of the past. Like a family assembled, together we are more than the sum of our parts.

The child compels us to recognize family for its primacy in our lives, as well as for its greater purpose in difficult times. Nina shared with me the story of her daughter, Jenny, whose questions helped Nina find her own sense of spiritual value in a painful time. Nina had learned from her husband that he had had a brief affair working out of town some three years earlier in their marriage. "My immediate inclination was to leave," she said, "even though he truly was devastated, remorseful, and it had been three years since he did it. Of course, I didn't tell my kids what was going on, but I did go off one night and checked into a hotel to blow off steam." Her middle daughter, Jenny, who was seven, had picked up on her anger and on something not quite right at home that involved her dad. When Nina returned the next day, "Jenny came to me out of the blue and said, 'Mommy, does Daddy not love us anymore?' Of course, that was the real question. It was an 'us' here, and yes, he really did love us. I made some comment like, 'Of course he does,' to which Jenny came right back with, 'So, Mommy, if Daddy does love us, then why are you going away?'

"It came down to her question," Nina told me. "It was my decision to make. I chose to stay. We are a family."

Jenny's question had awakened Nina to a question bigger than her immediate feelings toward her husband, or deeper even than their adult romantic relationship. What is family? Is it more than this betrayal or heartbreaking event? Does it endure beyond pain? Where is forgiveness and where is destruction? These are spiritual questions. The child was right to ask: Where and when are we still family?

When we listen to our children we hear important spiritual questions. When we follow them to new places, whether in conversation or literally into a church, on the way to the market or a graveyard, or viewing the backyard gutted by a hurricane, the world is far more vast and alive than before.

We know this from our own experience, as well as from a growing body of research. In one study that drew from a population of religious families in central Pennsylvania, a research team led by Chris Boyatzis, a professor at Bucknell College, asked parents of children ages three to twelve years old to keep a journal for two weeks of all the discussions of a spiritual nature that occurred in their homes. Parents recorded the content, as well as how often, when, where, and how the discussions arose. The study found that for the majority of families, about half of the time a child initiated discussions of a spiritual nature, whether at the kitchen table, during bedtime, or riding in the car. Only about once a week did the children tend to ask a question about the family's own faith tradition, but daily or every other day they asked questions about morality or good behavior from a spiritual view. This is the young child seeing the spiritual nature of morality and wanting to act accordingly. Some of the children's questions were compelling yet funny, showing vision and clarity.

"Is God a man or a woman?"

"Why do people not believe in miracles?"

This is just one of many pieces of research that show big questions, spiritual questions, originating with children, opening the door for further exploration by families. In my conversations with parents across the country, they tell me about the memorable questions they've fielded from their children, which have opened wonderful lines of conversation about matters of heart and spirit.

"I think that each blade of grass was created by God, so we should walk on the sidewalk."

"Daddy, when you sing you become like an angel."

"You know God is everywhere. God is even right in the post office."

"If bad people get forgiven by God, then why do we put them in jail?"

These moments open the door for parents. We pause from marching across the grassy lawn, or scowling impatiently at the post office, to see the world as the child does—with sacredness throughout. Important questions we may have pushed to the back very long ago return to the fore. These moments also flag an opportunity for us, as parents, to cultivate our children's intuitive spiritual curiosity before they enter the popular culture that socializes them away from it, as Tanzi and Chopra asserted. Knowing the voice of natural spirituality in your child, you can prevent its loss in the first place!

The child is born whole. This new soul arrives with spirituality intact. The developmental work of childhood and then adolescence is to integrate this natural spirituality into the changing capacities of cognitive, social, emotional, moral, and physical growth. We will see in the chapters ahead that in each developmental phase there is the danger of our material culture ramping up and crowding out or attempting to disqualify this natural spirituality. But we can create a space for our children to develop and thrive. We can raise strong souls.

The child is our spiritual guide, but we are not passive at all in this picture. We recognize the child's force and impulse that we want to encourage, that we want to help thrive, that may also—if we let it—help us grow and thrive, too. But we are not just watching experiences or even just reacting to our children's spirituality. Because we love them, and because this love awakens in us great reserves of depth of feeling and of awe, we create around them a space in which they will thrive. And this is what we will be examining next, this very special space we—parents and children—create: a unique space where the child grows up. An inspired place called the *field of love*.

HOW TO PROTECT AND ENCOURAGE YOUR YOUNG CHILD'S "SPIRITUAL SPACE"

1. SET YOUR OWN INNER SPACE.

Set your inner space to live your deepest spiritual values in everyday interactions with your infant or toddler. Realistically, we get very, very tired and need to groom our inner life several times a day, consciously checking in and connecting with ourselves, particularly if our sleep reserves are low. As parents we sometimes need to reset our own inner space whether through time in nature, prayer, or meditation. Setting your space allows you to attune more sensitively to your child. Once you feel in sync, you can connect with the powerful transcendence in your child.

2. WALK THE WALK.

Your infant's experience of you is her experience of the entire world. When you nurse or feed your baby, change a diaper, bathe or soothe her, play with her, take care to embody love, trust, compassion, acceptance, and a connection to a loving universe or God. Your touch is the touch of all life. To your baby, this is what life feels like. In stressful moments, when you may be short of energy or patience, it again helps to reset your inner space. You may find the transcendent space more immediately accessible with your child.

3. CULTIVATE THE CAPACITY FOR QUIET CONTEMPLATION.

Long, loving silences let the connection flow. This uninterrupted time provides you and your baby the opportunity to attune to one another. You're also helping your child feel at ease without a steady stream of distractions to keep him occupied. If you get home from a day away and the baby is asleep, you may find that your infant still finds a way to ensure this time by waking up for the love. This is great! Do not feel you need to foreclose this time to be on schedule: go with the baby. Honor the intent. With a toddler, it may include cozy-chair time, sharing a picture book, or playing gently. It might be lying down together for naptime.

4. WELCOME NATURE AS YOUR CO-PARENT AND YOUR CHILD'S TEACHER.

Play in the grass. Hug a tree. Spend time outdoors in natural settings so your baby or young child has the opportunity to form a strong, positive connection between who we are and what nature is. *Look how the bird builds its nest twig by twig—amazing! Let's pick up this litter from the good earth.* You are showing the sacredness in all living beings and the spirit that is through all of nature. When your toddler's eyes widen at the sight of a flock of geese or a picture of an elephant herd, draw the connection between all families in nature: *Look—a family all together, just like us!* This is quite a contrast to disturbing an anthill or throwing rocks at a noisy flock of birds.

5. USE YOUR WORDS.

Young children are listening and learning language long before they are verbal. Use words that hold your values of sacred presence in our lives. Speak of the "good earth," the "loving duck." Identify spiritual qualities in people you know or those you encounter: Katie the clerk becomes "Katie, the kindly woman with spiritual sparkly eyes." Language sets the tone for spiritual perception. When we speak this way with our children from the start, they come to see spirit in our relationships and in the natural world.

5

FIELD OF LOVE

Creating the Space for Spiritual Parenting

P arents often ask me, "So, how do you *make* your child spiritual?" Or, "What can I do with my children so they don't lose this original natural spirituality?" Or, "How do you push back to protect natural spirituality against the utter garbage that kids pick up online or through other kids at school?" In a world of sometimes shocking mixed messages, parents intuitively try to create a home in which values cultivate a deeper and more resonant life, one with higher meaning and purpose.

Parents often feel isolated and uncertain in this challenge. After all, we live in a culture that does not talk openly about spirituality. The entertainment and social media are focused elsewhere, and schools tend to avoid anything that might be confused with religious teaching. We may have conversations at our place of worship or we may have carved out our own meditation practice, but as a society, we do not have a common currency, a way of talking about spirituality that we all understand and work with. Those of us who have an internal spiritual practice, or are part of a religious community, could also do with a bit of vocabulary, a set of ideas about how to approach the transmission of natural spirituality. This is particularly true for parents who are meeting a soul at its very start in our world and want to give it an open and protected space to flourish.

Your positive influence as a parent is profoundly important to your child. As we also have seen, and we're about to see even more clearly, *you're not in this alone.*

Throughout this book we explore ways to support a child's natural spirituality so that it grows and strengthens to become the bedrock of resilience and success. Science offers encouraging evidence suggesting that this support extends beyond parents and includes family members, friends—all those concerned with children's well-being. We can distill a few basic points from deep science that take our understanding of human nature and spirituality from the lab to the living room.

First and foremost, humans are naturally social. Just like a flock of geese in flight and a herd of elephants on the Serengeti, we are built to be in groups. Most people are aware without ever needing to read the science that when we lack social interaction, it's easy to feel unhappy and to even slip into the blues or depression. Lunch or coffee with a friend can lift our mood or add logic or love to our perspective. Right down to our biology we are inherently social beings. Evolutionary biologists, such as the great E. O. Wilson and more recently Sarah Coakley, hold that the survival of the fittest includes the ability to collaborate effectively and live harmoniously together.

Our social nervous system—the neurological circuitry inside the brain—supports our collectivist nature. Mirror neurons allow us to feel what someone else is feeling, and, at the level of the brain, experience what someone else is experiencing, without actually being in the same circumstance. Mirror neurons allow us to feel firsthand the frustration of a friend on the telephone who is stuck in traffic, just as if we were stuck in traffic. As a parent, if your child is hot and frustrated, by looking at the child, it is easy to feel hot and frustrated.

Our emotions and even our physical bodies are regulated by the feelings and the nature of the people around us. Neuroscientist Stephen Porges at the University of North Carolina, a leading researcher in the field of neurobiology and social behavior, has identified in fifteen years of research the neurological wiring of the *social regulation system* that connects the emotionality of other people with our mind and inner body. In his work, Porges shows that the regions of the brain that govern social communication—such as facial recognition, facial musculature for making expressions, and spoken language—are linked (via the brain stem) to the vagus, which is command central for setting heart rate and the functioning of organs. Even when our attention may be focused elsewhere, our emotions, thoughts, and physiology are meaningfully shaped by our web of daily relationships.

That we are naturally social is true to our biology. We live in a relational field that shapes us, even while we also can be highly individualistic. Just as each of us is pulled by the earth's gravitational field, even highly individualist people are swayed by a field of relationships.

What does this mean for the spiritual growth of a child? When we link together the science on our collective nature with the science of spirituality, we find a promising world for a child. Into the child's daily field of relationship, her innate spirituality and support for this natural spirituality from parents and others can now be infused. Spiritual presence, guidance, and values can come from extended family, close friends, psychologists, youth workers and clergy, coaches, and educators. Each of these important adults has a personal choice to decide to be a spiritual presence and model of love, and as they choose to do so, the child's routine social world becomes what I call the *field of love*: a place to learn spirituality in daily life.

We've talked about the nod, the joint effect, and the spiritual seek-and-find of selective spiritual socialization. That a child is wired by nature for "quick absorbing" from relationships explains how she naturally gravitates to loving, spiritually significant others to find a supportive spiritual connection and how each generation "passes the torch" of spiritual engagement to the next. The nod is actually part of a broader field of loving relationships. Often the nod from a parent or grandparent is the center, ground zero, of a web of spiritually guiding relationships. Yet, there are other life-changing spiritually guiding relationships.

As parents, you, along with the spiritually significant others in your child's life, are key coordinates on her spiritual map. Parents, grandparents, aunts or uncles, as well as teachers, coaches, ministers, or mentors: each committed person who sends a strong signal of guidance, steadfast interest, and love may also hold a special place.

Hidden in Plain View: The Field of Love Supports, Surrounds, and Strengthens Family

The field of love is a *relational space*—a fluid, evolving, interpersonal space that we both discover and create in relationship with one another. We access it in our hearts. It is a sacred space that we inhabit together as a family or an intimate community. Often this shared sacred space holds joy, yet it can also buoy us up in times of sorrow. It can exist in a tightly knit school or youth organization, or even in an adult organization or group. For many children, however, the first experience of the field of love is the family and emotionally meaningful friends. It is a super-sized *we*.

Like a picnic blanket, the field of love spreads out to hold a "family"—everyone in a family and everyone who feels like family. But instead of fabric, this blanket is made of emotional connections consisting of spiritually based love. It is our natural social nature linked to our natural spiritual nature.

We can see how the family-centered field of love includes the "third piece"—transcendent presence—when we consider, as we saw in earlier chapters, that children experience their parents' love as embodying the love of God or a higher power. As George Vaillant asserts, transcendence is prominent in the positive experiences of compassion, forgiveness, hope, and joy that we share with one another. In studies, most parents, whether spiritually engaged or not, describe their role and their family as sacred. Loving family as an expanded field of love is infused with transcendent love, a natural extension of it.

Researcher Wan-Ning Bao and colleagues at Iowa State University studied 407 families and found that from accepting and loving parenting, the child experiences spirituality. This finding, replicated by other research teams, reveals the inherent blend of parental love and transcendent presence. This natural blend creates the field of love. Parents are ambassadors, whether we notice it or not, so that if we harness our inherent role, it greatly benefits our child's spiritual growth.

The field of love exists naturally but can also be a collective spiritual goal toward which a family moves. We do not need to be perfectly on the mark each day, but the field can become an ever present statement of how we aim to live as family and who we are as family.

When we lean into the goal of being a collective field of love, things change. Viewed as an interconnected whole, the relationships between our children and others affirm, support, and enable each and every one in the field. The field of love becomes both ground and guide to a spiritually rich and resilient life.

The field of love also serves as the foundation for spiritual parenting. Working from the field as a base, you can purposefully help your young child develop her innate spiritual assets into the spiritual strengths that will be so protective in adolescence and later life. By tapping into the field of love, the parent-child relationship gains support and guidance; the wind is at your back. Clinical psychologist and researcher Gina Brelsford at Pennsylvania State University helps families resolve conflict and move past impasses through psycho-spiritual family therapy. Brelsford's research has shown that when parents and children invoke guidance through prayer or contemplation by listening together from the higher power, there is a more rapid and stable resolution.

In the field of love, we are loved unconditionally and learn by example how to love unconditionally. We are not perfect, but love is the overarching sense of who we are, and what we do, as "family." We are fully accepted for who we are, and learn to hold others with this same compassion. We experience, we learn, and we practice spiritual values. Essentially the field of love is our lab, our incubator, our first run at living out spiritual values in the larger world.

However you envision it metaphorically, the field of love, if you determine to make it, is a real place in which your family lives. There is nothing imaginary about it. You hear it expressed when everyone at the dinner table laughs at the same time. Or when your six-year-old races to you to tell you that her younger brother needs help with his shoes. You see it glow when you Skype with Grandma and she waves hello and you and your kids wave back while one of them lifts the cat up to say hi, too. Your child shows it in her enthusiasm when together you look at a photograph taken of her years ago during infancy or toddlerhood. You feel it when you tell them for the umpteenth time the handed-down family story of when your forebears first arrived as immigrants in this country. The field of love is in us, and in the space between us, made up of love so strong that it feels almost physical to the touch.

The field of love represents our most expansive sense of family defined by love and commitment—by blood and by choice—and encompasses the love we feel for each other. The field of love holds all. On a daily basis within this space, a space that we hold in our hearts and inhabit together, your child can be sure of her place among the people she loves. She learns trust, learns to accept others in good faith, foibles and all, and feels she can safely explore life's questions, no matter how small or how imposing. There is room in the field for upset and disagreement, for all of the emotions, conversations, and problems a family has. The field isn't impervious to damage—hurtful words and actions can take a toll—but it can be repaired with deliberate and loving intention.

We catch glimpses of this deep connection throughout the child's first decade, exquisite in the way it reflects precisely where he is developmentally. When Isaiah was just two years old, his grandparents came to spend a winter weekend with us. Just out of the car, everyone was settling in. Grandma was arranging her cookies, Grandpa was stretched out and relaxing in the living room. Hot chocolate was warming on the stove. Suddenly Isaiah called all of us—Grandma, Grandpa, my husband, and me—and asked me to bring his new baby sister into the guest bedroom.

"Everyone sit on the bed!" Isaiah called to us, full of anticipation. We all followed his instructions and took our places in a row, sitting on the edge of the bed. "Now, lift your feet!" he said, with an excited grin and twinkling eyes. We followed the call. All the family had come together, held in this physical space. "There!" he pronounced with pride. Isaiah was putting all the people he cared about in one room—three generations in one place—demonstrating the specialness, the sanctity of family to him.

We'll see the field of love manifest in stories throughout the chapters ahead. For now, what's most important is to recognize it as the foundational piece of a child's spiritual experience from birth, and as such, a sacred space for spiritual parenting. We need to care for this space. This is the space in which our children grow up, and it is one that they create, as well. They are the catalyst for the field of love. It is within this space that we can begin to talk about our place in the universe, secure in knowing that those in the field of love also see those questions and conversations as valuable.

Much of what happens through the field of love may already be under way in your family. You may be having these conversations, may have created loving rituals spontaneously—in fact, I imagine that you have. You may find more reasons and more ideas here and in the chapters ahead, but for starters, just by bringing the field of love into your awareness and into your child's awareness, you strengthen the field with your intention.

When a family forms the field of love, the transcendent faculty in each member is primed to take that process a step further by charging the relational space—the relationship itself—with the "third presence," the spiritual presence. What makes a family a transcendent group passes through our neurological wiring. We can feel it right after we share a heartfelt prayer, or traditional grace, or light Shabbat candles, or when a parent finishes a blessing on a child. Just as lighting candles sanctifies the Sabbath, you can sanctify family by purposefully having your family acknowledge and cultivate the field, and by building from these spiritual principles. From cell to soul, through the field of love, family manifests as a spiritual space.

A Spiritually Grounded Childhood Starts Here

As the organizing principle for family, the field of love provides for a spiritually grounded childhood in three basic ways.

First, the field of love is predicated on many loving people in the life of the child. The spiritual space of family is enlarged by more attachments rather than exclusive or limited ones. Field of love makes the case for an expansive intimate world, more love, more points of lifelong meaningful connection and attachment. For example, the field might include extended family, community, beloved teachers, and "soul mate" friends who deeply shape the child's life. It also creates an intentional channel for closeness—a road to inclusion—with those who might otherwise, due to geographical distance or other challenges, be lost to the child.

Second, the field of love is a transcendent, inspired space—one defined by what I consider the miracle of family. In *The Art of Possibility*, Rosamund Stone Zander and Benjamin Zander write that when we live authentically in an affirmative space of inspiration, events "unfold in the realm of miracles." When it comes to family, $2+2=100$. This is the equation through which every family is formed. As Brad, the father of two young children, told me, "Love grows exponentially—you put a little bit of love in and you get twice as much back. When you have one child and you are really in love with this first child, you think, how could I ever love the second child as much? Then you realize that you can. I have two incredible children, and rationally I would think that I don't know if I could love a third child as much, but from this experience, I have to say that I could. It is great to know that I have that capacity for love."

Third, the miracle extends to however families are made: the unpredictable combination of individuals, circumstance, and serendipity: a right turn, a wrong turn, a pregnancy that ended in disappointment, only to be followed by the arrival of a beloved child, the many ways that the child can come. Through a spiritual lens we can see the formation of family as a series of miracles. This warm and stable world of relationship-plus-transcendent-love is the child's training ground for developing an awareness that we live in a sacred world.

As we saw earlier, researchers Annette Mahoney and Ken Pargament have shown a natural "sanctification" of family whether or not a family is part of a religious tradition, there is an inherent perception of family as sacred. Many religious traditions cultivate sanctification of family, viewing it as spiritually created and sustained. Even among people who do not connect with a religion and who have a mild to moderate sense of spirituality, a sense of sanctification arises in marriage and around pregnancy. Mahoney's and Pargament's research shows that when we acknowledge and honor the sanctification of family, this awareness fuels a broader spiritual awareness of daily family events, whether joyous or unpleasant. We bring more forgiveness and forbearance, commitment, and compassion to the moment. Learning to see into relationships as spiritual events stays with the child and profoundly affects the way they treat others throughout their life.

Togetherness is also good for us at a biological level. Researcher James Coan and colleagues at the University of Virginia, in an fMRI study tracking participants' response to an electric shock, showed that we anticipate and the brain literally perceives less physical pain if we hold the hand of our beloved spouse. Suffering is lighter when we are bonded together. This has been well documented by Harold Koenig, professor and director of the Duke University Center for Spirituality, Theology and Health, whose decades of research on the elderly shows that people live longer in a religious community that offers regular "spiritual social support."

Attachment Concept Expands to Embrace More Sources, More Love

In the second half of the twentieth century, the primacy of the infant-mother attachment (later partially expanded to include fathers) informed almost exclusively how we looked at the psychological intimacy and closeness of the parent-child relationship. Attachment theory has been and remains a helpful theory. However, we can extend and enhance it to be more helpful to parents and families today.

Attachment theory holds that a child needs at least one attachment figure, but it doesn't mean there's only room for one. You expect something entirely different from Grandma than you might expect from Mom; the strength of the field of love comes from its many connections of love and not from expectations of behavior.

The reality of family life and children's lives has evolved dramatically in the past half century. Today, most parents share parenting responsibilities, and often both parents work outside the home. Grandparents may help raise a child, or a babysitter may be a constant and truly loving presence. Divorce has created complex blended families. Adoptive parents and birth parents are often all present in a child's life. There are many independent or "single" parents, and grandparents, caregivers, and special mentors or committed youth workers can all be important to a child. Whatever the family structure, "close" family can be geographically far away, at times more likely to get together for a Sunday call or Skype session than for Sunday dinner. The times call for a helpful model to understand what children need and how they can thrive in these new family and social constellations.

The field of love makes the case for a larger perspective: more love—from many sources who bring different kinds of wisdom and expertise—with the flexibility to evolve with the child as he grows. The field of love as a context for spiritual development offers a more contemporary and expansive view of the potential for spiritually significant others in your child's life—and in your own. It positions all members of the family and committed adults as available to the child.

When we put together the child's natural spiritual cognition with the field of love we see that in this space, loving connection is magnified.

Supporting scientific evidence for the field's effects is emerging, most notably along two lines. First, studies from our lab and others show that the transmission of spirituality from parent to child is enhanced when it is through an affectionate bond or family style. It can come from a parent or from Grandma with a nod on the subway (or in life). But we are seeing that the strongest way to encourage spirituality in your child is through a positive, loving family connection, and the bigger the "family"—the bigger the field of love—the larger and more loving those connections are. The more people caring about a child, the better.

Second is the protective joint effect. When spirituality is transmitted through family it is more protective against pathology than when we come to it alone. Attachment theory would say the parent is enough or perhaps God is enough, but we know that the cojoined effect is more protective than either of those alone. So the more present the field of love, the more strongly it becomes a source of resilience and protective results.

WHO LOVES YOU? MAPPING YOUR FAMILY'S FIELD OF LOVE

How do we feel love in our family? Let us count the ways! With your child, describe the idea of the field of love and on a sheet of paper draw or make a list of all those individuals your child suggests belong on the map. Include those near and far, and those of this world and those who have passed on. Don't stop with people: include pets or wildlife, and all aspects of nature. This can make a lovely bedtime ritual, a nightly remembering of all the love and support that exists for your child, from Mom and Dad and siblings to family far and near, naming each one and, especially for those who live far away, naming where they live to help your child feel their presence. For those who have passed on, you can say "loved you even before you were born . . . and still do."

In the Field of Love, Important Features of Family Naturally Make Sense

From developmental theory and science, to a practical approach to parenting and family life, the field of love model reflects the contemporary world of family, relationship, and spirituality. It readily includes the range of loving adults in our families. It holds many configurations of family as normal and says that any of them can support healthy development as long as the family is built on a foundation of love and commitment.

Within the field we can reach out to different members for different reasons. A child can seek out whomever seems the best fit as good company or a helping hand, beyond the core contributions of mother or father. Grandma listens carefully to long stories. "Aunt" Betta, a close family friend, sweeps in for a day at the park. The caring babysitter or nanny is a loving constant across the day. So, too, in matters of the heart, the child can reach out for different reasons, and each adult is differently equipped to reach back. All this is done in, with, and through love. Everyone counts. People other than parents have extremely important contributions to make to our children.

As parents we can rely on the field of love for strength, like a sail that captures the force of spirituality. If we know it and explain it to our children, it can carry us along. As parents we cannot make or invent spirituality; we can only connect to it and guide our children to develop their own relationship to spirituality. Helping your child and relatives to think in terms of the field of love, to name this new space, brings awareness of the terrain and of the opportunity that comes with this shared sacred space. The field intrinsically brings unity to the family. By talking about the family in this way, we create an awareness and a bond—a bond that is held for each by all. That awareness and those bonds are the field of love, both a symbolic and very real space for your child to experience natural spirituality and for spirituality to grow and thrive.

Five Ways to Create the Inspired Space
That Is the Field of Love

1. Illuminate and engage the field

When family comes together we move together in a familiar way—our seats at the dinner table, the order at bath time, how birthdays are celebrated. As a parent we can deliberately make our family traditions and rituals spiritually focused, from Sabbath or Sunday dinner to a gratitude prayer or an offering of love. These rituals are powerful, as evident in studies of social behavior and its effects on the brain. Ritual conducted by one person in a close group fosters the spiritual awareness in another person. While true of people in general, this synchronizing of brains is most pronounced among closely bonded people—like family!

A shared family ritual invokes our felt certainty of the spiritual fabric that makes, sustains, and guides family. A child, as well as a parent, can be encouraged to lead the family in prayer, meditation, or a loving kindness image of good action. Around the table or following family ritual, be explicit in recognizing the sacred bonds within family. Talk about how these bonds stay clear and strong in our heart, as if we're all together at the dinner table, no matter where our day takes us.

"Family is sacred: the bond between our hearts is made of love."

"Family has a special glow. Can you feel it? God gives families that special love so they can pass it along to others."

"We're so lucky to have family to love, near and far. No matter where we are, we're always whole and together in heart. Family is always special."

2. Bonfire of love: gain-gain

A core spiritual principle in nearly all faith traditions tells us: love begets love. "When you give it away you gain," said a fellow four years into recovery through Alcoholics Anonymous. Remember Brad, the dad of two who described his delight to discover that "love grows exponentially"? In the realm of generosity and love, there is only more, never less. Children understand this bonfire model, which says good ignites more good. It is in clear contrast to the limited-pie model that suggests that your piece leaves less for me.

The spiritual space of family is about discovering and helping your child see abundance—the experience of *enoughness*—rather than the shrinking pie. *Gain-gain* means we have more than enough to go around. We don't need to compete as if love is a scarce resource. Love begets love.

Sibling competition is at its heart about the perception of one sibling not getting as much love as a brother or sister. It might come in packages such as "Who runs faster?" or "Who got more ice cream cake?" but it is usually about parental love.

The child says, "She gets all the attention. You love her more!"

You can say, "Actually, the more love goes into the family, the more it spreads and grows. The more love everyone gets and feels! And it's natural when we feel loved for us to also feel generous and want to pass that love along. So when you're kind and loving to your brother, you're adding love to the family and making more for you and all the rest of us!"

Children can be shown how to set bonfires of love or stoke them. Use the phrase "love begets love" freely to help your child see the common thread in actions that enrich the field of love. Find other opportunities to enlist your child in acting on this intention.

"There's your brother walking home from the school bus! Let's welcome him back home in love. Let's show him the big love!"

"Whatever you do that is good spreads through the entire family. It's as if you put your goodness into the family bucket, and everyone's happiness goes up when each person does the loving thing."

"Look, you fixed your sister's dollhouse—how kind. Think of how happy she'll be to be able to play with it again. Through that one simple act you've added to the love your sister will feel and it will come back to our family. Love begets love."

You will be teaching your child that love is not a zero-sum game, not a competition for limited resources. The child feels empowered when you make clear that "You are very important in the family space. You help to co-create the field of love." *Love begets love* is an expanding reality, not a confined or confining one. In fact, the core sacred purpose of spiritual family is to offer love and encouragement.

3. Acceptance vs. judgment: family offers a purposeful cast of characters

The spiritual space of family forges your child's vocabulary and perceptual lens for later relationships. By showing a child a more loving way to be with a sibling, cousin, or gruff grandparent, the child gains a more loving view of all people. Many religious traditions hold that family members are purposefully brought together to share life lessons and help each other grow. In a day-to-day way, regardless of belief about how we arrive, the work of acceptance and encouragement within the family generalizes to our child's kindness outward, to people in the world. Every person can tap into the field of love with awareness and intention. Like the grandmother-granddaughter royal couple on the subway, we can notice one another first and foremost as "souls on earth," rather than the label we might assign in a judging way—"the smart one," "the good-looking one," "the underachieving one," "the stubborn one." We can listen for one another's humanity and cultivate it within our family.

The child is empowered for the good by realizing her potential to be a helper. It ultimately weakens a child to be a judge and constant critic (as well as alienating other people!) because it separates the child from spiritual power to love and build. We teach acceptance versus judgment every moment of the day by our words and our own relationship to family. Do we as parents pick and choose favorites within our family or among people we know? Do we disenfranchise or marginalize certain members, perhaps labeling them as "black sheep"? Or do we empower our family as a field of love by welcoming to Sunday dinner or an outing the quirky cousin, the less superficially appealing relative, the side of our family with less outward success or money? Family models our core humanity. Judging, weighing, and measuring versus embracing, accepting, and appreciating—family helps us grow, evolve, and deal with other people in the world; it is where we practice human kindness and acceptance.

This is evermore true when our family is particularly annoying, has hit a rough patch, or is profoundly troubled. Family at its most irritating and distressing offers the opportunity to practice values of love and the embrace of acceptance. You can teach your child that when we are most annoying, most reduced, we most need love and encouragement.

An exchange with your child might begin, "Your cousin Lewis is coming for dinner tonight. Please help him feel included, part of our family and of our love."

Your child responds, "Lewis is rude, Mom. He's just weird. Lewis is such a loser."

You can then say, "Family is built as the perfect cast of characters to teach us deep love. True radical love is where we love even if we get nothing back at all, because we are sources of love. Remember last time, you were kind to Lewis, and it totally rebooted the way he acted? He stopped complaining about Mommy's cooking, and started making jokes and playing with the dog."

You will be showing your child that family teaches true unconditional radical love and love without expectation because no matter what comes back, this love is about who you are. This isn't about judging someone as worthy or unworthy of your best response; it's about who you are and staying true to that.

When we come from a place of love and acceptance, then suddenly other people are worthy, not weird. Suddenly, we are huge contributors to goodness and forming loving bonds.

"Daddy also had problems with sitting still for math, so he is the perfect Dad to understand how you feel and give you the hints he discovered."

"I always wanted to be more patient, and here you, with your big smile, are teaching me to be patient!"

"I prayed and prayed for you, and then Grandma and Grandpa prayed and prayed for you. And then, after many days and nights and weeks and years . . . you arrived! The universe brought the child we are so grateful to love. You are so loved."

4. Field of love care and repair: opportunity in collective spiritual renewal

In chapter 3, we discussed a child's tendency to take a parent's ways and stamp them right on the face of the transcendent relationship. When we err as parents, which is often, we need to fix it at both the emotional level and the spiritual level. When we do, both family and spirituality for the child can be even stronger than ever before.

Just as a mended piece of fabric can be strongest where the seam has been reinforced, when we repair the field of love, the mended portion can become the strongest. Fixing can be an apology, an act of restitution, or an attempt at new family footing. The child will likely remember the fixing as vivid and important—an act of love.

What does this sound like?

"The family, and our special field of love, is the most important thing in my life. Today I was tired and too grumpy. I should have taken a nap and not yelled at you. I am so, so sorry. What is far more important is you, our love as a family, and the presence of spirit that we feel in our strong family love. Can we fix up our field of love, so that we are closer than ever?"

"Love is so strong that it can heal up our mistakes in the family, if we all agree to it. I decide to forgive and love. Daddy decides to forgive and love. And all the children decide to forgive and love. Then when we all do this together, we ask God to forgive and replenish the family. Then there is an even stronger family field of love."

"I am going to do a loving kindness meditation to open up the love that is really inside our family. Will you join me?

5. Entrance and exits into the field

Spirituality heats up at the borders of life and death, and the field holds the intensity of our family bond through time and space. In very real terms, a baby's arrival into the family is a sacred event that affects the entire family. Welcome home a new baby with gratitude, special ceremony or prayer for the child, and formally recognize the new child as now entering into the field of love. Draw the members of your field of love together to celebrate that everyone is now bonded to the new baby: siblings, parents, friends, companions, aunts, uncles, and grandparents, whether near or far away, living or deceased.

The field of love holds many generations. The intergenerational bonds, including the "third piece" of sacred presence, is deeply affecting. Connecting through the field of love, children naturally feel at home with ancestors. Acknowledge the living presence of ancestors. Point out the ancestors' personality traits or unique behaviors now found in young nephews and nieces, grand- or great-grandchildren. Point out family practices and ways that extend through time.

The child naturally gravitates to ongoing relationship, and spiritual parenting supports this sacred relationship. I witnessed this most poignantly in a visit to meet with a mother, Sandra, and her eight-year-old son Jeremy, to talk about the boy's loss of his best friend, Tom, who had been killed in a school shooting. Jeremy and his mother welcomed me to their home in a quiet, wooded suburban neighborhood. Sandra showed me the place in her home where she and Jeremy prayed. "He likes to sit with me and we pray together here," she said. Deeply devoted within a Christian faith tradition, the family had attended Sunday services since Jeremy was a baby and had shared every major religious holiday, Sunday service, and family picnic for five years with Tom's family. At the church funeral for Tom, Jeremy came with two photos taped on his sweater, one a picture of Tom and the other of the two boys, arm in arm, proud of a LEGO creation they had made together. Sandra showed me the memorial service program across which Jeremy had scratched out the day of death, and written instead a date decades ahead, which he explained to his mother as "the day Tom was supposed to live until."

In the weeks and months following his friend's death, Jeremy would return to the woods behind his home where they used to play, continuing their games, and at times pausing to talk to Tom. His mother watched him from the kitchen window respectfully and would later ask, "What are you doing up there?" Comfortably, expecting to be understood, Jeremy replied, "Being with Tom."

As we sat talking at her kitchen table, Sandra explained that she and Jeremy had talked about the field of love and how he could continue a relationship with his beloved friend in this way. The religious community, too, had come together in many different ways to lend support to the families who were touched by the tragedy. Clergy, counselors, parents, children, teachers, and others had stepped forward to share the burden of grief. Religious and spiritual engagement through their church has been especially helpful to her son, Sandra said. "We moved to this community seven year ago to raise Jeremy and to be part of the church here. It has made all the difference in the face of Tom's death." Leaning forward, she added, "Build your ark before it rains."

PRACTICE APPRECIATION, GRATITUDE, AND CONNECTION AS A FAMILY

We can always start by giving thanks for our family, and then try to find at least two things to recognize that gave today a sense of specialness or that we recognize as spiritual moments.

In a simple blessing at the dinner table or at bedtime, speak directly outward (to the world, to God, the creator, however you envision the presence on the other end of the conversation) and express thanks for the gift of the day and the many ways those gifts presented themselves:

> *Thank you for blessing each of us today. For bringing Jeremy home from school safely on the bus, for watching over Steffie during the soccer tournament, for Ellie's great adventure with her class, and for helping Mom and Dad take care of us.*

At dinner, go around the table and invite each family member to show appreciation and gratitude for the others. This gratitude can be for something done or simply for the way they are:

> *Dad, I appreciate that you're funny and you helped me laugh about my mistake. Jason, I appreciate that you waited for me outside school so I wouldn't have to walk home alone.*

Expand to include others in the extended family who live at a distance or for other reasons cannot be present:

> *As we sit down to dinner (or tuck in for bedtime), it is already tomorrow for Aunt Eve and Uncle Ken in London. And it's only midday for Grandma Val and Grandpa Michael at their house. But we can send our love right now and they will feel it.*

Speak of the specialness of family:

Being together is special, and that's why we do "family dinner." You don't need to eat or even talk, but you need to listen and show your caring while we sit together.

The Field of Love Explains Thriving Despite Loss

The field of love explains thriving children even when children have experienced loss of or severe impairment to a parent. In chapter 3, we discussed my research on the children of addicted mothers, seeing the impact on children and teens who were able to find healthy spiritual support from a nonaddicted family member. With the field of love, the opportunity for parental love and spiritual guidance also comes from extended family, friends, teachers, youth group leaders, and others.

This phenomenon has been shown cross-culturally. In collaboration with a team of colleagues at Nanjing University, Diheng Zhang and Yakov Barton, two of my graduate students at Columbia, studied children in a collectivist culture in rural China. In Jiangxi province, as well as other rural areas, parents can be economically pressured to leave home for the city for extended lengths of time, sometimes even years, to earn money to send home. Sometimes both parents need to leave their children, who then live with grandparents, aunts and uncles, or sometimes simply another family. The culture has come to call these children "left-behind children."

Based upon traditional Western psychology attachment theory, these young children who "lose" a parent or parents would be expected to have worse mental health in adolescence. But far too often studies supporting this theory come from settings of extreme poverty, violence, and even war—in some case parents have been killed. Simply put, the factor of parental loss has not been isolated from other sources of childhood trauma. Few studies look at a peaceful collectivist culture in which parental loss is filled in by someone else of good mental health. What if the parenting was of high quality, no matter who was acting as "parent"?

As scientists we tested this question in the collectivist traditional culture of Jiangxi province. We evaluated the mental health assessments of 114 so-called left-behind children ages twelve to sixteen and of eighty-four children of the same age from the same school who lived with both parents. We looked at levels of depression and anxiety and at the incidence of the type of personality disorder that, according to one-on-one parent-child attachment theory, comes from damage to the psyche caused by absent or emotionally unavailable or hurtful parents.

The data was clear: There was no disadvantage in mental health between those children who had been "left behind" and those who lived with both parents. The love and support that the children needed to flourish was sufficient from any committed loving source. It need not be the mother or father per se. There was only one difference between the two groups: children who had been left behind were actually more comfortable in the world, somewhat less likely to be anxious in daily life—quite the opposite of what would be predicted by attachment theory.

In a collectivist culture the child finds many so-called secure bases—loving adults with whom to develop a sturdy grounding in a field rather than an attachment, and all significant sources of love, guidance, and discipline. The child feels sure that the vast outer world has many other secure bases toward which to journey. A child with many sources of love, encouragement, and healthy emotional connection feels encouraged to look outward for those same things.

Multiple sources of love in family, friends, and school exist in the United States, too—a friend of mine refers to her children's "other mothers" as a title of distinction. We still have room to more fully recognize and honor the important others in our children's lives, and to empower and kindle their potential in creating and maintaining the field of love. These "others" are much more important than mere "in a pinch" second bests to mom. When we actively acknowledge the transformative power of multiple sources of love on children's lives, we can live into many loving relationships: authorizing teachers as more than dispensers of curriculum, and inviting neighborhood friends, fellow parents, youth leaders, clergy, coaches, and mentors to be recognized as truly significant resources to our families and our communities. If we gather up all of our sources of love and support, and see the strong relationships between and among them for our children, what we see is the field of love. In that relational space our children find the spiritual values—generosity, compassion, acceptance, love—lived out, and their own spiritual development flourishes.

An absence of spiritual engagement represents the loss of trust, hope, and optimism, those qualities that science tells us our children need to flourish. What distances us from people, and breaks apart the field of love, are narcissism and cynicism, two prominent obstructions to personal relationships. A 2014 study in *Neurology*, the journal of the American Academy of Neurology, found that cynical people have a higher likelihood of developing dementia; cynicism appears to be neuro-degenerative for the long term. The study by Anna-Maija Tolppanen, a professor at the University of Eastern Finland, and her colleagues expanded on previous studies showing that people who are cynical are more likely to die earlier and to have poor health outcomes, including a higher rate of coronary heart disease, cardiovascular problems, and cancer-related deaths.

For research purposes, cynicism is defined as a deep mistrust of others. Remember, though, that we are wired to need other people, as demonstrated in James Coan's finding of less pain perceived when a loving spouse holds our hand. To this I add that we need spiritual relationships that are bolstered by sanctification and that bring us replenishment and guidance. We know from Harold Koenig that "spiritual social support" helps us live longer. It is therefore not surprising that cynical people also tend to have greater stress responses, which means they typically have a higher heart rate, a higher blood pressure peak, and a tendency to have greater inflammation of their immune systems.

Tolppanen's study and the related research show the importance of trust in a shared connection with others: connectivity as fortifying the brain, distrust as starving our connectivity and brain. The brain even acts differently if we sense we are with trusted people: we perceive more. An MRI team at Tel Aviv University showed that the brain had a stronger visual and emotional perception of a film if you simply told the research participant that there was a fellow participant in the next room, also watching the same film in an MRI machine.

Spirituality can be stronger when experienced in a group. People who meditate or pray regularly alone still often find it particularly deepening to participate in a collective meditation or prayer. Consider the glow of a family dinner or a walk together at sunset, the specialness of Christmas morning or a Shabbat meal shared, or even that Sunday-night Skype call to connect with loved ones. Something in the shared experience moves us.

Moving On: The Field of Love Expands

As early as the end of year one we see it: a bonk on the head to a sibling who has claimed Grandma's lap, retaliation for the perception of infringing on love. In Paul Bloom's puppet study, at one year of age—just a few months older than the infant who so generously gives candy to all, regardless of their merit—the toddler gives the selfish puppet less candy. We start to distribute candy based upon moral merit, no longer unconditional love, but contingent value.

The challenge has begun, and will continue our entire lives. On the one hand: connection, our natural spirituality known through our heart, or intuitive faculty. On the other hand: our reflective, evaluative mind. Yes, the greatest challenge of the human condition has begun: while we are part of the field of love, we are also distinct and separate from others, with very diverse appetites and personalities, sometimes different values, and divergent priorities and agendas. By adolescence and the quest for individuation, the field of love sometimes can be in for a lot of wear and tear. All the more reason to build it early, and build it strong.

Grab the moments in the car, at the dinner table, before bedtime, and engage the "third presence"—explain that you now speak with your higher self—that helps our kids see that we have choices to be made, spiritual choices that are loving, generous, and abundant, and that these are things we *do*. They don't always just fall in our laps.

I opened this chapter with the question I am asked so often by parents, "So, how do you *make* your child spiritual?" The answer emerging from all corners of science and spiritual study is, we don't "make" our child spiritual at all. We cultivate their spirituality when we recognize the field of love as ground and guide for spiritual parenting. We set our intention to make our home environment and communities, our actions and expectations, and our ways of interacting with one another to be consistent with spiritual values.

Family and the expansive field of love are our most important tools for building a spiritual life, for giving our children a spiritual grounding.

6

THE FIRST DECADE

The Education of Head and Heart

One Thanksgiving, when Leah was six and Isaiah eight, I took them to a homeless shelter, carrying pies and cookies. As we entered, a boy about Isaiah's age, with a big smile, held the door for us and we all introduced ourselves. This was Michael, who had been at the shelter for several weeks and was especially excited to see another boy his own age. He and Isaiah were instantly at ease together. Michael was polite and gracious—and one of the few boys that age who has ever held the door for me. We offered him a big tin of cookies. He paused, then asked, "Are you sure?" and was delighted when we insisted. As we talked, we learned that Michael and his mother had been sleeping at the shelter for five weeks. Michael's father was in jail and his mother was internationally born and undocumented, so Michael couldn't qualify for public housing. He and his mother had walked the streets for nearly four weeks before space opened at the shelter.

We spent most of the day at the shelter, much of it in Michael's company. Later that night at home I heard a wail from across the house. I ran into Leah's bedroom to find her sobbing uncontrollably. "It's so sad!" she cried. "It hurts so much!" She was completely overwhelmed by sorrow. She had been so immersed with the children at the shelter, and especially attentive to Michael during our visit, that it had been clear she'd been deeply affected by his suffering. Now, as she processed the day in the quiet comfort of her own home, she had been drawn back into those feelings. As Leah resonated with Michael's suffering, it was with a loving heart, not with the analytical eye of a detached observer. In young children, this visceral heart-to-heart experience of someone else's feelings—this oneness with them—is a natural response. Psychologists traditionally call this an *undifferentiated* emotional state.

"Do you mean you feel so sad about Michael?" I asked Leah. She nodded. We talked about the boy's situation and about her feelings, and as we found the words to give her anguish a context, she grew calmer. Her sadness was no less, but now she was able to feel her sadness and oneness with Michael, while also aware of keenly feeling *for* him in his suffering. She now was able to differentiate between her feelings and Michael's experience and feelings. This shift in awareness that enables a child to observe others' thoughts and feelings as separate from their own generally dawns around age four. It is a subtle but significant nuance of mind.

In the past this shift has been understood as an important milestone in children's mental processing and cognitive development. We recognize that when a child advances from picture books to short easy reader stories and then to chapter books, it is a sign of cognitive growth: the child has outgrown picture books and the brain is ready to take on something more complex. Similarly, the assumption has been that a child necessarily outgrows the undifferentiated sense of oneness with others and, with the addition of logic and reason, advances to a more mature differentiated sense of separateness.

Science tells a different story. As we've already indicated, current research shows that from birth, spiritual development occurs in tandem with the other lines of development. A child's natural experience of oneness, or *unitive* empathy, is not necessarily something she outgrows or needs to give up in order to advance cognitively or in any other way.

To the contrary, head and heart inform one another. You want your child to draw from both. The goal is to keep both "head knowing" and "heart knowing" expanding and deepening together—for the child to integrate both of these ways of knowing into how they understand and interpret the world. Through the first decade a child develops the cognitive skills to understand the world in differentiated terms of "I" and "you," or "self" and "others." At the same time, her heart knowing and capacity for empathy deepen naturally as she understands and then bridges the distance between the "other's" experience and a sharpening sense of oneness with the "other." Flash-forward to our house one morning three years after Leah's consuming empathic sorrow.

Our family had spent the morning preparing for an exciting day at the Connecticut State Special Olympics. Rosa, the elder sister of one of my graduate students, was set to compete in the 200-meter walk and we were eager to cheer her and the others on. As we were about to leave the house in a light drizzle, an e-mail arrived from the organizers, announcing the cancellation of the entire event due to rain. Leah let out the same crestfallen, spine-cutting wail.

But this time, Leah, now nine, could articulate on her own what this would mean to the contestants. "They worked so hard—Rosa and the others," she said. "Now they're going to be so disappointed!" At age six, Leah's powerful experience of Michael's suffering overwhelmed her. By age nine, she could feel someone else's suffering deeply, but now without the earlier lack of bearings. Her sorrow had a location—the contestants—and in the same breath, a unitive knowing of lost dreams. That's development. These are spiritual values taking shape: feeling the interconnectedness of all things, caring truly about someone else's loss.

Your child is right to tap into that deep compassion. It's the quality that so many of us, as adults, feel cut off from or strive to revive through meditation or other practices. It's where so many spiritual traditions and religions try to take us. The child starts there. Natural spirituality is in the bond of head and heart—each way of knowing informing the other—and this comes forward in many ways that we'll discuss in this chapter.

Kids Come to Life and Learning
Heartfully Engaged

As you know, the central theme of this book is that human development—and by that I mean the innate drive to learn and grow—is designed by nature to include a spiritual component. Our natural capacity to experience transcendence, as shown by the research in chapter 2, is a biological and psychological fact. Further, an emerging body of empirical research, including our collaborative work with the three-generational study of adolescents and their mothers, shows that in adolescence, personal spirituality—a vibrant engagement of that transcendent faculty—is the single most protective factor against depression, with positive lifelong effects on healing, health, and well-being. Adolescents who feel a two-way relationship with a loving universe are strengthened by it, whether they experience it through a relationship with nature or God or a deceased loved one with whom they feel spiritually connected. They are less likely to abuse drugs and alcohol, less likely to engage in high-risk behaviors, and are deeply fortified for their hard work of identity development and of finding higher purpose in life, work, and relationships.

Adolescent spirituality will be discussed in later chapters, but for now, the important point is this: the foundation for a personal spirituality is laid in the first decade of life. From birth through about age twelve, we're hardwired to learn about the world and ourselves in it as a spiritual experience and in the context of relationship. Love is the medium and the field of love is the context. When we feel love from our parents and others, we experience ourselves as one with a loving universe, connected with others and part of the larger world. We know all living beings—from the guinea pig to the oak tree—as kindred spirits. We also experience the transcendent directly through dreams, intuition, mystical experiences, and other dimensions of consciousness that science has only begun to document.

Just as our language for everyday communication develops naturally, we're also hardwired for the language of that ineffable realm: ritual, symbolism, dreams, and mystical experience. Children love ritual: the bedtime story and good-night kiss, the favorite Saturday-morning breakfast and afternoon playdate, game day, or Sunday school. Symbolism comes naturally to them, too. Children forever have been students of the oral storytelling tradition, mesmerized by stories told around a table or a campfire—no book or iPad necessary. They dream vivid dreams, love to talk about them, and are eager to find meaning—the message in the bottle—that a dream carries. They readily see synchronicity and reciprocity in a world that is built with inherent sense.

Geraldine Fox, a physician and professor at the University of Illinois-Chicago, taped her own two children for the entirety of their development, from birth to leaving for college. A number of medical schools show her video, "Normal Development in the First Ten Years of Life," to train psychiatry residents. In the film, they see her young daughter crying after a little bump not because of the pain, but because she felt that she was being punished for a moral infraction—being mean to her brother earlier that day. This is a child's natural sense of what-comes-around-goes-around karma. Wile E. Coyote and the Road Runner need no explanation, even to a toddler.

Mystical or powerful transcendent moments of awareness are common among children, and they know them as true and valuable. Without a strong spiritual life or religion that encourages an awareness of transcendent experiences, such experiences can feel completely imaginary or made up. But I ask you to consider for a moment the strong inner events you remember from childhood, and know that many, many children have mystical experiences—classic moments of illuminated reality. For instance, Jane, a management consultant now in her sixties, vividly recalls such a moment at age six when she experienced it with a child's simple wonder and acceptance, only later finding the word "transcendent" to describe it. As a farm girl who enjoyed exploring outdoors for hours at a time, young Jane was walking through the yard back to her house after playing one day, feeling "deeply content and happy," and looking into the grass as she shuffled along, feeling the sun on her back.

Suddenly, I felt a wave of energy wash over me, a sense that time was standing still and that the space I was inhabiting was somehow enlarged and more peaceful—as if I were at the center of some kind of energy field. And the blades of grass I was focused on seemed microcosmic. I had this sense that all the meaning of the universe was contained in that one blade of grass, that God himself was present there next to the sole of my tennis shoe. I was startled by this insight and didn't understand it at all at the time. But the memory remained vivid in my mind as I grew older, returning to me many, many times as I learned about life, religion, compassion, and finding one's own spiritual path.

Many children have these experiences, though they may not actually tell anyone about them. Yet, these memories are kept, tucked safely away in the mind, and are held for a lifetime as sacred and real. At an international science conference, Stefan, a neuroscientist in his forties, divulged over lunch with colleagues that just such an experience at age eight was responsible for the great sense of purpose and passion that has distinguished his career and his life. As a child, Stefan had always enjoyed taking walks in the forest near his parents' home. He loved the woods because they felt "so vibrant and full of life and mystery." One beautiful summer day, much like other days, he wandered into the forest and, growing tired, sat down to rest on a big gray rock.

While sitting on that rock, I watched the pretty trees surrounding me. After a few minutes, I started feeling connected to the rock and the trees. It then appeared to me that the rock, the trees, and myself were part of a whole much greater than "little Stefan." Following this experience, my purpose in life became clear: I would later become a scientist to demonstrate that the essence of human beings cannot be found in the brain.

Stefan never mentioned this experience, or others that followed, to his parents, grandparents, or the children at school. It was an experience beyond words for him as a young boy, something he intuitively sensed that no one would understand or even believe. But the experiences belonged to an intimate and profound realm as concrete and real as the rock on which he'd sat that day. Even as a child he recognized his experience as transcendent, a higher order of knowing.

Ritual, Symbolism, and the Unconscious Connect Head and Heart

Dreams, mystical experiences, and more common spiritual experiences are sources of direct knowing—direct, authentic, and uncommanded experience—that invite connection between a child's head and heart knowing. Experiences of direct knowing are when the details of everyday life are felt with a superbright punch of significance, and show us that everything is part of some bigger order, and that life matters. Ritual and symbolism—music, stories, incense—are sensory cues for such connection. Together they deepen your child's attunement to the transcendent experience. You want your child to develop that eventual cognitive connection between head knowing and heart knowing. How do these simple acts or stories hold such power?

Ritual creates a special bond that physically "holds" the transcendent, connecting body and heart. What begins as a physical or sensory experience, we invest with meaning and emotional content. We light a candle to honor a moment or a memory. We sing a song, share a meal, say a blessing. In this way, ritual also opens the moment to the "something more." From the most ancient rituals to the most newly created ones, ritual by definition invests a moment with meaning; spiritual or religious ritual inherently carries meaning that resonates with transcendence. Remember the study of parents who kept journals of their children's spiritual questions of wonder and why? The most common spiritual questions, next to questions about an ultimate God, were about religious ritual. Rituals provide intense spiritual experience a system of interpretive meaning. The great anthropologist Joseph Campbell considered the "language of symbol" a powerful way to hold and guide transformational experience. In my observation, the symbolic language is particularly compelling with children as a way to hold their experience—just look at a child's face as you read the Bible, a picture book, or a symbolically driven story of any sort.

Symbolism connects mind and heart. The symbolism of ritual and story allows the child to hold and understand her intuitive knowing, her heart knowing. In this sense, symbolic stories are the cognitive visual, the linkup between head knowing and heart knowing. Whether in nature-based myths like those from Native American or original Hawaiian cultures, biblical stories, or superhero characters, symbolism develops through a cognitive process in which we invest an image or an idea with meaning. For a child, the stories of Noah's ark and of Superman succeed as fantastical adventure stories, but also as stories of meaning and inherently spiritual values: courage, faith, determination, higher purpose, and victory against daunting odds. They have the force of goodness with them.

Children have the capacity to bring these two worlds together—mind and heart—and this capacity is innate. It has nothing to do with religion. However, the world's religions have brought the spiritual and the physical worlds together through ritual and symbolism through thousands of years of practice. As we'll see shortly, ritual and symbolism can deepen our experience of family, strengthening it as a spiritual unit bound by something beyond practical functionality. Ritual and symbolism help us know the transcendent aspects of events and of people, and allow us to see past the superficial quirks or rough edges—or the polished, perfected image—to what lies deeper. In ritual we gain respect for the deeper being of every member of our family or community. Together we celebrate the seasons of our lives (school-age confirmation, bar and bat mitzvah at puberty, birthdays), our inherently sacred bonds (marriage, anniversary, or baby naming), and the emergence of new responsibility and ability on spiritual grounds.

Religion is a valuable context, but not a prerequisite, for developing the language of ritual and symbolism. The opportunity is also there in great literature, in sweeping events of the day and through history, in conflict resolution and inspiring actions from the pinnacles of power to the playground. Universal themes of love, conflict, suffering, and healing all are inherently spiritual and invite us to bring those discussions into the conversation of the day, whether it is around the kitchen table or in a classroom. This is the field of love in action, creating a space where all feelings, all worries, all debate are examined through a spiritual lens, the lens that enables us to see the larger picture and the highest good.

Spirituality is most of all a felt connection with the world apart from the purely physical, the transcendent realm. The field of love, dreams and mystical experience, and the use of ritual and symbolism are all ways that children (and adults) experience the ineffable. The best possible outcome of your child's first decade is that these links to the transcendent—which occur to him naturally—stay with him, and are not stamped out or discouraged. For this to happen he needs to continue to know the transcendent, to name it and to inhabit it. And you as his parent are vital to this effort. You may feel distant from your own transcendent understanding, or you may have an active spiritual life, but either way you can help your child forge his own paths by honoring and drawing attention to his own knowing of the heart. So much of clinical treatment in adolescence and then adulthood is about restoring knowing of heart. We do not need to cut off the child from heart knowing in the first place.

With your help and intentional cultivation of your children's spiritual assets of love and heart knowing, these spiritual assets can remain strong. By supporting them, you can fortify them against the sea of socialization in the school years ahead. Just as you work to instill good eating habits, work habits, exercise habits—often working against what your child is increasingly exposed to out of your home—you can help your child keep a spiritual understanding of the world as known from birth.

The Best Education Builds Heart and Mind Through Science and Spirit

When we talk about educational curricula intended to turn out a well-rounded child, no one debates the need for children to develop their core faculties in reading, writing, and arithmetic. Natural spirituality just isn't considered one of them. And outside of school, the once clear and un-scheduled space in children's lives for quiet walks, solitude, reflection, and conversations about life's wonder, its mysteries and big questions, of-ten becomes filled with places to go and things to do: playdates, sports practice, homework, TV, computer games, social media, and other on-line activity.

We do children a disservice when we teach them that rational con-versation requires a split between logic-based learning and their direct experience and inner heart knowing. The split forms when we teach chil-dren that science and logic are the only sources of "real" or true infor-mation, and we dismiss personal experience or intuitive information as "unsubstantiated" and inferior. That split is unnecessary and foundation-ally untrue. At the very heart of science and innovation is the passion to expand knowledge, explore the unknown, and draw from all possible sources of insight and information—to think outside the box. Chance, intuitive hunches, and serendipity have always played a role in scientific discovery. Our children need to know that their emerging abilities en-compass both the analytical and the intuitive—head knowing and heart knowing—and that both are important.

Neuroscience shows the implications for spiritual development at the most basic cell level. Neuron by neuron, the use-it-or-lose-it principle ap-plies. The brain grows along pathways that are well used and it prunes away those that aren't. It is why your child speaks the language you do and not the ones she never hears. That's also why children who grow up in homes where adults use a rich vocabulary have a stronger early vocabulary than do their peers without that influence at home. It works that way with speech development and language skills, as well as with cognitive processes that enable children eventually to work with numbers and abstract ideas. The same is true for the brain's mirroring system that enables the wordless bonding between a mother and her newborn baby: the more robust the interaction, the stronger the connection.

As your child develops her capacity to learn and question and reason, her brain continues to change. She changes as a thinker. That's natural. It's normal and wonderful. And every bit develops even more richly if heart knowing stays in the mix. Intellectual rigor doesn't have to come at the cost of a vibrant inner life and keen spiritual senses.

How can we keep those neural connections of unitive empathy strong? Language, our own actions, and love are our most powerful tools. Children naturally see the interconnectedness of all things, and their worldview, as young and small as it may seem, assumes love, protection, and care. This is how they have understood the world with us from birth—as a context of love and caring—and this becomes the lens through which they continue to naturally see the interconnectedness of all things. We sometimes inadvertently chip away at a child's heart knowing when we create a distanced "about" or "as-if" quality to the experience or feelings of others that underscores the separation between us rather than the interconnection. In casting our child's concern for others as "none of our business," "not our doing," or "not ours to know," the take-away message becomes: *Don't think about it.*

"That's Charlie's problem, not yours."

"If she needs help she'll ask the teacher for it."

"Homelessness is a very big problem and yes, it's sad to see someone homeless. But don't worry, you have a home and family that loves you."

This emotional distancing disavows a child's spiritual attunement right down to the neurological level. Maybe we say these things to be reassuring, or perhaps to avoid an uncomfortable subject, but this is neither helpful nor healthful because it fragments a child's natural way of knowing. As we just saw with Leah's story, the child of four through six or seven years old still feels others' suffering directly, not *as if* they know what it's like, but *as* their own. Training them to distance themselves from those feelings, and from others' experience, is a mistake. When we steer children away from talking about their authentic experience, we curb their potential for heart knowing as they grow. They need to know that information doesn't always have to come through an external source or be validated by the group. (This becomes especially important when they hit adolescence and their inner voice could offer wiser guidance than the voice of the pack.)

With all the talk today about the need for children to develop empathy, it's as if we believe this is something they must be trained to do. Many activities designed to "teach empathy" do indeed create opportunities for meaningful shared experience. But children don't start from scratch. The innate love and unitive empathy of the young child are inborn capacities that emerge naturally. As we support and encourage unitive empathy and *cognitive empathy*—consciously choosing to see a situation from someone else's perspective—the two develop intertwined. When we neglect that early developmental scaffolding we make it all the more challenging to "teach" them empathy later.

Younger children not yet trained to tune out heart knowing "just know" some things on this deep level. They see a lone duckling in the park and wonder where its mother is, perhaps worrying that the duckling is lost or separated from its family. They put a crumb of bread down for the ants filing across the sidewalk. They fuss at us for trying to rid the kitchen of mice: "Don't kill the mice—they're only trying to eat!" They hand a crying baby a toy if they can. They often try to comfort us when they're worried that we're not okay; they pick up on our tension or the fear or sadness we thought we'd hidden.

As they enter school and develop their capacity for critical thinking, we teach them to ask themselves: *How do you know?* That's an important question. You want your school-age child to know where his ideas come from. They need to learn how to research something. From ages six to eight or ten, they need to learn to be critical consumers and creators of knowledge. But we don't need to do that at the expense of invalidating or tacitly shutting off their original channel of heart knowing and unitive empathy. They're going to need it for the rest of their lives.

Kids Aren't Squeamish About Life's Big Questions

Children are naturally at home with the seen and unseen dimensions of the universe and are open to the beauty and complexity and promise that it presents. Every child begins this way, as a deep knower. The child shares his dreams, talks to the birds and speaks of them as his friends, feels the comforting spirit of a deceased loved one, and intuitively senses shifts in the emotional charge of a situation or person.

You want to encourage your child as a knower. It is good for your child to have a full range of motion, physically, intellectually, emotionally—and spiritually. You want your child to see the interconnected nature of the universe, to use imagination, ritual, and symbolism to draw meaning from life's experiences, to look deeper for answers that aren't easy: none of this weakens critical thinking skills. It exercises them and makes them stronger. How much richer a child's critical thinking skills grow in service of life's big questions and puzzles!

When I talk with teachers about how children react to the world around them, nursery-school teachers will often say something like, "Oh yes, they're so spiritual. I see it in our nature walks—they're so in awe of natural beauty, so full of wonder." You don't hear that from many fifth-grade teachers. That's not because fifth-graders are not spiritual. They just don't get the encouragement to express spiritual knowing, or opportunity to gain awareness by dwelling in a contemplative space. They are not asked about their inner wisdom or knowing of the heart.

Heart knowing is far too often resuscitated only in clinical settings, when immense suffering makes the need for integration of head and heart so clear. This means that a child's heart knowing might lead him to ask an inspired question or assert something he "just knows" from the same inner source, but these insights don't fit the parameters of the typical class discussion. *If we're not supposed to hit, then why do some people spank kids? Why do we help some people and not others? If you tell a lie and it doesn't hurt anyone, why is that wrong?* Children aren't usually encouraged to think that way in school. They may even have been socialized out of the kind of heart knowing that leads to these questions. Nor have they been given language to talk about spiritual values. But if an adult encourages or validates the inspired inquiry, children rise to it quickly—they have the capacity and only need to be encouraged to use it.

It's not hard to raise the questions of right and wrong, good and evil, and create a safe and welcoming space for kids to share from their deep inner wisdom. We can ask, "What does your higher self say?" "Does your heart feel an answer?" Our interest and the words make heart knowing real and important. Children love the questions and will respond in whatever way they're developmentally prepared to do. We have only to invite the conversation.

For instance, racism is a complex and difficult issue to talk about. Like all forms of social injustice, it is fundamentally a spiritual issue, a moral question of right and wrong. One Midwestern suburban K–4 elementary school with very little racial diversity uses Martin Luther King Jr.'s birthday each year to create experiences that embody the lessons of prejudice and inequity for these five- to nine-year-old children. Among other things, the school tags all the water fountains and bathrooms with either a red or blue ribbon. Students are randomly assigned to one of the two color groups and, thus segregated, may only use those water fountains and bathrooms with their color ribbon. Class documentaries, discussion, music, and art round out the week of study. In ways tailored for each grade level, the children explore the civil rights movement not only as a historic event with legal and political implications but as a deeply human issue, a spiritual event.

An educator might consider, for example: How might racism be discussed as a spiritual issue, since factually, historically, the civil rights movement gained traction among people first as a spiritual movement? Martin Luther King Jr. was a spiritual man, a spiritual leader. Many of the activists came through organized efforts by faith communities representing different religions. The legal and political complexities may challenge children's budding analytical minds, but the symbolic experience of segregation, the spiritual implications, are instant and deeply affecting. Without these larger questions, the segregated bathrooms and water fountains would be a mere inconvenience. Through symbolism and direct experience, kindergarteners on up can grasp the wrongness of racism and social injustice. They are eager to talk about it.

Symbolic learning connects head and heart around moral issues, and even for young children guides natural awareness of right action. Children's literature is about the deepest and most profound questions and themes, good and evil, right and wrong, heroism and cowardice. During the nursery school's *Stone Soup* activity described in chapter 4, three-year-olds talked candidly about why they might be hesitant to talk to a stranger who knocked on their door or to give him food. They know that they're not supposed to talk to strangers. But when it came to whether they would want to contribute to the stranger's soup pot there was no question. No hesitation, only excitement at the prospect of adding their carrots or peas to feed the hungry. When we avoid or don't discuss the moral implications—when we talk only about the characters' actions and practical motivations—our children miss a chance to learn from their own reflections on the issues. We also pass up the easy opportunity to use the ritual of reading and the symbolism within stories to personalize the child's spiritual learning experience.

We can bring the big questions home by inviting children to connect with the issues and the questions. Point out how the story themes are present in everyday life around you. For example, reading the *Stone Soup* story you might ask the following questions:

"Have you ever wished someone would help you but nobody did?"

"Have you ever wanted to help someone but were afraid to? Or worried what other people would think?"

"Do you know anybody who is hungry?"

"Have you ever tricked someone to get what you wanted or needed?"

Because life's big questions *are* personal*: Who am I? What is my mark on the world? What gives my life meaning and purpose? What can I do about the suffering of others?* Through adolescence and the rest of our lives, we continue to grapple with the big questions. Children do so every day, too, from the playground to the kitchen table. You don't have to be an expert in literature to ask questions that pique children's interest and stir discussion. Children so rarely get to be experts on anything, and they love to be asked: *Have you ever felt that way? What would you do in that situation? What do you think?*

Put heroes and superheroes to work for you. Harry Potter and Hermione, Spiderman, Superman, the Avengers, and Princess Elsa in *Frozen* already inhabit your children's lives. Bring them home during dinner or drive-time chats. What motivates a character to act selflessly for a higher good? What about evil? Characters in these stories also collaborate—some for good and some for evil. Every school-age child recognizes this. Children are built to know good and evil; they simply need your encouragement to reflect and take stock of their own feelings and ideas so that they can connect head and heart. You can ask:

"Do you ever feel this is true in real life—that sometimes people get together to work together to do good things and sometimes to do bad things?"

"How have you seen this in your own experience with friends
or classmates?"

We all see the presence of good and evil in the world and should be
riveted, with plenty of questions about it. We all have questions about
our place in the world and the meaning of life. These are legitimate questions for consideration, for personal reflection and open discussion in
which a child's full, personal, and direct experience is real and relevant.
The conversation about spiritual values isn't a conversation that should
be segregated from the rest of a child's learning experience. If our child
tries to engage, we need to acknowledge. Why did that witch steal that
magic box? Why was the Beast so mean to Belle? Why did Hansel and
Gretel's mother leave them in the forest? Don't say, "Nobody would ever
do that to you, it's only a fairy tale, only a story." We don't need to dwell
only on the disturbing parts of literature, but when the child is open to
conversation, then engage, and let him explore these ideas so they don't
become foreign or "off limits."

How could we possibly wish for children to leave this innermost, questioning, morally striving part of themselves out of their learning as they
move into more and more challenging situations and decisions in life?
Whatever aspirations you may have for your child, there is not one field
of study or career or relationship or endeavor for which this inner voice
is best silenced. Peter Benson's international and wide-ranging study on
adolescents and young adults (which we have mentioned previously)
identified spiritual development as a "universal aspect of positive youth
development" that translates directly into benefits in relationships, work,
and personal meaning and purpose. This and other research shows that
spiritual qualities of character, including openness, empathy, compassion, and conscience, are among the most important factors in lifetime

success and satisfaction. Study after study from across disciplines and around the world report similar findings. All of this begins at the beginning—your child's earliest years.

We can cultivate children's natural spiritual assets into richly developed strengths for a lifetime. Math is a good analogy. You're not born knowing addition, subtraction, multiplication, and division; you're born with the capacity for mathematical thinking. Your child is born with a capacity for spiritual knowing. Rather than leave it to be winnowed away by neglect, we can support their natural spirituality, hold open the space for expression, provide a language for it, and help their spiritual assets grow into these six core spiritual strengths:

1. A spiritual compass for trustworthy inner guidance
2. Family as a spiritual "home base" and sustaining source of connection, unconditional love, and acceptance
3. Spiritual community as an extension of the family's field of love, a shared experience and a lifelong "road home" to spiritual connection
4. Spiritual "multilingualism" that broadens their access to a world of sacred experience and inspiration
5. Spiritual agency that empowers them to right action that expands the field of love into a culture of love
6. Transcendent knowing: dreams, mystical experiences, and other special knowing

These core strengths build out, like nesting dolls or concentric circles, from the most singular, intimate inner compass, extending and resonating through a child's spiritual experience of family, community, the multicultural world, and ultimately into their own sense of spiritual agency and transcendent experience. As we'll see next, these strengths give our children the power to shape their world for the better, from the playground to any path they travel in adult life.

7

THE SIX SPIRITUAL STRENGTHS

f you encourage your child's natural spiritual assets—trusting heart knowing and validating direct transcendent experience; encouraging natural love of nature, of spiritual ritual and prayer and right action, and the sense of family as special—these assets will develop into spiritual strengths with lifelong benefits. These are the spiritual strengths that science now tells us provide the most impressive protective benefits in adolescence against depression, substance use and abuse, and other high-risk behaviors, as well as a source of thriving. And to repeat, parents are especially important to this process. You can nurture your child's spiritual relationship with the people and the world cultivate these core strengths—or shut them down.

It is a delightful moment when as parents we witness with wonder and awe a pop of natural spirituality in a child—something our child says or does that shows a great soul in a little body. When this happens, we can offer developmental backup with validation or interest, or ask our child to take us into their experience even further. Sometimes the moment just calls for our own appreciation. We do not need grand theories or perfect answers to honor these moments. We really just need to show up. Often a parent's own intuition kicks in alongside and reawakens our own spirituality.

Simple parental attention, as we've seen in the science around the nod and the joint effect, is more than simply supportive. It is a catalyst. In the Chris Boyatzis study (in which parents kept a journal of their family spiritual discussions for two one-week periods), it was in the second week, after parents and children had been paying extra attention to spiritual discussion, that children made more spontaneous spiritual remarks throughout the day. It seems to me that the child quickly senses and responds favorably as the family shows greater intention to listen and honor the child's natural spirituality.

More from the child leads to more from the parent—this is the family discovering its own pace, gently turning up the level of family spirituality. Boyatzis shows in scientific terms what I see routinely in my work with children and families, and what we know full well from our own families: when we show an interest in what our children think and do, they welcome our attention and want to share more. When we take a loving lead, they follow.

When we acknowledge, embrace, and help build a child's natural spirituality, we build a pathway through which children can access their knowing from the heart, even develop a transcendent sense of themselves, other people, and dynamic relationship with a higher power. With a felt awareness of transcendence built in, life becomes more. At the very least the child now has a lifelong passage to his natural spirituality. If in the first decade you support your child's spiritual development, cultivate these assets into the following six strengths—they become a reliable source for guidance, clarity, and a sense of purpose.

1. A child's spiritual compass: trustworthy and good for life

A child's inner life is an instrument of spiritual knowing, a trustworthy inner compass that aligns itself for health, and orients toward the truth and spiritual values.

Through heart knowing our children sense the inherent worth in fellow living beings, events, and nature. Granted, in the blink of an eye or without a nap the sacred child may bonk a sibling on the head or "share" her cake by carving off just the tiniest crumb, but these are quick and occasional notes of childhood before the executive functioning of adolescence kicks in. Through the first decade, as her cognitive skills grow and her social and emotional development continues, her inner compass evolves, too. Its "true north" setting naturally orients toward spiritual values.

Remember the studies of children of opiate addicts that showed the propensity of the children, at even the youngest ages, to align themselves spiritually with the healthiest spiritual adult in the home or among other caring adults? Even a single powerful childhood experience of spiritual awareness can be a lasting source of guidance through adulthood.

We often speak of a "moral compass" that guides us to choose right over wrong. That moral compass is built upon the spiritual compass, which finds direction from the higher self guided by the transcendent relationship.

You can engage your child's heart knowing and help her develop her spiritual compass to navigate just about any situation in life. Your job is to offer her the language to talk about this inner guidance. Help her practice using her inner compass in everyday ways so that she comes to understand that it's there for her, and trustworthy.

"You want to skip your cousin's party, because it might be boring. What does your natural spiritual compass say about family commitments?"

"I can see why you would be annoyed with that clique of girls for gossiping about your clothes. What does your spiritual compass say about gossip—or for that matter, talking that way about things like clothes? Can you 'live and let live'—accept that they do it their way and you are on your own path?"

"You went an extra mile to make sure the new girl felt welcome. Your spiritual compass sure guided you in a beautiful direction."

Children often show a stronger spiritual compass than we might expect, enabling even young children to sense adult hypocrisy or prejudice—and to act on it.

Celine, a mother in her early thirties, had severed connections with the church of her childhood and religion in general, after a hurtful experience surrounding her teenage pregnancy and her eventual divorce from her daughter's father. But she let her six-year-old daughter Rya attend Catholic school because the child liked to go to church with her grandmother, who remained quite observant. Celine worried that Rya would "be brainwashed" by the prejudice and hypocrisy of which she herself had been a victim, but she kept quiet about it because the personal history was so complicated. One day Rya came home from school very worried but wouldn't tell her mother what troubled her. "Then all of a sudden she says, 'Mom, just so you know, I don't think you're going to hell. And I don't think I'm going to hell, either.' And I looked at her and said, 'Well, that's good. Why do you say that?'

"Rya replied, 'In school today they said it's bad to be divorced because you're breaking the bonds you promised to make. They taught us that if you're divorced you're going to go to hell. And I don't think that's true.'"

Celine's worst expectations of misuse of religious doctrine were confirmed, but she was inspired by her six-year-old daughter's response. Rya's inner compass was as strong as her mother's. Rya knew her own spiritual truth, and at the same time could incorporate the church as part of her loving bond with her grandmother. Kids can surprise you. Helping your child read her inner life as a spiritual compass can lock in natural spiritual values. A spiritual compass and language with which to talk about it also helps children as they face social challenges. School is hard for little people, and their inner compass can become a ready intuitive tool with which to navigate the often-choppy waters.

Beyond a navigational tool, your child's spiritual compass is the synthesis of her core values, expressed as inner guidance. The social and emotional terrain of childhood is full of challenging moments when kids can easily get lost in the thick of emotions and impulses. Kids pick on each other, hurt one another's feelings, take sides. They feel ashamed, angry, inadequate, left out, scared, and confused—often by their own feelings. Especially when they're very young, you may be there at the time to help them get centered and bring their heart knowing and spiritual values to the task of sorting things out. But you won't (and shouldn't) always be there as chief navigator. If they've learned to access their inner compass themselves, they'll come to use it reflexively. As they near adolescence and the challenges grow more complex, even if they're drawn to explore unknown territory in the process, they'll be prepared to draw deeply from inner resources for guidance—equipped to find their own true north.

2. Children are hardwired to hold family sacred and sustaining

Allison was among a half-dozen nursery-school mothers at a parent coffee I attended one morning. They were sharing stories of children and family, and the conversation turned to the magnetizing effect their children just naturally seemed to have that pulled family together. Some described how the birth of their child had brought extended family members closer. In Allison's case, her son Peter had helped heal a rift between Allison and her father—more than two decades after his death.

Four-year-old Peter was fascinated by a photo on Allison's dresser of her father, who had died twenty-some years earlier, long before her son was born. It was a snapshot taken on the beach in the 1980s, when she was about ten years old. Peter would frequently pause by the picture, studying it intently.

One day Peter asked, "What was he like? Was he like you?" In the days ahead he posed dozens of questions. These were a bit difficult for Allison because as an adult she had been somewhat estranged from her father. One morning as Allison was getting him ready to go to nursery school, out of the blue Peter asked, "What was Grandpa doing with the kite?"

Allison was bewildered. "Kite?" she asked.

"Yes, there's a kite in the picture of Grandpa in your room."

Together they peered closely at the photograph. Sure enough, on the far side of the picture was a tiny image of a kite flying high above the beach. Seeing it reminded Allison that she and her dad had taken the kite flying that day, thirty years ago. Peter's hunger to know everything about his grandfather reawakened Allison's connection to her father, prompting her to take Peter to her father's graveside. It was her first visit after all these years.

Peter's natural curiosity and his desire to know his grandfather embraced a fading piece of his mother's past, infused it with new color, new life, and the spirit of his grandfather. That Grandpa Joe had died years ago wasn't relevant. Peter knew that he had passed on, but he wanted to reel in this kite-flying, beach-loving, playful grandfather and make his presence felt in their home and family. Peter's spiritual compass had drawn him to what mattered most. He wanted his grandfather in his life. It was, in a sense, also what was needed to mend a tear in the fabric of family. The field of love was made whole, as Peter mended what Allison hadn't managed to mend for herself earlier.

Young children are naturally drawn to the specialness of family. Remember the research that young children experience parents as omniscient beings, loving and protective? The child's trust in what we say and do is complete. They show us in so many ways what psychologists talk about as the "primacy of family," the family's role as the defining context for a child's development. The field of love is the basis for what I call the spiritual primacy of family, a child's defining context for spiritual development and values.

The field not only nurtures a child in the here-and-now family but also connects them to the loving presence and transcendent connection across generations. As children develop more advanced language and cognition, they carry that connection forward firmly in mind and heart.

Liam was ten years old when his Grandma Joan died. She had lived nearby and from birth he had had a very close and joyful relationship with her. She picked him up from school several days a week. They baked cookies and took adventures to the children's museums, aquarium, and swimming pool. As Liam started getting homework, Grandma Joan would help him study. On family vacations the two would take quiet walks in the woods or by the water. Nearly every significant event included Grandma Joan.

More than two years after her death she remains a loving presence for him. Sometimes he sits and thinks about her, especially when he's had a bad day, he told me. He recalled how on one such day, "I was just thinking about my grandma, and that thought went to another thought of just thinking of my grandma and how I love my grandma so much. There is so much of her that I wish I still had. Sometimes if I am lonely, I think of her. So I talk to her. It's like a prayer and kind of a conversation. It helps."

"Sometimes I ask her for help," Liam says. "If I have a hard time learning something, or trouble with a test—I ask her for help so I can get through things. Sometimes I feel like she answers back. It's like simple little things—not like big things—that I ask her for help on. Most of the time she's right there for me. I ask Grandma for help. She helps."

This spirit-deep relationship with family is one of the core assets of a child's natural spirituality. They draw life lessons not only from the strengths, but also the foibles and failings of various family members. They may not have a vivid personal memory as Liam did. For Peter, the simple photo of his grandfather was all the cue he needed. A friend tells me how stories of her mother's struggles to learn English as an immigrant have impressed her six-year-old daughter, an avid reader, who feels her grandmother's pride in her granddaughter's love of books. Children find their own meaning and value in the family experience on a spiritual level, often despite complicated relationships within the family. The aunt or uncle who bucked family expectations to pursue their own dreams, the difficult or complicated family members, the funny or outrageous or adventurous ones: your child wants to know them, if only through their stories, and wants to know that the field of love is big enough and strong enough—loving enough—to hold them all.

The child hungers to know all relatives, living or deceased. The natural sense of family bond with relatives who are no longer alive is culturally supported in most countries around the globe, often as some form of ancestor honoring, prayer, offering, or appreciation. Many cultures and religious traditions have ceremonies that recognize a crucial place of relationship with ancestors in our lives. In Mexican culture it's the Day of the Dead. Ancestor shrines and offerings are common in China and other parts of Asia. In Jewish tradition, the mourner's kaddish prayer is recited each Sabbath to remember departed loved ones and in the same moment celebrate life. At weddings, baby namings, christenings, and other life cycle events we invoke the memory of those who have passed on. We draw them into sacred moments through ritual and symbolism to consecrate the moment and keep their presence alive in the field of love, in the family story.

Whether celebrated explicitly or more privately, this "sanctification of family," as researchers Annette Mahoney and Ken Pargament call it, reflects a quality of family that has lasting value to our children. Mahoney's and Pargament's expansive body of research has studied family patterns of spiritual engagement and their effects. Using surveys and interviews with self-identified religious families and spiritual but nonreligious families, findings in both groups show that when we perceive our family as sacred we (1) are more committed, loyal, and try harder in relationships; (2) are more forgiving and appreciative of family members as individuals; and (3) see daily work as daughters, sons, parents, and spouses as an opportunity for spiritual growth.

How do we "sanctify" the family to strengthen this experience for our children? We don't do it by lecturing a child on how to be a good person. We do it by creating everyday moments of focused attention to qualities like commitment, forgiveness, resilience, and loyalty, all held in the field of love. It might be in a two-minute family huddle in the park, a walk on the beach, or around the breakfast table, or a regular Sunday Skype session with loved ones far away. We can pull together around a family member who is feeling badly and express love and support in words: *Let's rally around Jeffrey in encouragement, he had a hard day with his math test, and the family wants him to feel total love!* We define our family's spiritual values—we say *this matters deeply to us; you matter deeply to us.*

Bring the ancestors into the picture. Children yearn to know, *What would they think of me?*

"Grandpa Louie would have loved the craftsmanship you put into your project. He'd be so proud of you."

"Mama Mac always listened to the birds and talked to her plants—we laughed about it, but she always just laughed back. She'd smile to see you in the garden now."

These impromptu minirituals and recognition *en famille* mean so much to a child. Not only as a personal embrace by the family, but as a celebration of the family itself. Whether you do it with a family cheer, with hands held around the table in prayer, or that weekly video chat, a child feels the all-affirming love that family is. Our purposeful sanctification of family strengthens the spiritual primacy of family and nourishes the deepest core of a child's being.

Circumstances can break down families and tear the field of love. Divorce, death, loss, trauma: the tear can seem irreparable. But families can purposefully reconfigure and use sacred intention to resanctify and mend the field of love. Most important, this means that families can remain "together" or spiritually whole even if someone is physically absent, whatever the reason. The transcendent experience of a higher good, a higher awareness embodied by your family, also strengthens your child's two-way relationship with a loving universe. We so often pool family efforts for external and relatively inconsequential things— to organize busy activities, get everyone new clothes or equipment for a vacation, or in the many ways as adults we allocate money and other resources. It takes only a few minutes each day to celebrate our families and family members and to make the field of love a felt reality for our children.

3. Spiritual community gives your child an expanded family of kindred spirits

Beyond the solid foundation of family, a spiritual community gives your child the people and places to help cultivate these deep values. The idea of spiritual community is often assumed to be a religious community. A religious community that is open and loving can be a spiritual home for your child, as we'll see shortly, but it is by no means the only place where your child can cultivate the sacred space within and find spiritual connection. An affirming collective of people, shared values, and shared experience can spring up spontaneously around a very loving family down the block or an inspired leader of any organization or group. It might be a close-knit cul-de-sac or neighborhood where adults and kids genuinely care about one another and show it; an extended family that includes close friends with whom you create traditions, perhaps consistently celebrate special occasions and holidays; a youth group, community service program, or other special-interest group in which your child feels a part of that "something larger," feels unconditionally accepted and appreciated.

Sports can be a natural mind-body-spirit experience for kids, packed with passion and purpose. Sports teams tap into kids' hardwired spiritual values: for selfless commitment, collective practice, ritual, play, and higher purpose. They revel in the rhythm and demands of practice and the sport itself, push themselves to their personal best, sacrifice to help teammates, and aim for a common goal and a common good. The support and encouragement of coaches and parents who frame the game, the teamwork, the winning and even the losing, the athleticism or "heart" that kids show: the sum of it all registers as something greater than mere physical performance. It is often a push beyond themselves into a transcendent connection with teammates for a bigger, higher purpose. Whether or not they are aware of where that feeling of oneness comes from within them, they are, in essence, connecting through the transcendent faculty. Team spirit truly is an expression of spirit, and in its own way it enlivens them, fortifies them, and can buoy them up when things get tough.

Nature is the original spiritual community, the most fundamental and enduring one for our children. Bobby Lake-Thom, a Native American author and healer, writes that the Native American system of spirituality "is one of constant bonding with the earth matrix." Specific myths address the four essential stages of life (childbirth, puberty, vision quest, and burial) interspersed with a variety of everyday rituals and ceremonies. Children's awareness of these rites of passage, as well as the everyday ritual have such a profound effect, Lake-Thom explains, because they provide "an opportunity to synthesize the conscious and unconscious, logical and intuitive, the masculine and feminine and the physical and the spiritual." These different aspects of our spiritual selves are wedded in ceremony, a lived, enacted form of transcendence.

Whether it's on the sports field, in a church or temple, at the community center, or on the street where you live, spiritual community also gives your child the place and people to build out the field of love. In spiritual community, all three types of the transcendent relationship are strong and present: relationships of unconditional love, relationship with the higher power, and a child's engagement with the higher self.

This communal embrace of values forges the spiritual inroads in childhood that will forever remain a path back to this childhood endowment. A shared world where we embrace, celebrate, and indeed come to rely on heart knowing sets up the child for life. Head and heart are connected. Natural spirituality is linked into the rest of life, which becomes much more—more filled with joy and awe, love, meaning, and purpose.

What does spiritual community look like? From camp grounds to the sanctuary, all of these spiritual communities create opportunities that are beneficial to our children: intergenerational company, support, memories of those who have died, time for quiet reflection, ritual, song, friendship, and other spiritually engaged families. A spiritual community adds to the field of love, is an extended family-by-choice that shares spiritual values, celebrates you for your spirit, and cheers or prays you through challenges. Together we sing, play, pray, learn from and tend to one another. We express our shared humanity in food or clothing drives, community service projects, car washes and benefit performances, meals, or visitations to the elderly or homebound members of the community. Spiritual community commits to the well-being of all, embraces each unconditionally, values all for their inner being, and includes them irrespective of outward merit.

Kids love all of this. They are naturally drawn to the ritual and ceremony sensory experiences: music, movement, and imagery; spiritual story, myth, and symbolism; and perhaps even the feel of ceremonial robes or objects. Religious communities are very appealing to children because they've been doing this spirit building full-throttle for a long time and with great success.

Children's natural curiosity and magnetic draw to religious ritual and community may be unnerving to you as a parent if you've had a negative experience or no experience with religion growing up or in your adult life. You may worry that precisely because children are so open, so receptive, they will be inculcated with dogma or prejudice—the "my God is better than your God" mentality. Here's something to keep in mind:

There is great diversity in faith-based communities, from traditional theistic religions to humanist congregations. You don't have to settle for one that presents a conflict in ideology or practice for you. The search for a good fit is a perfect opportunity to have rich conversations with your child that you might not have otherwise. What core values are most important to you? What services or activities might you try to explore in different faith communities to see how those values are expressed and practiced there? You can help your child learn to separate the valuable message (love, acceptance, and a relationship with God or universe) from the imperfect messenger. Talk about how to tell a true spiritual community or spiritual leader by the qualities of love, acceptance, and contribution it represents. The bottom line: How does this community extend or strengthen the field of love?

Whatever misgivings you may have, becoming part of a spiritual community, or even the search to find one that feels like a fit for your family, presents opportunities for inner growth and a feeling of connectedness that are so important to children. We can ground them in the natural spiritual values we want to guide them, encourage them to develop their own inner compass, and support their desire to find a place or group of people where they feel that quality of spirit.

One can always play or pray alone, and that, too, is meaningful and sustaining. But to feel your voice resonate in a chorus of voices, to feel held or uplifted, inspired, soothed or healed with and through others who care about you: this is the unique gift of spiritual community. It is the collective "nod" and commitment to higher purpose that invests these moments or practices with their special meaning. Your child may find that in the ritual campfire at summer camp, a weekly shared meal with family or community, or the team's ritual pregame chant in the huddle.

When I was growing up, my family's spiritual community was a temple in Des Moines. I can still remember my six-year-old self, so excited to go to temple with my grandparents on Friday nights. My great-grandparents on both sides had been settler Jews in the Midwest, part of the region's first Jewish community and of the generation that built the temple I grew up in. This was the temple in which both my parents were confirmed, as well as all of my aunts, uncles, and cousins. It was the temple in which my parents were married and in which I was named. It felt like home. It was a small synagogue and small, warm Jewish community and it was a natural and deeply felt extension of the field of love. I remember one particular moment as a six-year-old with photographic clarity. It was Shabbat services and I was sitting in a pew, flanked by all four of my grandparents. At one point I glanced up and saw them, all four leaning over and smiling at me. As the cantor sang with deep emotion, I was so deeply moved with the soulful connection through body and spirit, I cried. My grandparents, and the community of Temple B'nai Jershurun: they were the carriers of Judaism for me. Religion can be sacred; it can hold that.

4. Spiritual multilingualism is your child's passport

If these first three strengths—a spiritual compass, commitment to family, and spiritual community as a sustaining source of love—are must-haves for children's life journey, then spiritual multilingualism is their passport. Having our own spirituality and sense of community, whatever that may be, is important to a child. But you want your child to be able to see the sacred in others. Spiritual multilingualism enables us to cross familiar borders and embrace the essence of spirituality in its many cultural narratives.

Children come to understand that diverse spiritual traditions share common themes and often have parallel ideas and observances: the rhythm of the seasons, the birth of a baby, ceremonies of commitment, or rituals around death and mourning. Having your own spiritual or religious orientation but being able to hear and understand others not only makes it easier to engage with other people, it also enhances your own access to sacred experience by making these universal inner connections available to you wherever you go. A child who is conversant in the "many names, many faces" of spiritual practice can find the sacred in others—engage more meaningfully with other people in our diverse global culture.

"The biggest mistake people make when first beginning to look at unfamiliar perspectives is immediately to make comparisons between the familiar and the unfamiliar," writes Buddhist feminist theologian and author Rita Gross. "The power of the comparative lens comes not from making positive and negative comparisons; rather, it comes from seeing each perspective clearly, in its own right. In other words, one gets a deeper understanding of one's own perspective by understanding how others understand their own perspective."

In childhood, natural spirituality of the heart very quickly attaches to the names, stories, and rules to which our children gain daily exposure. Starting as early as age four and certainly by age seven, children absorb the language and customs of thought used to express spirituality in their family or spiritual community. Research shows that for children these names are prioritized as spiritually "more real." A team of Harvard psychologists led by professor Mahzarin Banaji investigated whether young children already had in-group versus out-group—*my God is better than your God*—perceptions around the names of the higher power. The team found in controlled experiments that a child as young as age six will rate "God" as named by her faith as more omniscient than "God" as named by another geographically remote unfamiliar faith. No matter what we may think about religion, we want to be sure children are open to the spiritual presence in all people. You want your child to be as attuned to spirituality as possible. As parents, we want to act early, deliberately, and swiftly. We do not want a child to build tribal superiority, which has nothing to do with a clear and open pipeline for natural spirituality. Theological competition is a misguided form of accidental socialization that ultimately distorts access to transcendent love.

The early mental packaging of a child's natural spirituality makes imperative—read *urgent*—that our children become, in essence, spiritu-ally multilingual and multicultural from an early age if we genuinely want them to have respect and appreciation for natural spirituality in other people and cultures. This "many faces, many names" perspective is the opposite of religious chauvinism and all other "isms." Offer your child a window into the religions of other families and peoples. As ambassadors, offer the opportunity to feel transcendence in many places and ways.

Well before kindergarten, but certainly by elementary school, kids are primed to want to learn about spiritual expression and they are hungry to learn. Walk by any house of worship—a mosque, a temple, church, a cathedral, or a spirit hut—and a child will be curious and want to explore inside. They see a house of worship built for prayer or contemplation, or spiritual community life, and they want to experience it, too. They are already little universal beings. Explain to them that God and spiritual-ity has many faces as seen by humans. Teach them, too, that all people of genuine, loving spiritual nature share a fundamental sense of good-ness in how they view others and the world we share. Your child is ready to understand other faiths, traditions, and cultures. Speak about other religions with interest, share what you know, learn more together, and see where your own natural spirituality can find expression in other faith traditions. Talking together will provide the language to speak about other forms of spirituality and also offer words to discuss personal choices and views.

Jane (who earlier shared her epiphany of walking with God through the grass as a six-year-old) had grown up in a tiny farm town of one hundred people and attended a small community church and Sunday school most Sundays. There, she said, "I had imbibed a sense of a boundless and loving God—no dogma, just a belief in an all-powerful divine being whose presence made the universe fundamentally good." That open and loving religious backdrop "permanently changed my view of spirituality, and gave me confidence to know that our connection with the universe, or with God, or whatever we define as the uniting energy, is a deeply personal one, and that it doesn't have to be bounded by any sectarian rules," Jane said. "I have been grateful for that many times, because I believe it helped me remain open to learning about all faiths—including the Buddhism embraced some thirty years later by my husband at the time, a lapsed Catholic. It has also given me hope in times when I felt alienated from religions of all kinds."

Spiritual multilingualism isn't only about accepting others. We also grow as spiritual beings more able to fully engage our human experience. Rolland, a young man of nearly thirty, told me how his grandmother died of a sudden illness when he was eight. She lived in India, her homeland, and—unlike Rolland's family in the United States, who were Baptist—she was Hindu, something he heard for the first time when he heard his parents talking about her funeral arrangements. His grandmother was much beloved, and as he felt the loss reverberate through his family he also found himself thinking for the first time about aspects of his religious upbringing that he had never really thought about before: how death was explained in his Baptist community, and other religions' different views of the life, death, and an afterlife. Learning of his grandmother's Hinduism inspired Rolland to feel and know transcendence through the path of his grandmother's spiritual practice.

As children grow and take in more and more of the world—events, debates, conflicts at home and globally—a foundation of respect and an awareness of universal spiritual themes will help prevent them from seeing fellow human beings as distant others or inherently wrong because of different religious or spiritual expression. Fluency in many spiritual languages can deepen and permanently strengthen their capacity for heart knowing, including seeing the transcendent in people who look and pray differently.

More schools are venturing into spiritual multilingualism as part of their curriculum in global, multicultural education. Foote School, a progressive and culturally diverse day school in New Haven, Connecticut, sends its sixth-grade class—eleven- and twelve-year-olds—on a series of field trips to augment their study of world religions. The program is part of the humanities curriculum, designed to give students experiences to help them be global citizens in our diverse world. I was invited to accompany the class on a field trip, focusing on the Abrahamic traditions of Judaism, Christianity, and Islam.

To get to know these faiths at least a step beyond classroom study, the students were taken to three landmark houses of worship in New York City: St. John the Divine, the largest cathedral in the United States; Temple Emanu-El, generally considered the most architecturally spectacular Reform synagogue; and the Islamic Cultural Center Mosque, spiritual home to the city's Muslim community, all of these houses of worship accommodating countless international visitors each year. Each structure is breathtaking, exceptional, and vast.

From the grand cathedral to the grand synagogue to the grand mosque, the children craned their heads up and around and a breathy universal choir of "Wow!" echoed through each sanctuary. At each stop our school guide and the welcoming clergy took the students through these great halls of worship and pointed out architectural highlights that reflect aspects of the faith's spiritual foundations. At St. John's, the crucifix and the stained glass windows depict the biblical roots of Christianity. In Temple Emanu-El's historic hand-scribed Torah scrolls the students could see the durable expression of an ancient spiritual story and people. And at the Islamic mosque, the sea of men kneeling in midday prayer was a vivid reminder of spiritual devotion embodied in each and the many gathered together.

At various points along the way these children on the cusp of adolescence asked the clergy respectfully about different prayers, rituals, and symbolism. They listened intently, absorbing the distinguishing features, and the commonalities, of the different faiths. Their questions and comments reflected their growing capacity for reflection and a probing desire to connect this practice in this place of worship, with their own inner knowing of the heart. In one activity, the teacher asked the children to draw in a journal something from anywhere within the great structure that touched them with personal meaning or significance. A Jewish girl drew the votive candles at St. John the Divine. A non-Jewish boy drew the Torah scrolls from the sanctuary at Temple Emanu-El, and a group of nearly a half-dozen children stood attentive and respectful for quite a while before they drew the kneeling men at the mosque.

As we stood outside waiting for the bus, a chaperoning teacher explained to me that the school hoped the children would "respect the differences, but more fundamentally find the common ground between faiths," she said. "We want them to truly feel at home in all three spaces, rather than just passing by on the street, wondering what goes on inside." Judging from the students' enthusiasm, the trip accomplished that. Equally important, as evidenced by their responses to the drawing assignment, all of the children found something of personal meaning or significance, and many did so in houses of worship and religious contexts that were not familiar to them previously.

You don't have to wait for a school field trip to broaden your child's spiritual horizons. You can go on those walks together, visit houses of worship and respectfully explore, or search online sources for information and commentary, or virtual tours of historic religious sites and spiritual communities around the globe. You can encourage your child to hear at the level of his heart the wisdom contained in a world of faiths, as well as from those on his own spiritual journey.

You can't order up moments of transcendent illumination, but you can open the space for them by supporting your child's sense that spiritual connection exists everywhere and at all times—and that they can find it in people everywhere. *You have your own inner spiritual wisdom through which to experience the wisdom in traditions around us. Even if in our family we have a strong one of our own, we can learn different things from other spiritual traditions. All are valuable to our own understanding of spirituality.*

If you welcome questions, they will come. The child is making sense of messages from without, trying to link up these messages with experiences of the heart. The child also is a keen empirical scientist of spirit, making observations that are consistent or inconsistent between family and cultural messages and knowing of the heart. Sometimes these are moral questions, sometimes they are big structural cosmic questions, sometimes they are picking up something within their own hearts.

So they will ask you foundational questions: They will hear about something—let's just say reincarnation—and the questions bubble forth: *If you were born a rabbit, can you come back as a human? Could I come back as a rabbit?* You don't have to be an expert in world religions to honor your child's questions, welcome the conversation, and explore the world of ideas together, whether that's through online resources or from your own—and your child's—perspective. You can ask: *What do you think? Have you ever sensed you may have been a rabbit? How so?* Let your child's curiosity drive the exploration. If you hop on board to visit these questions together, you give importance to the discoveries for both of you.

Silence is the worst thing you can do to your child's spiritual development. Silence sends the implicit message that a child's transcendent experiences and feelings are "off the map," not "really real," or are not important enough for your family to discuss. This can be the accidental side effect of a parent's own avoidance of spiritual questions, or a sidestepping of cultural or religious blending within a family. But losing the place of natural spirituality in the home is a loss to the child. A young teen girl explains it this way:

> My mother was raised Hindu. Well, sort of—that is what she really is. But she went to Catholic school, and she believes in Jesus, so officially she is Christian. My father was raised Jewish, but did not really observe as a child. So because they did not have the same religion we got rid of it as a family—and we are atheists. Well, not really atheists. We just don't talk about it.

This highly articulate girl went on to share that she felt joy and felt uplifted when visiting a beautiful cathedral on a class trip, but she had no frame of reference for understanding these feelings as coming from a source of spirituality within her. Her parents' rejection of religion had prevented the recognition of spirituality as a natural, personal faculty of direct knowing and connection to a larger universe. Spiritual multilingualism can hold on to direct knowing, far better than silence, if a single religious "language" does not make sense for a family.

No matter how complicated or ill prepared you feel approaching this spiritual conversation, there is always a way to do it. In a religiously "mixed marriage," it's less important in *which* religion or spiritual language you land. The essential point is that you provide your child with a way to explore natural spirituality. You don't even have to have a clear stance on your own spirituality. You simply need to show that you respect the quest and support the exploration. Spiritual multilingualism opens up things, broadens the conduit to heart knowing and a child's inner compass. Now is the time—in this first decade—to sustain the spiritual conversation in the way you welcome questions and conversation. As learners and as spiritual beings, our children need to be free, not locked in place by limitations of language and socializations.

5. *Spiritual agency empowers children to create a culture of love*

Our children venture forth every day into the nitty-gritty human experience. They confront the good, the bad, and the complicated, from home turf to the playground and school cafeteria. When they encounter inconsideration, nastiness, or selfishness, young children often reflexively choose to be kind and generous, to be helpful and to step up and speak up when they see someone in need. Through the first decade, as they become more socially aware at school and in their worldview, they also become more self-aware of their own power to act in the world. The field of love isn't just there to support them; they can create it. You've showed them how to do it in everyday life at home—and they have the power to create it, expand it, wherever they go.

This growing awareness of spiritual agency becomes the practice ground for cognitive empathy—consciously choosing to understand a situation from someone else's perspective and to respond sensitively. In so many ways children are perceived and treated as having no agency, no power. And in many ways it's true: They can't drive a car, they don't control family decisions, and they can't put you in a corner for time out when you lose your temper. But spiritually it's a very different story. Spiritual agency comes from within, and no matter what their age children have opportunities each day to make choices that exercise that power for good and that deepen their sense of ownership over their own choices.

If you have ever watched (and listened to) a bunch of kids through a school day, you know that they recognize cheating, meanness, and hurtful behavior by classmates. "That was mean!" one child calls out in a foursquare game as the server takes obvious pleasure in smashing the ball out of reach of the short child. The impossible serve isn't technically against the rules and it earns points for the server's team. Some would justify it as merely a competitive advantage—tough luck for some but part of the game. But children recognize the hurtful impact of an unbridled, punishing competitive spirit in a setting that doesn't call for it. Head knowing says that it's within the rules; heart knowing says it's just not right. As we know now from research on bullying prevention, there is enormous power in educating children about social cruelty and in helping them recognize their authority to speak up in the moment or to an adult. With an inner compass that points to right action, and having been encouraged to trust it, a child feels empowered to act. If you can stand up for yourself—and others—on the playground, you're solid.

Foursquare is not just a game; nothing is, really. Yet within the school day, foursquare is perhaps the most representative moment of the setup of our society. It is played collectively with rules made by the players, and it is competitive. Yet, like every moment of adult life, it is inherently social and, as in all of life, ultimately our values dictate how we play. Is the punishing, aggressive server within the letter of the law to target a short, slight classmate with his high-power drive? Sure. Is it unkind to exploit someone's physical limitations, even, to quote the observing child, "mean," as in taking a bit of malicious delight in another's downfall? Well, yes, I think so. The spiritual meter always runs alongside the laws made ad hoc by our collectives. The sixth-grade child knows that there are always two games running, and the "right" play meets both laws: the letter and the spirit.

We know that the way a child acts can be profoundly shaped and guided by spiritual values. As parents, the choice about whether to cultivate those values and build that foundation in our child is our choice to make. A child can feel the urges on both sides of a choice: sadistic satisfaction versus an empowering love. They also know the urge to turn away and ignore, to be a silent bystander to wrongdoing when the right action is to come to one another's aid or tell an adult. They know themselves as powerful to make a spiritual choice, particularly when we highlight their power—their *spiritual agency* to act in the world—and we say that they are responsible. Children rise to this self-awareness and agency readily—it is biologically and developmentally there for us to cultivate.

I find when I work with educators and youth advocates that the "culture of love" is a term that makes intuitive sense to people of all ages. It normalizes a higher standard of conduct, raises the bar of social interaction. Within a community, forming a culture of love is less like erecting a building and more like setting up a system of conducting rods, a system that creates potential for compassionate connections. The culture of love is about extending the field of love from family to the wider world. Not only at home, but at school, on sports teams, or later on at the frustrating weekend job, our children can practice seeing everyone they meet as more than a winner or loser; they can see them first of all as a being, a spirit. Culture of love is about encouragement and helping each other move through life together. It sees that everyone has need of one another. We commit to get across the finish line together and recognize that everyone has a contribution. Ultimately, it's more about celebrating and investigating life than controlling and "having for myself." The culture of love makes for a much bigger life. It's about sharing the journey and appreciating that we have each other and we're not alone.

The children in the *Stone Soup* discussion knew the difference between mean and kind—and they were three years old. "Mean" is not part of the culture of love. Mean is not socially cool if a school actively promotes the culture of love. Children are naturally eager to co-create a culture of love. They can hardly wait to put their carrot in the pot to help others. When the field of love within the family is extended into a culture of love, our children themselves set standards derived from their core spiritual values.

This is the power of spiritual agency.

6. Transcendent knowing: dreams, mystical experiences, and other special knowing

Children have a natural and engaged attitude to that which matters most in life: love, connection, and oneness. Their heads and hearts engage strongly around transitions and at the borders of life, birth, and death. For the young child, dreams, mystical experiences, and extraordinary knowing are simply a part of reality; they make sense, and feel significant. The child values these moments of transcendent experiences and may report such special events to parents with enthusiasm and wonder. As a psychologist, scientist, and parent, I refer to children having these moments as "special knowing." This is the native spirituality of the not yet socialized child.

Dreams and other transcendent experiences and ways of knowing remain in the pioneering stage of scientific exploration, but for your child, they are fully developed and realized. They are one way the child has of processing the many internal changes and the everyday circumstances that may be stressful or otherwise intense.

Transitions are big in the first decade; titanic, really. Take, for example, the developmentally normative progression through school. Imagine having a new boss, with new rules and different organizational culture, and mixing up colleagues every year. That's what your child faces in the progression through the grades. These are tidal waves of psychological shifts. On top of these constant transitions are the major milestones, such as "leaving home" for elementary school, with developmental shifts around separation, bonding with peers, and agency in the world. A child may be apprehensive or confused about this radical growth. A dream often brings clarity to the new landscape, integrates the many facets into a cohesive symbolic narrative—a storyline—and even points one or two steps ahead in the direction of the child's inner growth.

Dreams often confirm what a child intuitively knows about the meaning of a transition. The kindergartner might dream of walking across a bridge with his classmates, leaving his parents behind. The child preparing to leave middle school for junior high school might have a dream with a similar theme—unfamiliar surroundings that are a mix of exciting and scary, and a separation from the cozy familiarity of grade-school teachers and friends. Dreams offer a deeper developmental narrative of the transition, helping the child take just one step beyond. This is what a dream does: it illuminates our path.

Some dreams are transition dreams that help children know and feel comfortable with their path. Other dreams bring clarity around the recent encounters that are hard to metabolize. An unpleasant or manipulative person they have met may surface as a scary clown or trickster in a dream. The images and ideas of dreams are infinite, as conscious, unconscious, and transcendent knowing shape the story. Regardless, the child naturally loves and honors dreams. The fact that dreams don't occur in physical space doesn't weaken their meaning or impact on a child. As parents, we must honor this. Dreams are a lifelong inroad—make that a highway—for growth and clarity. They are prophetic in the true sense of the word: "to teach" along our path.

A child is not wedded to concrete literal interpretation and is ready to symbolically read into dreams. We can partner in that exploration. Take the most shocking: a death in a dream. These dreams are not uncommon, and children typically tell us if someone dies in a dream. You can help them search for the symbolism: *Did a part of you get old and out-*

dated? Did that person in our lives fade away? Did something deeply connected to that person change in our life lately? Children live into the entire world symbolically; dreams are perfect fodder for their growth.

Making dreams count means showing interest and clearing the space for reflection. Each morning might start with a loving welcome and sense of genuine interest:

> "Good morning! Welcome back from the dream world to Mom and Dad."

> "Did you dream?"

It is important to hear the dream. If mention of a dream comes up in the car, let it roll. Work on it together with the child as vested authority for its meaning.

> "Was there a feeling attached to that person or that part of the story?"

> "What feels that way in life? What is going on that reminds you of that right now?"

As the child grows older, the practice becomes one that the child can guide. The child can become conversant in engaging dreams to gain self-awareness and knowledge. In doing dream work, you are helping your child to read the symbols in life and to pay attention and enjoy the deep meaning in life. Other special ways of knowing include mystical experiences, and children do have these. They will readily tell you about them if they feel comfortable doing so. (They're waiting for your nod!)

Mariah was three when she mentioned to her mother, Ellie, that when she played in the playpen she wasn't alone—that a woman often came and kept her company. Ellie was always near the playpen working, so she knew Mariah was alone—no one was sneaking into the house—and she assumed this was her daughter's version of the classic "imaginary friend" of very young children. Then one day as they sorted through some attic boxes of photos, Mariah went to a picture she had never seen before and said, "That's the woman, Mommy—that's the woman who comes to play with me." It was Mariah's great-grandmother.

It's important to understand that all of this is part of the field of love. It's nothing to be scared of. It's not dark. It's not weird. Ellie was able to say to Mariah, "That's beautiful—it's about love and Great-grandma's love. How wonderful that you have that relationship with Great-grandma. I know she's so delighted by you and loves you so."

As mothers and fathers, we can be encouraging and supporting. We can weave transcendent experience into a very positive bigger picture that honors and makes it special while also showing the experience to be good and normalizing, as part of how the world truly works. The child pushes open the door and the light comes in. How will we use it to illuminate the darkness? Trust your instincts. See what emerges in you as a parent. I am certain that we must meet these moments with deep appreciation and interest.

As we'll see next in the life of the adolescent, dreams, intuitive guidance, exceptional knowing, and other transcendent experiences continue. If in the first decade we support our children as knowers, then in adolescence they will readily integrate this source for guidance, clarity, and a sense of purpose. They have infinitely greater resources if they can access their direct knowing, spontaneous intuition, and deep inner wisdom.

If your child has developed these six strengths through the first decade, you can be sure that the transcendent relationship is alive and well, and we can say without a shadow of a doubt that you've laid the foundation, built and fortified it. Now it is theirs internally as they move through the adolescent's hard work of becoming a freestanding individual.

PART II

ADOLESCENCE AND BEYOND

8

WINDOW OF AWAKENING

The Science of Spirituality in Adolescence

Adolescence awakens in the child a world of intense, passionate intrigue. The adolescent's curiosity, emotional sensitivity, and attraction to adventure grow. However, these developmental aptitudes for discovery also bring elevated risk. Parents often view adolescence as a time of trial and error for their children—a time when mothers and fathers anxiously hope that their son or daughter won't be the one to drive into a wall after a party or cheat on the SAT. Generally, parents allow adolescents some room for mistakes, provided that the subsequent marks aren't indelible. A teen's judgment related to danger and risk is generally assumed to be weak, so a certain amount of darkness and strife is expected throughout these formative years. All too often, though, the suffering that adolescents feel is far greater than we realize, and the risks associated with this suffering are far more severe than most of us wish to acknowledge.

In part, teen pain exists because it isn't understood properly by our culture. We see the behaviors but we don't understand what the teen needs from us to navigate this fraught passage. Adolescents are generally viewed as testing the waters of independence. They deliberately buck authority and frequently act against the wishes of their parents. To a parent, the strength of feeling, emotional outbursts, and sound of defiance can ring familiar from a decade earlier, during the last oppositional stage of the two- and three-year-old. "You really don't know what you're going to get from one moment to the next," a father shared at an evening program for parents of teens. "My wife and I will brace ourselves and then look at each other, as in, *What now?*" The mother of a champion high school athlete said, "My son's insistence on saying no against me, doing it his way, reminds me of how he used to refuse his car seat!"

These behaviors are commonly accepted as a phase of the teenage years. What is overlooked, however, is the extraordinary importance of the teen's inner work under way, which forms the early foundations of adult life. The tumultuous period of adolescence is when values and priorities are forged, meaning and purpose are discovered, and an inner compass is honed. This critical work of crafting the self helps the teen determine how to engage with the world.

However, the most important and untold story about adolescent pain in our culture is that underlying the most prevalent forms of suffering lies a fundamentally spiritual struggle. This precept is especially critical in our understanding of adolescent spiritual development. Adolescence is a time of spiritual awakening: a crucial window of engaging with spiritual reality.

As we'll see shortly, research from my lab, as well as by labs at other leading universities, shows that a direct and personal relationship with a transcendent higher power—universal spirit, God, Allah, or the universe, whatever the language or name—can be the most powerful protection against suffering in adolescence. Spirituality is the bedrock of a young person's sense of stability and meaning in the world, whether he or she is an affluent adolescent in Palo Alto or a homeless teen living under the Brooklyn Bridge.

In fact, my lab's research and a growing body of scientific literature about adolescent development shows that spirituality is *the* most robust protective factor against the big three dangers of adolescence: depression, substance abuse, and risk taking. In short, adolescents who have a personal sense of spirituality are 80 percent less likely to suffer from ongoing and recurrent depressions and 60 percent less likely to become heavy substance users or abusers. Girls with a sense of personal spirituality are 70 percent less likely to have unprotected sex. In the entire realm of human experience, there is no single factor that will protect your adolescent like a personal sense of spirituality. The totality of recent, cutting-edge research paints a definitive and unambiguous picture: the adolescent brain is a spiritual brain, primed for development and responsive to the protective benefits of personal spirituality. This research, along with the extensive science we've seen earlier regarding the nod and the field of love, offers insight into how all parents, whether religious or not, can support their adolescents on their spiritual paths and help them avoid the pitfalls so common in the second decade of life.

The benefit of personal spirituality is so strong that I consider it the legs on which adolescent (and future adult) physical and mental health stand. Depression and substance abuse, even sexual risk taking, can be seen as ill health, the symptoms and behaviors of spiritual struggle. As we'll see shortly, breakthrough findings have shown that a teen's heightened vulnerability to spiritual struggle is part of a spiritual awakening. This awakening is grounded in a developmental surge of the biologically based faculty for transcendence.

This means that teens' struggles aren't just physical and psychological, they are also fundamentally spiritual. In fact, many of the difficulties teens face are expressions of or can be linked back to spiritual questioning and drive. The hard news to hear as a parent is that your teens must have those struggles to become adults. The good news is you can help them be prepared as they go through the challenges, and thus prepared, they will greatly benefit from this passage. In this chapter I'm going to introduce the science and research that sets up these ideas, and in the next chapter we are going to delve into adolescence and its spiritual quest more deeply. But first we need to understand why adolescence is such an important window of opportunity.

The Big Job of Adolescence: Individuation and Spiritual Individuation

The story of how a teen "gets spiritual" bears out the developmental science that has long been part of our understanding of the inner work of adolescence. The adolescent's characteristic emotionality, raw sensitivity, and at times oppositional defiance emerge in service to the most important inner work of the human lifetime: *individuation*. Individuation is the process through which the adolescent forms an aware core self, an inner map of the world, and a game plan for living in that world. The teen takes all that she has learned over childhood, as well as all that she now encounters, and tests for its me-or-not-me quality. Based upon direct personal experience (and some amount of experimentation), the teen begins to develop a distinct sense of self: I am someone who . . . studies hard/ is straight or gay/loves and cares for animals/is nice to all members of the high school class/wants to be popular/only dates this kind of person, never dates that kind/has the power to lead a clique/plays for the team/wants to be the funniest in the class/is smarter then everyone/is going to be wealthy/stands for justice. The adolescent embraces only that which she feels is true to herself; anything that feels inaccurate or false is dismissed. The soccer career you may have envisioned for your athletic child gives way to her own zeal for international studies and the debate team. Whether you are deliberately nonreligious or quite devout, your teen is having his own experiences and bringing home his own view of the spiritual domain, decidedly (and sometimes defiantly) independent of yours.

The adolescent's apparent utter self-centeredness, which may be interpreted as selfish, isn't at all. Rather, it is crucial for the development of the self. This self isn't simply an amalgam of likes and dislikes; the self is the teen's instrument for knowing the world—*Who I am, what I feel and perceive, what I want and value. This all equals me.* To do this authentically takes great work as the adolescent forges a view of morality, relationships, identity, and passion for work. This tooling up of emotion and perceptiveness allows the teen to sense and feel, to hold a stake in life, and to know the world through the emotional faculty. The needing to know, being the one to decide, are signs that the teen is hard at work on individuation.

A primary form of individuation, one that often goes unrecognized by parents or community, is spiritual. *Spiritual individuation* is the personal determination of spiritual views: about the self, about fellow human beings and reality, the me-or-not-me assessment, all of which the teen evaluates through inner experience, but now through a spiritual lens. *This is who I am spiritually. This is who you are spiritually. This is how I perceive the world as a spiritual place. What is good, worthy, full, or empty? What is life-giving, and how do I join and become part of what is good?* Spiritual individuation is the adolescent's drive to find deeper personal meaning and purpose, in himself and in life. Because this is a spiritual question, it takes on a larger scope and opens the teen to greater and deeper dimensions of life. For instance, teens seek something deeper than simply to know their talents or measure their worth by their GPA. They seek to find a deep sense of calling, to discover how to deploy their talents for a greater good, and can come to see their gifts as indication of an assignment for a higher purpose or from a higher power.

We've looked closely in previous chapters at the presence of natural spirituality in childhood, a child's innate spiritual assets, and how, when supported, they grow into strengths: a strong inner compass, a deeply felt sense of family and the expanded field of love, spiritual multilingualism, spiritual agency or the power to make a difference in the world, and transcendent knowing. These strengths become the tools with which the teen engages the spiritual self in adolescence. The hunger for transcendence, the quest for meaning and purpose, the driving sense of what is evil or hypocritical in contrast to who or what is "truly good"—this is the work of spiritual individuation. These spiritual drives and emotions can be heard as a revving-up of the engine, right alongside sexual drives and emotions of empathy, trust, and rage.

Spiritual individuation is foundational to development in the second decade. In my opinion, it is the most important work of adolescence, and the highest priority for a parent's energy and attention. Its success forms the bedrock of health and wellness, as dozens of studies on mental health and wellness in teens now show. The intensive high-stakes process of individuation sets up the teen for much of adulthood, right down to the development of the brain.

A High-Performance Brain Boots Up
for the Big Questions

The process of spiritual awakening is triggered by puberty, literally ignited in the brain by the same rush of hormones that trigger sexual growth. As found in Laura Koenig's twins research, the surge includes a dramatic 50 percent boost in genetic expression for spirituality, an unlocking of the genes that contribute to the inherited capacity for spirituality. The heightened desire for sensation and thrills soars, while the deep search for meaning and purpose carries an intensity never felt before. This surge can set a teen reeling. *What on earth is happening?*

The neural capacity of our children's brains, once thought to stop growing by age five, we now know continues to grow well into adolescence. Synaptogenesis is the growth of new connections between neurons and occurs steadily but more dramatically at certain biological and developmental moments, such as adolescence. The actual mass of the brain shows rapid increases in both white and gray matter in adolescence, with accompanying increased neural sensitivity and conductivity. If the physical surges of adolescence can be likened to the takeoff of a 747 airliner, the accompanying increased neural sensitivity and conductivity of the brain will be a clear challenge for the novice pilot in the cockpit. Their brains are growing and interpreting the world like never before.

A twenty-year-old student shared of her seventeen-year-old self and that roaring 747 feeling of adolescence, struggling with the powerful emotions of awe, wonder, and urgency that uplifted yet drove her:

The vastness of the universe suddenly became too much for me to conceive of. I was overcome with the desire to know more, travel, and embrace as much of the world as I could before it disappeared from right underneath me. There was a sense of urgency and a feeling of loss at the same time, and I found myself grief-stricken at the thought that I would never be able to see all that the world had to offer or take it all in. I felt like an insignificant speck in a galaxy that was just too big for me.

This is spiritual awakening in adolescence. It was at once a wonderful yet tumultuous start "filled with emotion and uncertainty," she tells me. But it was not without its gifts. "It also made me more aware of the world around me and more willing to step outside my comfort zone in order to experience it," she says. Experiences like these are typical of teens and offer a window on the dramatic growth under way in the adolescent brain and the transcendent faculty.

Jay Giedd and colleagues at the National Institute of Mental Health discovered at the turn of the millennium that the adolescent brain grows rapidly and gains gray matter in specific regions: new, fresh cells starting at age ten and continuing into and through adolescence. The surge of new cell growth includes the frontal lobe, the "problem solver" and "decision-maker brain," which forms new gray matter until age twelve. The sensory and spatial region of the parietal lobe grows new cells until age fourteen. The emotion-processing region of the temporal lobe grows until age sixteen. And surprisingly, in the occipital lobe, which is associated with direct perception, new cell growth continues to age twenty. When your teen has a burst of risky behavior, an irresistible attraction to people, places, or things, misperceptions of people and motives, or struggles to manage his emotions and feels overwhelmed by his inner life, you're seeing the outward uneven burst of expression of this growth in the frontal lobe, parietal lobe, temporal lobe, and occipital lobe. The expanded capacity of what amounts to the brain's hard drive and increase in processing power needs to be formatted and customized. The brain regions need to become interconnected and synced so that they learn to efficiently talk to each other.

The teen brain must integrate this burst of neural capacity into a smooth operating system for physical, cognitive, social, and emotional processing and regulation. That is the work of the second decade. Through a process of pruning less-used neural connections and deepening more frequently used ones, the teen brain sculpts the profusion of synapses and neural networks that are developing within all regions of the brain. The brain does this through a process called *myelination,* a layering of tissue around the nerve fibers that both speeds transmission of the electrical impulses and serves as a protective sheath so that these impulses aren't lost and instead are transmitted more effectively and efficiently.

Then, add to this high-performance adolescent electrical system a new turbo-charged engine capacity plus high-octane fuel in the form of a dopamine-rich neurochemical mix bathing the brain. Dopamine is the neurotransmitter that regulates the brain's reward and pleasure centers and affects emotion regulation. The dopamine in the areas of the brain associated with experiencing—feeling, perception, and drive (the temporal, parietal, occipital regions, and the subcortical areas like the insula and striatum)—is wildly up-regulated.

The frontal lobe matures at a steady rate while the centers for feelings, connection, and the transcendent capacity accelerate dramatically, such that the gap between the "experiencing brain" and the "interpreting brain" is wider in adolescence than it will ever be in a healthy adult. So, as the regions that process feelings and experience are experiencing dramatic power surges, the frontal lobe that makes sense of it all is pretty taxed as it moves along at its steady pace of development.

Neuroscientist B. J. Casey's innovative team at the Sackler Institute at Weill Medical College of Cornell University synthesized findings from over a hundred MRI studies to date on the adolescent brain. The findings show that the rapid acceleration in activity (and reactivity!) in the brain regions, as I described above, create strong emotionality and motivation for reward (in the subcortical regions of the limbic system, accumbens, and amygdala), while the brain's control and restraint center (the prefrontal cortex) grows at a steady linear rate. This pronounced gap between the teen's felt surge of emotional motive or purpose—intense friendships and crushes, challenge to authority, risky behavior—and his or her lesser capacity for restraint and control explains why teens tend to act impulsively or react with strong emotion despite better judgment.

Not only is the teen brain receiving and responding to more stimuli, but the heightened sensitivity and speedier transmission amps up teen reactivity, as well, while the controls are still spotty. The child of ten may seem more self-possessed and reliable, with better judgment, than the teen of fourteen, fifteen, or sixteen. The work of adolescence is to hone the new gray matter into a well-functioning system appropriate for the teen's environment. The critical step here is to build fibers expanding white matter tracts for connectivity, specifically for connecting the prefrontal cortex with other regions of the brain, such as those that handle motivation and emotion. The sculpting of this raw material, the developing of wiring between the neurons within regions, and the connection between regions is critical. And it is open to your influence.

Neurons and Neuronal Networks: Use 'Em or Lose 'Em

The focus and form of the brain is based largely on use—the greater the use of neural networks, the greater and deeper their growth. This makes adolescence a crucial time because the brain is altering itself. If your teen doesn't use a capacity—for example, he avoids math or reading, or even face-to-face conversational skills—the connections between that region and others begin to be pruned away. Connections within the region itself are pruned, too. This intensive growth and pruning process makes the brain effective and attuned to the specific environment in which the adolescent grows. To a large extent, after adolescence the growth and pruning ceases, and the brain becomes more set and fitted to a specific environment. Environment includes cognitive tasks, values and culture, tendency for reflection, the nature of relationships, the emotional tone, and the practice of spiritual transcendence.

The scholarship of Ronald E. Dahl, professor of psychiatry and pediatrics at the University of Pittsburgh, highlights the impact of parents and community on the adolescent brain, as well as the teen's own personal practices or habits of living—inner and outer life activity. He calls the combination of these factors the neuro-psycho-social pathway of brain development. Dahl holds that the family, school, community, and personal choices of the adolescent create the environment that shapes the adolescent brain. This is a serious responsibility for all involved, foremost the adolescent and parent. The adolescent has tremendous impact on her own brain development by how she chooses to use her brain. For instance, Dahl cautions against long hours of couch-potato video games in favor of reflection, math, and sports to cultivate the connective wiring. Dahl urges parents, teachers, and teens themselves to be thoughtful in the environment they create around adolescence, and to be aware of the direct impact of those choices on the developing brain. If we look at Dahl's work alongside research on spirituality, it highlights the developmental impact of spiritual practices, cultivation of inner life, and pathways and access to transcendence.

The other key issue neurologically is that the brain's "command central" front brain (prefrontal cortex) and the surging "under and back" regions of the brain that register experience are just starting to talk. The brain builds connective fibers between command central in the prefrontal cortex so it can hear from the back (limbic system, accumbens, and amygdala) and reply with ways of processing and directing strong experiences.

In a fascinating study by an innovative neuroimaging team from Washington University in St. Louis, researchers showed, using fMRI, that neural fibers in the prefrontal cortex can override the usual communication between brain systems. These neural fibers in effect "hotwire" the brain-wide structural mechanism, enabling the prefrontal cortex to act as command central for the entire brain. The Washington University team showed that the prefrontal cortex takes over someone experiencing major depression in exactly this way: affect and cognition become ruled by dark, anxious rumination.

The study was not looking specifically at spirituality, but this executive override power carries significant implications for the spiritual brain. MRI research on meditation shows harmonization of brain regions initiated by the prefrontal cortex. Science has already shown broad and pervasive measurable benefits from foundational integration of transcendence into daily life. This includes effects on mental health, compassion, relationships, thriving, risk and resilience, and inner meaning and purpose. It is reasonable to posit that the entire brain might function entirely differently when transcendence and spiritual awareness are built into the system as a central organizing point. The teen lives each day in a different experiential world when transcendence informs perception, affect, and emotion, all of which are driven by the prefrontal cortex. Shaping via a "hotwired" connection may very well create quite a different intersystem experience when imbued with transcendence.

The developmental opportunity here is to set up the wiring—the brain's connective white matter—that supports this dialogue between regions. You want your teen's brain to establish a strong, positive link between the region that governs her perception of reality (frontal lobe), where she "tells the story" of her experience and uses it to inform her focus and direction, and the back brain (parietal and occipital lobe), through which transcendence appears to be perceived—opening up the link for travel. If this connection remains undeveloped or if it develops to reject or block messages of a transcendent nature, then it can atrophy or grow thin, blocking access to transcendent experience itself. The impasse, or incomplete neural path, leads to an adult some twenty years later who makes statements such as, "I would like to feel spiritual and I've tried, but I just don't feel it."

As we've learned from previous chapters, if the spiritual interface is supported, it enhances all other aspects of development. It can become the organizational hub for other aspects of development. For instance, as the frontal cortex expands the capacity for critical thinking, a corresponding deepening of the spiritual faculty brings far greater capacity for nuanced moral reasoning. Teens often get into trouble when they know the right thing to do—head knowing would say *don't do it*—but they just do not feel compelled to act in accordance with their heart knowing, their moral standards. This can represent a disconnect between front- and back-brain dialogue. When head and heart are connected, there is a resource—a guiding inner voice—that helps answer the questions and can actively respond to help the teen resist temptation. It might, for example, lead your teen to pass up casual sex in favor of a loving relationship that embraces a healthy sexuality, to opt for honesty over cheating or manipulating the truth, or to consider how a personal choice or action might affect others.

The brain's front-back connection also allows for the body to relax and to find peace through abstract or symbolic practice. For instance, fMRI research shows that seeing a religious symbol of great meaning to you—a neural process that requires recognition by the front of the brain—reduces the experience of physical pain, a back-brain function. Research has shown that for some, seeing a religious symbol also improves cardiovascular functioning through a similar process that connects the front and back of the brain, a form of mind-body-spirit integration. Symbols associated with a participant's faith can also increase persistence and hard work at tasks.

The emerging picture from research is clear: the brain's front-back connectivity is critical in helping adolescents process their experiences and feelings, modulate impulses, and make good decisions that are informed by head and heart. Spirituality enriches this process. Not only is spirituality helpful for the adolescent, but we know that the teen is in fact primed to have a burst of spirituality-seeking behavior. This is the most important conversation for the adolescent brain, and once that connection myelinates, it is secured to a great degree. This period of front brain–back brain connection, conversation, and myelination is a critical window, meaning that during adolescence all systems are go and the work is most intense and productive *now*—synaptogenesis is on your teen's side. Once the window closes, this process is possible but is harder.

To recap, the take-home implications for parents are clear. This rapidly growing adolescent brain responds exquisitely to use, practice, and environment. Essentially, form follows function. The brain wires itself as needed to meet the physical, social, and psychological demands and opportunities of the teen's experience. When the adolescent learns an instrument, meets a new friend, or navigates conflicts with friends, the brain is wiring up to bring this experience and insight to bear on new situations. With practice, the brain is building capacity and pathways between regions, preparing for success in handling the ups and downs of life. As parents, we often focus on the obvious concerns arising from the teen lifestyle and environment: Are they developing the motivation and study habits to be successful learners? How about the friends they hang out with—what if we're concerned about the company they keep? Those are important concerns, certainly, but they can obscure an even more important point: environment includes the inner life, how your teen uses the brain for inner practice. Conscious reflection, introspection, and inner experience all shape the adolescent's brain.

What does this look like in your home? Likely, a small group of teens in your basement rec room would be chatting about events of the day: observing how someone is treating someone else, who has hooked up with whom, who cheated on the quiz, and what about that snarky Facebook post, or the taunting tweet. These conversations also slip easily into what life is about, from cruelty and love to fears and faith, religious beliefs or nonbeliefs, doubts about a family faith tradition, or a desire to try a taste of different spiritual traditions. Adolescents are attracted to this spiritual work and will dig in for hours.

If access to transcendence has been built in the first decade, then it is there, ready and available to respond to the inquiry of the adolescent's driving mind. The question asked by the front of the brain can seek and find an answer from the back. The analytic and conceptual front can recognize the felt knowing of the back as real, with a name, and a long-standing practice of integration into daily life.

A later start to spirituality does not signal a disaster. It means that the teen, and parent, simply have two jobs at once: spiritual individuation, plus naming and accessing transcendent experience. Parents can listen closely to a teenager to hear nuances of transcendence, name them, invite the teen to share what answers may come to the spiritual question at hand.

As the teen tests inner life against theory, culture, and opinion, there is far more chance of success with our support as parents, educators, and community. The adolescent needs—and we can help provide—a user language for spiritual individuation. Just as with other language development, this is built in childhood, but the opportunity for growth continues in adolescence.

Whether or not spirituality was part of your home during childhood, it is crucial to support this work during adolescence. Continuing to come back to their transcendent nature will help teens forge pathways that will benefit them for the rest of their lives. Just as we want them to get in the habit of physical activity, good food, strong study habits, and good friends, we want them to get in the habit of a strong inner life, a practice that makes explicit their spirituality, and continued work toward asking and understanding the big spiritual questions.

The Severed Spirit: The Disconnect Between Life and Life Illuminated

Developmentally, the adolescent is laying the foundation for erecting her house of life. This house in which she will live is based upon the bedrock of identity, work, values, our way of leaning into life, personal and professional choices, and relationships. When spiritual individuation occurs, it becomes the central organizing principle to life, such that by adult-hood your teen will have built her spiritual house.

Severed spirituality occurs when transcendence is not infused into the developmental process of adolescence. The foundation is built without the strength, connection, and direction of spirituality. If we have sev-ered the spirit during groundlaying work, the house is colder, darker, and less sure. The structural integrity is compromised.

A 2007 Pew Forum shows the cultural outcome of the minimalist support teens get for spiritual individuation. It seems the number of teens who are supported in the work of spiritual individuation to derive its full benefit is relatively low. Attention and energy are no longer channeled into spiritual emergence as was more common in the generations who came of age in the twentieth century. "A Portrait of 'Generation Next'" re-ports that in a cohort of late adolescents and emerging adults (eighteen to twenty-five years old), 80 percent had texted within the last day, the median number of texts per day was twenty, and about 75 percent of re-spondents were active on Facebook. In contrast, less than 4 percent said that people in their generation view becoming more spiritual as their most important goal. At the same time, a related Pew Forum report, "Faith in Flux," published in 2009 and revised in 2011, shows that about half the people in the United States change religious affiliation, usually be-fore the age of twenty-four; reasons for affiliation changes varied but show the hunt for spiritual fulfillment and a need for spiritual support.

Our culture-wide neglect of natural spirituality in adolescence is start-ing to show in the low prioritization of spiritual life and lack of spiritual home. I see this culture-wide "drop of the spiritual ball" to be *the* fore-most health liability for our adolescents and young adults. Given the ro-bust protective benefits of spirituality in mental health, this culture-wide dip among eighteen- to twenty-five-year-olds in spiritual goals may ac-count in large part for the high current rates of depression, substance use and abuse, and conduct problems involving risk taking.

As we've seen during the connective phase of adolescence the brain must connect the natural transcendent faculty in the under-and-back of brain with the frontal command-control central, the prefrontal cortex. This allows the regions and capacities of the brain to all work together, and transcendence stays in the mix of your teen's daily lived reality, interpretation, and even perception of life events, felt self, and relationships. Thus a two-way street is formed: command central elicits spiritual feeling; spiritual feeling, sensing, and perception gains recognition by command central, such that we become spiritually aware.

For an adolescent, when transcendence is not guided to connect with the rest of lived experience, the teen loses hold of the innate capacity for spiritual awareness. Sex is disconnected from love. Social perception lacks empathy. Solitude is felt as lonely isolation. The world is empty instead of full. A severed spirit is transcendence lost from the broad view of life. The world is different without the knowing of the heart, without the sense of being part of something greater and good, without the added glow of family or the field of love, or without the intuitive awareness of the wisdom in nature and all living beings. As we'll see in the chapters ahead, adolescent individuation informs your teen's relationships, her standards in living, her map of reality, as well as who she is on earth, her identity as calling and meaning and purpose, for better or worse, full or empty. In severing the spirit, the hunger for ultimate connection is unmet. The faculty for healthy spiritual development atrophies, and worst of all, there is no mechanism for truly sensing and then being able to metabolize the presence of good and evil.

In spiritual individuation, the platform of transcendence comes to inform the very broad range of daily choices and overarching developmental work. The entire world looks different from a spiritual view. And your teen's innate capacity for transcendence, and the neurological interconnectivity of this natural spiritual endowment, tends to get locked into place for adulthood. As we have discussed, adolescence is a precious window for locking in a fluid front-and-back brain capacity for spiritual awareness, the transcendent relationship, and integration of transcendence into relationship, calling, meaning, and purpose. Together these create your teen's *spiritual identity*. Identity formation, as we know, is another hallmark task of adolescence. Spiritual identity is a deeply felt sense of *Who I am spiritually, how I set course and navigate, see my guideposts and calling in the world spiritually*. As spiritual identity can become such a deep and lasting aspect of the self, this central developmental task needs to be a top priority. This doesn't mean a forced march to religious services. It means engaging the spiritual dimension in everyday life, cultivating your teen's capacity for engaging the Big Questions, as well as the seemingly smallest or subtle wonders or complexities of life. The fully integrated command-control process and spiritual identity may include religious involvement or it may not.

A Study of Teens on the Brink:
Positive Psychology vs. Sociopathy

Severed spirit carries great moral and ethical costs, and often the price of a purposeful life of fulfillment. There are trends that have been associated with some cultures of affluence in the United States that cultivate severed spirit rather than spiritual growth. We see this in narrow goals for success at all costs, blindness to moral development, and a total abnegation of inner life and spiritual fulfillment. The increasingly common teen with a polished persona on the outside, yet suffering inside, was brought to public attention by Yale-trained psychologist Madeline Levine in her book *The Price of Privilege*. She writes of the moment she greeted a talented, affluent teenage girl for a therapy session and saw carved on the girl's arm the word "empty." I hear this as a case of severed spirit: without awareness of a spiritual presence within us and throughout life, life looks desolately empty.

As parents, educators, and caring adults, what can we do? Research says that we can parent our adolescents for spiritual individuation, with a strength and presence that ultimately outweighs the surrounding culture. This is essential. When an entire community's norms eschew spirituality, the lives of teens grow grim.

Psychologist Suniya Luthar, a highly distinguished developmental psychologist, has for more than fifteen years studied the suffering of youth who from all outward appearances would seem to "have it all"—affluent kids primarily from suburbs around major cities. Her research tracks parenting styles, the societal messages received by children and teens, and the effects on development over time.

In a landmark study, Luthar followed a cohort of 252 students in an affluent commuter suburb of New York City, from sixth grade through the completion of high school. After graduation the students continued to hear from Luthar and her team; the vast majority of the students stayed involved in the study all the way to the present day, when they were several years past college and into emerging adulthood. In a series of research reports Luthar portrays the developmental path for teens in this and other geographical areas of affluence in the United States as riddled with anxiety and suffering, due primarily to culture-wide parenting styles. Luthar found that fathers were largely absent, and available primarily around weekend events involving accomplishment. Mothers, the majority of whom were full-time parents, were found to be perfectionistic, over-extended to meet the many activities of the children, and anxious to meet the mark of outward success. Luthar noted very little concern with goodness or morality in family goals and time together. This is family as a breeding ground for skills and competition, without including the spiritual presence that makes family a field of love.

The effect of being parented without feeling unconditional love and spiritual direction is a striving for outward success to please parents. The child courts a sense of parental-contingent love. Little interest is paid to inner life or reflection, nor to morality or spiritual values. Instead enormous resources are put into performance goals. The net effect is neglect for spiritual development in children and teens.

The cost of severed spirit is clear in the teens' social culture. Luthar's data shows that physical appearance was the most powerful factor for predicting a girl's popularity, with a girl's hostility or "mean girl" factor being the second greatest predictor of popularity. For teen boys, substance use was the greatest predictor of popularity, followed by their exploitive attitude or behavior toward women.

Within this harsh and exploitative world, Luthar's data further documents rates of substance use and abuse that surpass teens in the inner city. She proposes that this may be an attempt to ameliorate equally elevated rates of depression and anxiety, which she suggests are the result of the outward chase to please parents. Feeding a child on raw outward ambition, without unconditional love, does not make for success in any way. Rather it creates inner suffering that can be damaging to long-term adult relationships, ethics, and even sustainable practices at work.

Viewed through a compassionate and realistic lens, these affluent youth, who might be said to have everything, often exist in a spiritual void, striving, even craving, to meet an outward mark in a culture of judgment and superficial gain. Talent is viewed as a gold coin, not a doorway to a personal purpose or calling to serve. Girls are evaluated for their bodily form, by both boys and girls, rather than for their strength of character or spirit of kindness. In such an empty and annihilating world, it is little surprise that these affluent teens followed by Luthar had higher rates of depression and substance abuse than the matched inner-city teens. I read the research as saying the epidemic of severed spirit in large part accounts for our unprecedented rates of depression, anxiety, and substance abuse in youth.

To test this directly, I joined up with Suniya Luthar, along with Sam Barkin, to ask, In such a culture of judgment, can parents who try to support spiritual development actually succeed?

We looked at the 12 to 15 percent minority of teens in Luthar's sample who upon high school graduation had a strong transcendent relationship with a higher power and who saw their lives as being purposeful with contribution to the world. We then asked, How did they get this way?

We found that most of the spiritually thriving adolescents were involved in a family practice of spirituality and in steady participation in a spiritual community outside of school, often a religious denomination but not always.

These teens looked very different from the norm of their community, with lower rates of depression and substance abuse. And this difference lasts far beyond graduation. Seven years post–high school, these teens still held on to a strong transcendent relationship and viewed themselves as being of service to a higher power. The peers from high school who had shown low rates of spirituality senior year now showed increased rates of sociopathy (exploitative and manipulative behavior to a clinical degree)—more than eight times the national rate—and elevated misuse of prescription drugs.

The ring of family and chosen spiritual community trumps the broader culture of judgment. The adolescent inhabits an immediate world of warm meaningful connection and light, even when surrounded by a cold, dark, and empty culture. As parents, as spiritual communities, our worth is immeasurable. This should sound like a five-alarm fire! Spiritual individuation is the foremost work of adolescence. If we leave them in a state of emptiness, unsupported in developmental depression, they can remain lost for a lifetime.

More than any skill or asset, spiritual individuation will set up the teen for a much healthier, more meaningful, purposeful, and thriving adult life. Lacking spiritual resources, teens search for the transcendent experience wherever they can find it: risky behaviors, including reckless driving or casual or unprotected sex, and substance use.

Substance Use and Abuse

Developmental depression is a natural component of the inner struggle for spiritual individuation, and we'll turn to that discussion in chapter 10. But our epidemic of substance abuse is much like depression in that it comes from a failure to engage the surge of natural spirituality in adolescence, an abandonment of the adolescent during spiritual individuation. There is a difference, however, in the focus. Developmental depression is about answering the knock of spiritual awakening, ideally to engage in spirituality individuation. But if that has been ignored or shut down, then the severed spirit shows itself, in a downward spiral of depression. Substance abuse in adolescence is showing a very specific spiritual need: transcendence. The adolescent surge of biologically triggered capacity for transcendence offers tastes of illumination, total oneness, and connection and makes the teen want more of the transcendent experience. How the teen learns to access and return to transcendence tells the story of substance use during adolescence, which is the setup for a lifelong relationship to substance.

The first psychologist in the United States, William James, in 1904 viewed substance use as emanating from a spiritual hunger. "The sway of alcohol over mankind is unquestionably due to its power to stimulate the mystical faculties of human nature . . . drunkenness expands, unites and says yes. It is in fact the great excitor of the Yes function in man."

The problem is that this particular road to "yes" does not build a true connection between head and heart to sustain a strong ongoing spirituality or transcendent relationship.

Current research supports this view of substance use as a misguided attempt at transcendence. Synthesizing a review of over 1,300 research articles on addiction and spirituality, a team of scholars led by Geppert showed spirituality as a consistent force in recovery, as well as in prevention. Substance abuse is a spiritual struggle, and its resolution often comes through spiritual emergence and growth.

Our fMRI study with the team at Yale, introduced in chapter 2, showed that activity of the craving part of the brain (insula and striatum) went quiet—the craving stopped—with engagement of the transcendent relationship. This craving part of the brain applies to cravings of all sorts of things, including gambling, sex, alcohol, or drugs. The craving brain is particularly active in people with addiction. The fMRI research of our team and other labs suggests that the transcendent relationship alleviates the activation of the neuropathway of craving, reducing the draw of all objects of insatiable desire, including substances.

Patrick M. Flynn and colleagues, in a study published in the *American Journal on Addictions*, found that 63 percent of addicts in recovery from cocaine dependence claim that spirituality was essential to their recovery. Spirituality has also been associated with maintaining abstinence from drinking or using drugs, be it for the short term or long term. Anne Fletcher, in her book, *Sober for Good* (an extensive study of addicts in successful recovery), writes that spontaneous acknowledgment of spirituality was one of the five more important components of breaking free from addiction.

However, when it comes to teen onset of alcohol and drug use and addiction, our culture has been shockingly slow to consider that the mass doping reflects our spiritual abandonment of adolescents.

My lab did a study that compared the protective effects of the transcendent relationship against substance abuse in adolescence versus adulthood. In each population, we looked for the presence of the transcendent relationship, demonstrated by statements such as, "I turn to God for guidance in times of difficulty," or "When I have a decision to make, I ask, What does God really want me to do?" We found that the stronger the teen's transcendent relationship, the less likely she was to use drugs. Specifically, the adolescent who has a relatively strong personal relationship with God is 80 percent less likely to abuse substance than the adolescent with a "weak" (meaning vague or absent), transcendent relationship. The samples for this study were a Judeo-Christian nationally representative sample. The findings were right on target with the spiritual developmental model: adolescence brings with it an erupting hunger for transcendence, which, if not embraced, can devolve into a shortcut in the search for it. And the transcendent relationship was twice as protective for adolescents as compared to adults! In other words, the transcendent relationship is more protective when a person is more vulnerable—during adolescence.

Since our study was published in the *Journal of the American Academy of Child and Adolescent Psychiatry*, fellow labs around the globe have consistently shown the strong protective benefits of spirituality against onset of heavy substance use and abuse. A meta-analysis of more than twenty-two studies published worldwide was conducted by Jerf Yeung and colleagues at the Public Policy Research Institute in Hong Kong Polytechnic University. Their meta-analysis showed that, drawing from populations across the world, adolescents with a strong spirituality are less likely to use alcohol, nicotine, marijuana, or other illicit drugs.

Drugs, alcohol, sensation seeking, risky sex, and other high-risk behaviors are often viewed as an expression of the experimental curiosity or recklessness characteristic of adolescence. Looking at these behaviors through the lens of spiritual development and the natural quest for transcendence gives us a different way to understand the teen's motivations and experience. To the teen, the high of drugs or alcohol, the thrill of driving fast and taking high-stakes risks—all are shortcuts to an experience of transcendence. And our popular culture encourages and promotes this kind of experimentation—TV and music encourage drinking, sex, and thrills. You don't hear adolescent culture (or much adult culture, for that matter) encouraging introspection, inner questioning, or spiritual practice.

As teens take ownership of the self, rules can provide a helpful structure for their moral life, a kind of scaffolding for spiritual identity or practice. But rules are a thin substitute for a personal spirituality that incorporates the teen's own direct knowing and inner moral guideposts. Strictly observed, rules can keep you out of trouble, but they don't help once you've taken half a step into uncharted waters. Specifically, once the teen has tried the alcohol or the drugs or the high-risk behavior, and if they liked it—if only for the peer approval—then the rules that most teens have been given by parents or religious strictures (such as *Just say no* or religious moral absolutisms) don't do much to help. Once they've tried it, they are alone, outside of the rules.

The substantial research showing spirituality to be highly protective against substance abuse is consistent with the writings of psychologists and researchers, as well as those of recovering addicts themselves. Alcoholics Anonymous supports authentic spiritual connection (however each person defines that), and this treatment approach has resulted in accounts of many recovering addicts who have described their drug and alcohol use as a shortcut at an attempt at the transcendent experience.

When I contributed a short piece about adolescents searching for connection through drugs to a *New York Times* blog forum devoted to the issue of drug addiction, I received some personal and very thoughtful responses of "that's me!" and "I feel understood" from adults and adolescents. While some adults posted comments that were critical or unconvinced, there was not a single young adult or adolescent whose correspondence in the forum or in personal notes to me dismissed the connection between the desire for spiritual connection and the slide into addiction. Many wrote to me of their experience developing a personal relationship with a higher power and including spiritual values as an essential part of recovery.

"Spirituality was the first thing I lost when I started drinking at age fifteen and the most important thing that gave me hope I could stop drinking when I was in treatment at age forty," wrote one reader. "Over the years since I've thought that (along with running and hanging with sober people) going to church is a vital part of my continued sobriety."

A middle-aged woman who described herself as a well-educated and successful health care professional said that her alcoholism had wrecked her career and personal life and inflicted incalculable wounds on her family. Writing from being one and a half years sober, she said, while "the God thing in AA is quite off-putting to many . . . the love and compassion that is palpable in the fellowship" proved healing for her.

Spiritual Individuation and Positive Psychology

Much has been discussed lately about youth and positive psychology. Positive psychology looks at our finer side, focusing on grit, forgiveness, optimism, and a large host of internal assets. How does spirituality interface with positive psychology in teens? Might a spiritually individuated teen look different in terms of these highly functional assets?

Originally this question was asked within research by Peter Benson, who led the Search Institute in Minnesota, dedicated to understanding youth assets. Benson and colleagues published more than a dozen articles and reports on thousands of youths showing that for youth, spirituality was related to a very broad range of personal internal assets, such as commitment, dedication, and persistence.

Once science identified the transcendent relationship as an exceptionally active ingredient in spirituality, it was possible to ask whether much of positive psychology might actually rise up from the personal transcendent relationship. Together with Yakov Barton, a Columbia researcher, we recruited more than four thousand late adolescents and young adults in the United States and in India, whom we asked about a sense of transcendence. The questions focused on their transcendent relationship and on measuring traits generally considered within the purview of positive psychology, such as grit, optimism and forgiveness, and positive relationship; these traits matter because they have been shown to predict a life of fulfillment. Then we looked in the data for patterns, and we identified five groups. Four were essentially the same story: transcendence went hand in hand with various positive psychology traits, and the level of each varied in parallel: Very High Transcendence–Very High Positive Psychology; High Transcendence–High Positive Psychology; Medium Transcendence–Medium Positive Psychology; Low Transcendence–Low Positive Psychology.

This is not surprising since the traits of positive psychology (persistence, grit, and optimism) grow out of transcendent values, a spiritual worldview and sense that our direction and relationships have ultimate value. Living a spiritually guided life means that everything takes on more significance, a higher purpose. For instance, playing baseball or working for academic achievement become more about the thrill of playing or striving for knowledge, rather than playing to be a big shot or collecting As. A strong and supported spiritual life simply pushes the teen to greater perseverance, determination, and focus from within. Ideas of compassion and unconditional love help us cultivate commitment, push us to forgive, and encourage us to create meaningful relationships, rather than focusing on hollow ideals of popularity and coolness. Because everything takes on greater significance, for teens, there is more reason to persevere. Because everything is endowed with spiritual presence, there is reason to feel valuable, optimistic, and hopeful, to work for the long term, whether or not in the short term we win or lose. There was one group that was an exception to the pattern of level of transcendence as indicative of level of positive psychology traits. About 16 percent of the late adolescents and young adults were low on transcendence but still high on positive psychology. I call them the "virtuous humanists," people who perhaps derive an implicit spiritual fulfillment through "right action," or perhaps simply walk a different path.

Science tells us that adolescence is the launching pad into biologically predetermined spiritual seeking. Furthermore, much of the troubling adolescent behavior we have come to expect—thrill seeking, substance use—is part of the journey (though misdirected). From previous chapters examining spiritual development in the first decade, we know that a supported spiritual life is important. We know from the nod, the joint effect, and the field of love that parents and community also have a role in shaping the brain. Now we see that the teen's brain is growing, that shaping the neural pathways is the teen's job during adolescent. Now we've reached the most critical point: in adolescence, continuing to incorporate spirituality into his or her life is crucial to your teen. And my research and others' shows it's much more likely to be for the better if you're there to help. Just about the time you may feel you have become irrelevant to your teen—dismissed, ignored, or out and out aggressively pushed away—you need to know that science of adolescent spiritual development says you are absolutely essential.

9

THE QUEST

The Adolescent's Search for Life's Calling, Meaning, and Purpose

magine that you live in a peaceful home in a cul-de-sac with a quiet backyard where you spend long relaxing afternoons. Life feels spacious. Nature is a lovely backdrop for life as it unfolds in its timeless, seasonal rhythms. Your family is loving and warm, however naturally imperfectly human at times. You've got nice neighbors and, beyond that, you're surrounded by people who are generally kind, generous, and helpful. For the most part, everything is familiar and comfortable, even serene. Metaphorically, this is the child's natural spiritual experience of the first decade.

Now imagine that suddenly you awake one morning and discover that it has all vanished; you're blindfolded, and you've been transported somewhere new. You peel back the blindfold and *slam!*—you are standing on Forty-Second Street and Broadway, smack in the center of Times Square.

Suddenly you see things you have never seen before, and even familiar things show up differently: vivid, chaotic, jarring. The sidewalks are jammed with humanity, most people rushing past you, some impatient, some looking right through you as if you're invisible. Homeless people ask for money; some people toss change their way, others don't. You see couples making out on the sidewalk, throngs of bustling workers, a glimpse of a drug deal. Bike messengers dart between cars, dodging yellow taxis and pedestrians crossing the street. Families cluster in lines to see Broadway shows. Protesters for human rights wave signs. Visitors from China, Japan, and Germany stroll slowly, taking in the sights, their languages adding to the street symphony of voices, traffic, and construction.

The place is astonishing and mesmerizing, ramped up and bursting with adrenaline. It's exciting, but equally confusing, and even a little scary. How did you get here and what are you supposed to be doing? How do you fit in? Who can you trust and how will you make friends? How do you stay safe and feel connected in this world that is suddenly yours? These big questions are new to you, nothing that ever crossed your mind in the cul-de-sac. Then, although no one has actually told you a thing, it dawns on you that this is your new reality. You have no idea what this is all about, how long you'll be here, or what you're supposed to do, but you get a clear sense that this is it for now and you've got a lot to figure out.

There are many different ways to build your new life in Times Square, with wildly different consequences. Plenty of trouble is available: drug use and addiction, risky sex, and other dicey situations. At the same time, if you can get oriented and stay focused, there is enormous opportunity for creativity, expression, and connectivity with other people.

Your old cul-de-sac self is beset with new sensations, new feelings: suffering, desire and sex, love and joy, bolts of sudden happiness. The thrill of the world, its vividness and glorious diversity, is wondrous. Yet, it's also big. The chaos and intensity of it all is disorienting static jamming your perceptual faculties. It can be hard to know how to navigate each moment here in Times Square.

As we've seen, the developing adolescent brain burgeons with new capacity. The teen brain is more full of feeling, more full of drive: more of life shines vivid and strong because there is more capacity to perceive. In his book *Age of Opportunity*, psychologist and distinguished professor Laurence Steinberg speaks of the "exquisitely sensitive" adolescent brain and how normal sex hormones and the related downstream bio-chemistry spark such intense emotion that an experience may easily be remembered for the rest our lives. This powerful imprint of emotional memory in adolescence is due to the high surge levels of dopamine, the same neurochemical surge associated with the heightened sensations of transcendent experience.

So here is the teen, suddenly seeing and feeling the world in Techni-color, shocked by the waves of new, intense emotion and ideas, con-fronted with political, social, sexual, and moral choices, and *bam!*, all of a sudden—right here, right now—he has to make sense of it all. His slowly growing prefrontal cortex, the analytical decision maker that inhibits the impulse to "just act," is growing at a chug-chug steady rate, while surges of emotion and perception, including that of transcen-dence, charge full steam ahead. For the next several years the teen will be a "work in progress" as front and back brain sync, and as the bio-logically based surge intensifies senses and emotional perception and fuels the adolescent's capacity for transcendent awareness and spiritual growth. As these developmental energies emerge and converge, they launch a developmental phase that is nothing short of heroic: the spir-itually driven quest.

Ready or Not: The Adolescent Search for Self, Meaning, and Purpose

When an adolescent starts 80 percent of comments with "I," it is not out of self-centeredness in the adult sense of the word, but rather due to the serious demanding work of individuation. They are compelled to figure out who "I" is. *How do I live? What do I know and believe? Who am I?*

Psychologists have long spoken of individuation as the cornerstone of adolescent development, since the best-known proponent of its im-portance, Erik Erikson (who renamed himself Erik son-of-Erik as an act of self-definition), defined it over half a century ago. Individuation is the process of asking, *What is me and what is not me? Who am I by my own terms?* The teen tests her inner sense of truth against the "three Cs"— the culture and custom of community.

What the teen cannot bear, as Holden Caulfield from *Catcher in the Rye* declares, is "phoniness"—hypocrisy and inconsistency—in their hunt for a harmonious truth, a felt wholeness of personal values and reality. In my work with parents and teachers, I sometimes share that "me, me, I think . . ." or "not me at all . . ." can sound irritating, self-centered, and self-obsessed. It isn't. It is the cultivation of the only instrument that teens—or any of us—have for knowing: our inner instrument. At a surface level, in our everyday lives with teens the questions and debates of individuation may sound overdramatic. But given the deep stakes of the developmental work under way, the emotion is appropriate.

In ordinary life, your child's external surroundings from early to middle to late adolescence rarely change so dramatically as being dropped into Times Square from a cozy family cul-de-sac. But the sudden shift in your teen's inner view of the world can feel just that radical, and often is. The new territory of adolescence is yet uncharted for them. Through a variety of experiences, the adolescent starts to assemble a new, revised map of reality in which he plots himself and his direction. The teen has choices to make, decisions of many kinds.

Some of these choices arise as moral choices about personal conduct.

Is it wrong to drink alcohol? What if I have to lie to my parents to do it? Is it my responsibility to keep my friend from getting drunk at a party?

What is my moral view of sex? Am I going to have sex, or say no to my new boyfriend (or boyfriend of a year) for now?

Is it really a breach of the school honor code if I help my friend with her take-home exam—just a little?

The questions can shift into bigger personal postulates and questions about the nature of morality, the self, relationships, and reality.

Is there a God who knows what I am doing?

Are we morally accountable to a higher power?

Am I accountable to myself, to my own standards? What are they?

Do other people have a right to try to influence me?

Would I have the same morality if I were raised in a totally different culture?

Is there an ultimate moral code to the universe?

Why are we put on earth?

It is not always the all-encompassing questions that grab hold of the teen. In a first brush with autonomy, everyday decisions or priorities, particularly choices in relationships, reflect much deeper values.

Should I do sports training camp or make the trip to see my grandparents?

Should I care about trying to fit in with the popular clique? What if it means I have to stand back from the kids they don't like?

Choice by choice, big and little, the new map takes shape and with it comes an emerging concept of identity based upon a deeper spiritual worldview. *Who am I? What do I want my life to be? What is my purpose?* The natural work of adolescent individuation is foundationally spiritual and deeply challenging. Individuation can progress without *spiritual individuation*, but it is a weakened version based too often solely on performance, accomplishment, and material success. Given the broad and pervasive protective benefits of spirituality found by science, I hold the view that as human beings we are designed with spirituality as the central organizing principle, the *spiritual hub* of our makeup. Full individuation in all areas of life ultimately rides on our asking and answering the big questions.

Quest is not just intellectual; it comes through the channels of human experience as intellectual, emotional, relational, and physical. Every adolescent has all channels, but for each teen, quest comes in most prominently on a different channel, depending on their individual makeup. All four of these channels for transcendence are open and active for all adolescents. In brief:

Intellectual. For some teens individuation is a highly intellectual struggle, driven by a working teen-based philosophy, theology, or existentialism. This quest is conducted through the inquiring and driving hunger to know and is resolved in intellectual terms.

Emotional. A strong emotional component is present for most teens, a sense of urgent hunger for transcendence. The hunger can be felt as a hollow emptiness, anxiety, edgy hankering for more, with the quest being about finding love, warmth, and the feeling of being part of something more.

Relational. Relationships are spiritual events, the ground of spiritual experiences for many adolescents. Love and daily interactions become a ground for spiritual connection and fulfillment. The quest can be for relationships that make the teen feel totally embraced, fully accepted.

Physical. For other adolescents, individuation is a physically felt sense, lived in the body and in the natural world. Here quest can push forward as a felt bodily frustration, irritation, or anxiety. This physical sense of urgency may be resolved through a sense of awakening or joy in the body, or a physical journey, or the need to push beyond previous limits, or a natural spiritual awakening received through the senses, often in nature.

Through all these channels the transcendent hunger emerges. The natural biological surge that pushes forward in adolescence not only adds new powers to perception, but it creates a hunger for spiritual transcendence, for knowing the world surrounding us and within us as a spiritual reality. Most of all, this drive has us seeking to know ourselves as spiritual beings and to identify our job or purpose in relation to the ultimate universe. This is the quest.

Unfortunately, a great majority of adolescents are utterly unprepared to do this work, much less identify its nature.

Spiritual Assets and Strengths Become the Teen's Tools for the Quest

Teens experience this passage in the second decade as a storm of feeling and questions without answers. They feel lost in a sea of strong feeling and frustration with the outer world (parents often included) for failing to respond to their upset or addressing their deeper hunger. When the cogent unifying rubric that they seek—transcendence and spiritual knowledge—is absent, they only feel the pangs of hunger.

The most helpful way to support an adolescent is to frame the quest as spiritual, and as an essential, core part of their emergence to adulthood. The unifying notion of a spiritual quest provides calm, focus, and rootedness. A parent can convey that ultimately this passage is an opportunity created by the teen's tremendous perceptiveness and capacity for spiritual awareness. The difficulty will pass and answers will come.

A basic language and understanding of spiritual life set up in decade one is extremely helpful in decade two, when the teen's capacity for spiritual awareness burgeons. However tumultuous the journey may become, the teen has an underlying confidence that he can know transcendence directly because that has been part of his life experience. His channel of knowing is far greater and can respond to those dogged questions from a deeper level.

Confronted with new ideas or situations, he can bring spiritual awareness to the big questions: *Is this what life should be about? Is this what I want my life to be about? Is this who I want to be?*

This is the challenge of spiritual individuation. But the teen can be equipped with the building blocks: knowing of the heart, direct knowing, field of love, parental endorsement of a higher power, and an inner compass. With these, the teen can know and see from the higher self. Rather than feel caught in the chaos, teens will have a sense of a greater spiritual reality within the self and beyond the self, accompanied by a language to hold these experiences.

Spiritual awareness going into adolescence offers the teen essential building blocks with which to build the edifice of individuation. Without this awareness and knowledge of spiritual life, the teen often attempts the quest for transcendence through undirected, unsupported shortcuts—tuning out, or tuning in to potentially destructive sources of information or inspiration. The surge will happen, whether the adolescent is ready or not. The fleeting taste of transcendence in sensory shortcuts—such as wild, soaring risk taking, hot and quick relationships, drinking or trying drugs—can gain dangerous momentum.

The Surge Fuels the Quest for Spiritual Identity

As brain science shows, the adolescent brain is built for the tasks of individuation and spiritual individuation in the second decade, even more so than in adulthood, when neural networks and patterns of thought have become more deeply entrenched. Adolescents have a fleeting and precious window in which the brain and mind are equipped to invest in the work through highly sensitive attunement and strong emotions, a burning hunger to know and discover, and a new set of perceptual tools for reflection.

For the teen, then, the Times Square experience is inherently a spiritual awakening whether it is labeled as one or not. The fundamental aspects of the adolescent surge previously explored together create the powerful drive for adolescent individuation, which we now know by nature includes spiritual individuation. The core features of that biological and developmental engine are:

- The adolescent brain is a spiritual brain. The transcendent faculty—the ability to feel and interact with a world beyond the physical world—is biologically based and is designed to be integrated with all aspects of adolescent development, just as in the first decade it is designed to be integrated with all aspects of childhood development.
- A genetic component in the surge primes teens for spiritual focus and transcendent connection on a biological timeline, as well as a psychological one.
- The surge in adolescent brain development includes metacognition, the higher-order thinking that allows adolescents to reflect on their inner experience to find meaning. This capacity to "think about how we think" includes questioning, reexamining and rethinking childhood assumptions about life, the world, and reality. Through this active, thoughtful, and at times life-changing work of reflection and making meaning, the adolescent sees the world as full, or sees the world as empty; the teen finds meaning, purpose, and calling, or feels lost and striving against the odds.
- Personal spirituality—a teen's own chosen path of spiritual engagement—becomes a cornerstone for lifelong personal growth, success, satisfaction, and happiness. As we saw in chapter 2, research has found that personal spirituality not only is linked to empathy, forgiveness, resilience, and other facets of what noted researcher Angela Duckworth calls "grit"—persistence plus passion to succeed. Personal spirtuality is also the most potent protection known for lowering the risk of the most common serious adolescent health concerns.

With the lessons from Times Square in mind, we can look more closely into how these defining features of the adolescent brain and development emerge in real time in our children. We'll focus on the capacities that support the adolescent's striving for a meaningful identity and for the hard work of integrating the various emerging selves—the student, the family member, the achiever, the dreamer—to achieve individuation. The quest is how the teen grabs hold of the surge and, through the transcendent faculty, channels that energy into a personal spirituality.

A large body of science shows that spirituality and lived spiritual values protect against a broad range of mental and physical illness, even down to the cellular suppression of genes associated with illness and the selective transcription of DNA for "healthier" protein expression. Stepping back from the big pattern of spirituality and health, the effects at every level of analysis—from overall feeling to neural correlates, to cell health, and throughout broad outcomes of physical and mental health—suggest that spirituality touches nearly everything. My read of the science is that this vast reach of spirituality establishes it as the central organizing, highest level of executive functioning. The spiritual hub is central to health, and it is our natural constitution.

For your teen, every experience registers through this newly emerging capacity as an event with personal meaning: *What do I think of that? How do I feel about that? What would I do? What should I do?* She observes those around her at school, at home, and in the community and reflects: *Do I say hello to the new kid? Do I welcome a chance to work on a project with a kid I don't know rather than rush to team up with my friends? Do I go to the movie with my kid sister like I said I would instead of "forgetting" our plan when my friend calls? What if my friend does something I feel is wrong?* With every new experience, the adolescent wonders if this particular experience really is their thing: *Is this a "me" or a "not-me" experience?* The new and varied sounds and opportunities of Times Square come fast and furious—there is so much to process and so much that can happen.

As parents, if we could pack one thing along with our adolescent son or daughter before they were swept off to Times Square, what would that single most essential thing be? Based on the research of the past fifteen years, the answer is spirituality.

The Spiritual Brain Becomes Developmental "Command Central": Core Spirituality Becomes the Organizing Principle for Identity and Individuation

We have long understood the adolescent tasks of identity formation, integration, and individuation as developmental imperatives, but without regard for the centrality of spirituality we've only understood them partway at best. We recognize adolescents' mercurial experiments with identity, their bids for independence as they pull away from us, their deepening friendships and first loves, and their desire for mastery of tasks and recognition. Yet along with this development and new capacities—critical thought, autonomy, sexuality, and a heightened awareness of the wider world—also comes a hardwired hunger for and spontaneous glimpses of being part of something more.

Life's deepest questions suddenly feel pressing to teens: *Who am I? What am I here for? How do I matter?* This is where our culture has basically fallen flat in its understanding of adolescent development. We hear the angst fraught with confusion or discontent, and we figure they are stubborn, difficult, or "moody." We think: *Oh, teenagers, they are never happy, can't do anything to please them,* or *It's their job to drive us crazy,* or *They'll get over it.*

The teen's turbulence is actually a spiritual awakening and the spiritual quest for meaning and purpose. It is teenagers coming online with all of their inborn and developing spiritual abilities, with a hunger for transcendence, and a driven search for connection and an inner coherence. It is spiritual individuation.

As we've seen in previous chapters, natural spirituality has been identified as a powerful and pervasive part of our emotional and psychological makeup. Biologically, psychologically, and developmentally, it permeates our being, acting as a catalyst and central organizing principle for growth.

If we think of development as a spider's web, then spirituality at the center determines the strength, scope, resilience, and continuity throughout the entire web. From that center, spiritual values and principles shape and inform all other aspects of your teen's self. *Who am I in a relationship? How do I treat "the other guy"? What are my values and how do I live them in everyday life?*

This spiritual hub is the transcendent self, the seat of the higher self: a teen's sense of relationship with the universe, a sense of being part of something larger. Through the transcendent self, your teen is able to reach out and speak to a world beyond our physical one and to discern guidance, through God or nature, for example. The transcendent self transforms the process of identity development and individuation. Everyday interactions become contexts for the spiritual self to engage and express. This is how the teen's personal spirituality spreads its wings.

The science of the spiritual brain tells us that when a strong personal spirituality exists at the executive level of the brain, it can often override other genetically based risks, such as the genetic predisposition for losing control and acting out aggressively, or for depression, substance use and abuse, and risk taking. Spirituality enhances a broad range of positive assets and helps override an extremely wide range of genetically based risks factors; its impact is unmatched and reflects its central role in our development.

More than that, spirituality's role as executive organizer at the center of the web means that it draws upon and affects all other capacities. This includes how your teen perceives the world and himself within that world, how he learns from experience and in a school setting, how he uses judgment to temper impulses, and intuitive skills to size up situations, people, and opportunities. If developed, our connection with spirit is the most central organizing principle of our psyche. As adolescents make their journey through the developmental passage ahead, you want them to have that transcendent self, that stabilizing, fortifying, organizing faculty guiding their way. Especially given the performance- and acquisition-driven culture and the hypercompetitive academic and professional environments in which our children live, research shows that the positive effect of this organizing spiritual core has become increasingly apparent. Long-term, a spiritual core affects everything, from their most intimate relationships to their aspirations for work and life, to patterns of behavior that have them engaging socially in ethical and positive ways, versus an antisocial or exploitative orientation. Spiritual development is the most important work we do in the second decade, and most deserving of our support as parents and community. Without support for forming this foundation, teens are left on a shaky base.

Having the spiritually engaged psyche in the director's chair gives a wise, bigger picture. This grounds the adolescent for the quest through this tumultuous passage. Without spirituality as the central organizer, the emotional, social, and cognitive assets are disorganized, lacking cohesion, coherence, and sense of purpose. Research shows that to leave that chair empty works against the adolescent, increasing the risk of depression, substance use and abuse, and high-risk behaviors. What's more, the empty chair can stay unoccupied for the rest of life, and the teen who suffers a lingering sense of not being rooted, of feeling anxious and without deep bearings, carries that into adulthood. An empty chair creates an empty life.

Personal spirituality, cultivated as the core through the quest phase, infuses each of the central tasks of adolescence with meaning, purpose, and life-affirming connection in ways that transform the long-familiar developmental tasks into rich spiritual experience, as shown in the center column of the chart on page 246. With spirituality, identity grows from ideas of meaning and purpose; without spirituality, identity can be dependent on acquiring "success" (in the far-right column). With personal spirituality in the mix, work becomes a way a teen harnesses inner resources to fulfill a calling; without, work's purpose is to feel talented and narcissistically special. Teens tell me that with an underlying spiritual sense in their everyday lives, they "feel alive" with a sense of oneness with the purposeful universe, not at sea in a random universe.

For every major development task, spirituality brings a positive structure to development, as you can see in the following chart:

A SPIRITUAL CORE SHAPES DEVELOPMENT: MEANING, PURPOSE, CALLING, AND CONNECTION

Developmental Task	With Spiritual Core	Without Spiritual Core
Self Is	Inherent Worth	Abilities Based
Identity	Meaning & Purpose	Acquiring Success
Work	Calling & Contribution	Talents & Gains
Relationships	Sacred, Share Love, & Grow	Pleasing, Meet Needs
Path	Buoyed Up and Guided	Unsure, Instrumental
Place in World	Always Connected	Ultimately Alone
Existential Reality	Purposeful World	Random World
Nature of Reality	Love, Life-giving	Unknown
Good Events	Blessings	Deserved, Luck
Bad Events	Opportunities, Learning	Random, Failure

A spiritual core changes all else into an inspired life. Spiritual individuation sets a teen up to value himself (and others) as more than just a winner or loser, more than someone who gets top scores in school or, as an adult, the big bucks, big house, big name. A spiritual view has the teen investing personal talents, traits, and accomplishment with a higher purpose and a higher good.

The process of spiritual individuation involves building a strong dialogue between the analytical mind and the intuitive or transcendent faculty, head and heart.

We can prepare children ahead of time for the adolescent awakening into Times Square. After all, it would have been helpful if someone had told you that you were going to Times Square, given you a map of the place, and taken the time to show you how to use your compass and the navigational tools to find your way on this journey.

Teens suffer when they don't know that this is the work at hand for them. When nobody tells them about the surge of spiritual awakening, the power of it can be overwhelming. Their crucial questions of meaning and purpose, calling, relationship, and the ultimate nature of the world are naturally overwhelming, too, when no one has told them that their relationship with the transcendent can help. Our culture has abandoned adolescents in this regard, and we need to do a better job. Fortunately, we can look to some long-established cultures where the adolescent rites of passage are imbued with spiritual significance.

Traditional Templates for an "Education for Transcendence"

Many cultures do indeed give adolescents a heads-up that they're about to embark on this important and exciting journey of integration of mind, body, and spirit. In these cultures, young teens are not only handed a map; they are given a gift pack of tools, and training in the skills they'll need to survive the passage and thrive wherever they go from there. In fact, it's understood that parents and other adult mentors have a responsibility—a sacred duty—to prepare their children for this developmental passage.

In his book, *Boiling Energy: Community Healing among the Kalahari Kung,* the psychologist and anthropologist Richard Katz describes one African community's spirit-based culture as "an education for transcendence." Central to the Kung's community life are the ritual drummings and dances, some for healing, others for celebrating aspects of male or female ways of knowing, or to engage and celebrate transcendent energy, or *num.* Kung children, brought up experiencing the transcendent energy force through these communal rituals from an early age, move into puberty fully aware of their innate spiritual faculty and encouraged to use it. Theirs is not a sudden round of instruction, packing in information from an external source. The Kung's education for transcendence is woven into the fabric of their everyday lives from birth. This is the ultimate "integrated curriculum" and a great deal more helpful than a wish for success and a new laptop to take to school.

In many indigenous traditions, including those in North America, puberty is commonly recognized as an awakening capacity for spiritual connection and readiness to receive generational knowledge. The Native American sun dance and lacrosse rites of passage for adolescent boys, and the spirit hut, sunrise, and balas chonas puberty rites for girls, all mark the passage to adulthood through sacred rituals that underscore the primacy of nature as the source of divine wisdom and the young person's spiritual birthright emerging with new power and responsibility.

Among world religions, coming-of-age practices include the Catholic sacrament of Communion, through which the adolescent is sealed with the Holy Spirit. In Judaism, the bar or bat mitzvah marks the adolescent's new role as an adult in the religious community and the broader duty of *tikkun olam*, or the duty to partner with God to heal and repair the world. In Hinduism, the Upanayana or Dvija marks the passage through which the adolescent joins the religious community as an adult. In Islam, at puberty the adolescent begins the formal prayer practice of *salat* (prayer five times a day) and other sacred commitments. At the "age of maturity," the Baha'i adolescent publically states a personal decision to observe that faith's religious laws. The Buddhist Shinbyu ceremony initiates young people into the temple as novice monks. In a Shinto ceremony, an adolescent boy is given adult clothes and a haircut, and then taken before the shrine of his patron deity to mark arrival into puberty. Through all of these ceremonies the adolescent is recognized as a spiritual steward of her or his own life and is called to contribute to the community as a spiritual adult.

These traditions are not simply symbolic gestures of collective identity, or elaborate rituals to preserve ancient glories or theologies. Coming-of-age ceremonies honor the emergence of heightened spirituality through which the adolescent steps up to honor spiritual knowledge and embraces the transcendent relationship. The rituals and cultural support for them are also a time-tested mechanism for the integration process needed for spiritual individuation. The quest enables the teen to more fully integrate experience across all developing faculties—biological, sexual, cognitive, social, emotional, and prosocial—so that all are infused with spiritual significance.

These longstanding cultural and religious traditions understand what Western science only recently has identified: the growth surge through the second decade of life sparks an inner quest and prompts the adolescent to seek transcendence and a relationship with the divine, whatever form and whatever name that may take for them. This is not a new idea to civilization, just one that has been forgotten by our contemporary Western culture, at great cost to our children. What we see as a surly, unsettled teen is more accurately a teen on a quest to bring mind, body, and spirit into alignment, to integrate those parts of the self into a coherent whole.

Every adolescent is on a hero's journey toward individuation. In mythic terms, they have to go out, slay the dragon, and come back with the dragon's head to rejoin the community in a new way, benighted. Psychologically, we understand the quest as the process through which an adolescent faces inner tests and trials, arriving into adulthood on their own terms. Sometimes they need to go out very far before they're ready to return and reintegrate into family and community, with their now strong sense of spiritual self. Whether they do this in a ritual vision quest or religious rite of passage, or on their own terms in the family culture, they struggle to go out, accomplish what they need to accomplish, and come back and rejoin in a deeper, more individuated way. Not only do they come back, they come back more evolved, suited for an adulthood of greater awareness and thriving.

Friends and School Environment Strongly Influence a Teen's Spiritual Quest

The adolescent accomplishes the integration of physical, mental, and spiritual selves—head and heart—through hard work and independent decision making. To a large extent it is a solo act. However, research suggests that for the inherently social teen, the surrounding social world of parents, friends, the school tone, and popular culture has a significant impact on the individuation process.

Sam Hardy, a developmental psychologist at Brigham Young University, studied the identity development of students from sixteen high schools over six years to see the potential long-term contributions of religious community and community service. His findings were pronounced in showing far greater individuation in general, as well as specifically greater spiritual individuation in students who were involved in community service and/or religious community. For these teens, questions of *Who am I?* and *What is the point of life?* were not avoided, ignored, or set aside. Their deepest questions had been actively addressed and, whether or not fully answered, at least were seriously considered. Because by actually doing good actions, they are de facto making themselves into a person who operates with spiritual values and can discover the feelings of the heart, and transcendent relationships, that come through service.

A teen's spiritual individuation is facilitated by participation in a well-intentioned community of people of many ages, such as a religious community and/or a service-based community. The teen's questioning of how to balance head and heart in the nitty-gritty of everyday life, central to the individuation process, finds answers through experiences of prayer, good actions of service, and relationships of service. Hardy highlights that the personal journeys of fellow community members are a rich source of guidance for the adolescent, since typically many fellow members in these communities have achieved spiritual individuation themselves. A twenty-something in a religious community can talk to a teen about their own spiritual individuation, as can an elder in a community service setting, each sharing his own pathway to spiritual values. This is the material from which the teen draws. Teens are less likely to abandon the hard work of individuation, or leave it dangling and unanswered, and more likely to find support and guidance when surrounding by caring adults who have faced the same challenge of spiritual individuation.

A study on the power of environment on spiritual individuation (based on a well-known University of North Carolina survey of thousands of adolescents) measured the impact of peers and of the general school culture on the successful spiritual individuation in adolescents. The contribution of peers turns out to be equal to that of parents in facilitating spiritual individuation, but the general ecology of school is even stronger. The comings and goings of school peers, the norms and rules of conduct in the school culture, and how to survive and thrive under the implicit values of the school: all of this matters as much as parents and close friends. (This is the field of love extended through the social engagement system of school and friendship, as we saw in chapter 5.)

This study also found that teens whose parents are loving—who are giving them the nod—have a much easier time forming a spiritual map of the world during individuation. To a large extent it is a map that mirrors the love, commitment, and care in their own home. A home that feels full of the field of love, of spiritual bonds between family members, is the lived emotional reality from which the teen draws to build a sense of self in the world.

As our children separate from us—which is what they are supposed to do—spirituality gives them another resource, another someone to talk to, to turn to for advice and direction. They aren't quite ready to do everything on their own, but they do want to call the shots and not be turning to their parents all the time.

Teens inherently feel the need for this internal process of reviewing and clarifying their deepest values, finding their inner guiding voice, and whether or not it is supported in any other way, they do it de facto through friendship. The data from the above study showed that friends, and the culture of a school determined by schoolmates, facilitate or inhibit spiritual individuation. But between two adolescents in the same high school, the adolescent whose spirituality is fostered and then supported by a parent may have a very different experience from the norm. A study from my lab, headed by clinical scientist Alethea Desrosiers, now a professor at Yale Medical School, suggests that to some extent the teen has a hand in fostering relationships that support spiritual individuation: in other words, they pick friends whose tendency for quest and examination of spiritual values mirrors the original spiritual parenting from home. In conversations and interactions with one another, teens share their views on moral issues, challenge one another's ideas about right and wrong, good and evil, and share other serious and important material that addresses life's big questions. Among friends is where much of this work gets done, but sharing this way was originally learned from parents.

In our interviews with hundreds of adolescents about the place of spirituality in their relationships, we asked when or with whom among family, teachers, teammates, or friends from school they discussed spiritual questions. Not surprisingly, the most spiritually minded teens expressed a preference for finding friends with whom they could talk about their own spiritual inquiries. These discussions were considered very private and significant, and the teens considered their discoveries very cutting edge. Out of respect for the confidentiality of their peers, these teens did not usually share these discussions with their parents.

However, we then asked the same teens about the frequency and openness with which their own parents discussed personal spirituality with them. A parent might be heartened to know that there was nearly an identical match: parents who talk about spirituality in a personal way with their teens can be sure that their teens continue the important work of exploring big, spiritual questions with their peers. In fact, the research proved that a teen was much more likely to do spiritual work with friends if parents got the ball rolling at home.

Our research also suggests that peer relationships often follow the same spiritual thread of curiosity and questioning that you created with your child in the first decade. This dogged inquiry happens often in the privacy of sleepovers or hikes or time alone between adolescents. So it's meaningful that your adolescent comes to you to have that discussion, but know that they are also likely having it with their peers. Do everything under the sun to support those relationships.

I know from work and research that most adolescents are delighted to talk about and to share insights from their heightened spiritual awareness. They're excited, curious, and full of energy when asked about the topic. They seem to know that their new awareness marks the beginning of a new adventure. However, they also notice that nobody but their friends seems interested in their discoveries. Few parents ask, we found in the course of conducting our research. And since many parents may not yet realize that normal adolescent development includes a spiritual component, their teenagers may not understand that spiritual experiences are a normal, intrinsic fact of adolescent life. Once asked, they launch into discussion knowing full well the presence of spiritual quest, questions, and hunger, and are delighted that someone finally asked. Teens are keenly aware of the reality of a sacred life force; they speak of it as something real.

Teens Talk: The Spiritual Brain Boots Up

As we saw in chapter 8, a growing body of research, including MRI and other studies, shows the remarkable changes in the brain as it builds the circuitry that supports the transcendent faculty and the interconnectivity between the front and back of the brain. Think of these changes as a free upgrade from a landline modem to high-speed Internet service. Your teen's bandwidth for picking up and processing experience is suddenly hugely expanded, with heightened sensory perception, a heightened drive for social connection with peers, and heightened emotional resonance and reactivity. Life in high definition! The teen is individuating and is often aware of this integrative work. As the front brain–back brain connectivity begins to set up, the teen struggles to get the analytical/questioning front brain to receive feedback from the intuitive/sensory back brain. You can hear the fine-tuning process in these two earnest "but" statements by girls who spoke with me. Their uncertainty matched by their breakthrough awareness is so familiar in teen reflections. Heart knowing and head knowing move disjointedly at first to develop the analytical/intuitive interface:

> I love every person on our hiking trip—each one seems so special to me now—but do you think that it's real? (Ellie, sixteen)

> I feel God exists, but is that scientific? (Jessica, seventeen)

Or this, from an eighteen-year-old boy obviously grappling for words to express his take on the timeless big questions of meaning and where we find it:

> I think everyone wants to find meaning in life and stuff, 'cause they want to justify their existence, but I think that sort of lies in the individual, because it does mean stuff to the individual—but that's sort of a more *inward* looking than *outward* looking.

The emerging self-observing metacognition of adolescence and the inner dialogue between the brain's front and back are audible here as Hannah, fifteen, expounds on the question of whether God exists:

> There are so many things bigger than us, how can there not be something else? Not like a God, but I don't know, how am I supposed to know? This stuff is kind of scary. We are not like the highest beings or anything. I don't know what it is but there has to be something. . . . Like how can the brain be so amazing and something spiritual or God not exist, you know? So many amazing things happen to people and sometimes you just get so lost in these moments, and science doesn't create moments like that. But I am a firm believer in science and it's not like I don't know evolution and all that stuff—I do, I believe in that. I really, really do.

These are all voices of the adolescent spiritual quest to transcend the ordinary, to experience the "something greater," and to engage the complex questions of life. Complex confrontations with life and big questions await teens no matter where they find themselves. Sometimes spiritual awakening is hard earned through questioning, often in the company of friends, sometimes by spending time in nature, or simply in contemplation on a bus ride or in your car waiting for the light to turn green. That's just how the mind works—and the spirit, too. The quest opens the space for experience, and an adolescent's openness is inevitably answered. For many teens it comes with confrontations at life's edges, a birth or death, in struggle or suffering, or trauma, whether their own or that of someone else. In my research interviews and other conversations with teens, many describe their spiritual emergence not so much as a dramatic breakthrough or "peak experience," but as a road of trials or self-discovery.

In our research interviews, asked if they have ever had what they would consider a spiritual experience, teens' range of defining moments is diverse, always genuine, and poignant. In these interviews and in my conversations with them I am always moved by the depth of their inquiry and self-discovery. Their perceptions of their journey are alive with consciousness, creativity, and resourcefulness as they shape their own personal spirituality from whatever their life has given them to work with. Each one makes a distinctive hero's journey, but their reflections carry a common theme of self-discovery and growing spiritual awareness. These are their voices:

> I'm developing into an adult now and my mind has changed. I was really just a follower, believing what people told me, never really questioning anything. I just assumed that God existed because people told me so and I never really thought about it. And then I thought about what's going on in the world today. I'd never thought about it, never compared it to what the Bible says. Now I feel just much more in touch, much more intelligent. I understand the world

a lot better. And I've come up with a different interpretation of laws and spirituality. (Luis, sixteen)

I feel that from people I meet, I tend to take things. Like, my parents: they believe that they're soul mates, so I have taken that belief and brought it into my own belief system. From my yoga teacher, I've taken stuff from her. And from the church I've taken things, and from the Bible and from my friends and family. (Katherine, eighteen)

I did a lot of questioning when I was close to seventh grade. I went from having been told all these things to being told by our parents that it's okay to pursue things in this way. I'd never really thought about it myself and I never really experienced it and at that point, I really started questioning what was valuable in my life [and] I made my own conclusions. So I've kind of taken what I liked and discarded what I didn't like to make who I am and what I believe spiritually. (Zach, fourteen)

Some teens feel compelled to explore other spiritual traditions or possibilities. Others don't need to venture away from their family's faith system. Instead, they feel drawn to dig deeper to find their own sense of connection and meaning in it. Rebecca, sixteen and Jewish, shares her family's religious identity but has clearly stepped into ownership of her own individuated personal spirituality.

My spirituality is definitely something I have evolved for myself. It wasn't given to me or instilled in me by any other person, because my parents aren't very spiritual people. I'm probably the most religious person in my household. I maintain it pretty much on my own. I go to synagogue for the high holidays, and several years ago I started praying every night before I go to sleep . . . it's not any particular prayer, it's just my own personal prayer. I find that spirituality infiltrates my day-to-day consciousness, and it has forever, since I could remember. It's been an integral part of my identity.

Annie, fifteen, a Buddhist, explains her thoughts.

I think all religion is finding out who you are, not just in physical terms, like I'm Annie and I'm a girl and I'm Korean—it's not like that. I think religion states who you are. I think all religion has the same origin—like, be a good person and have integrity—but with Buddhism, it's about guiding you to who you are and why you're here and what your purpose is.

Tom, at fifteen, drew from the Christian foundations familiar to him to connect with the God of his childhood, but reached out for what he felt he needed from other sources.

I had to know things and those little pieces of knowledge came in small chunks when I was ready to receive them. I didn't necessarily [understand] what I was dealing with [in the moment] but God was building me a foundation, very slowly, because he says we've gotta *work* our way out of this. I got that life is process and I'm in process, and little pieces come one at a time, from different teachers, different sacred or memorable moments, relationships, or books that came along the way.

Tammy, sixteen, attended a faith-based summer camp as the only non-Jew among her friends. Her spiritual multilingualism shines through here, enabling her to access her own spiritual experience in the context of a different spiritual community.

I experienced a new religion . . . made new friends, kissed a boy for the first time. I just remember feeling myself open up in so many ways—I felt my world expanding, I became hungry for excitement, hungry for new things, hungry to learn and seek and fulfill. I realized that life was full of opportunities for exciting new events, encounters, fateful incidences, and I wanted to take full advantage of all that life has to offer—see as much, learn as much, love as much as I possibly could.

Your teen's questioning is almost certainly going to be directed toward you, at times seeking, at other times challenging. Parents often take the challenge personally. We think: *You're angry at me,* or *You're disrespecting our family's religious tradition.* Maybe we suspect their friends are leading them astray, or something they are learning at school is undermining their spirituality as we have always known it. Or we fear that they may totally abandon a relationship with a higher power and never come back. Whatever moves your adolescent children to explore, they are not falling from faith. They're doing the essential developmental task of coming into their own faith; it can take time—sometimes years—and questioning, but the illumination will come. Wherever their spiritual yearnings lead them, teens find spiritual growth through the quest process. My concern is that so many adolescents aren't guided to the journey at all, or aren't encouraged on their way.

Religion can still offer that spiritual grounding today for many teens, and for some it already does. They seek the spiritual road map through their faith's tradition or one of their own choosing, in a personal and authentic way. This is not a matter of receiving and accepting a "belief system" imposed by parents or others. Teens often creatively take whatever resonates for them spiritually and use it to discover and then cultivate their transcendent selves.

For Tammy, the last night of camp, the farewell bonfire, offered a glimpse of the transformative power of the transcendent experience for teens and their capacity to draw so much from it.

It was bittersweet, taking in the sense of community while anticipating the impending separation of going home. I felt an electricity inside of me, transcending me and taking me to this realm where we aren't our bodies; we are energy, we are momentum, we are vibrations. I realized that this is the essence of humanity, its most raw and limitless crux. I was awakened to a sense of connectivity and unity—linking all people and things—and I could feel the energy around me emanating from others' emotions, permeating from the fire, diffusing the air through the sounds of the bugs and the songs being sung and the atmosphere of the night lit up by activity. This was a moment of clarity for me—I saw the world without physically seeing it. I saw it for what it truly was, the energy and the exchange of energy that propels this universe. I knew that this is where I wanted to reside spiritually, in that moment, in that juncture of connectivity.

Derek was eighteen, a college freshman hanging out with his dorm friends, when they decided to watch *Bowling for Columbine*, a documentary about the 1999 Columbine High School massacre. In an essay, Derek wrote that watching the film was a spiritual turning point for him.

There was a moment in the film when the 911 emergency audio recordings were played from the various students at the high school when the shooting began—you could hear the pain, the innocence, the fear. I asked myself the questions—*Why? How?* I was raised to believe if one does good things, good things will follow. And yet, these . . . children . . . were shot dead. . . . I found myself struggling with the concept of good and evil, and its relationship to God. If God is all-knowing, all-powerful, and all-good, and if we are truly made in God's image, how could God allow bad things to happen to good people? Why would God allow evil to even exist?

Tyrese, nineteen, now a Christian rapper at an urban hip-hop church, describes a turning point when his friend was killed in a shooting as they stood together on a street corner. He'd gone to church begrudgingly before, just to appease his mother. But on the day of the funeral something happened that shook him to the core and changed his life.

> I was, like, searchin' inside myself, like, wow, that could've been me [killed] . . . 'cause I stood right in the same spot where he was at, as far as stayin' on street corners, drinkin' with him, smokin' with him, laughin', jokin' with him. That could've been me. Thank God it wasn't. So I came to the funeral. And about two, three Sundays later, the preacher was preachin', and he said, "the doors of the church are open." And I looked inside, and it was like movin' me to get up there. It was like God was sayin', "If you take five steps, I'll take twenty steps. And if you take twenty steps, I'll take a hundred steps."

He felt guided—not so much by the preacher or a voice from above, but by "in here, the intuition in my heart," he says.

> And I stepped up there, and I'm takin' them steps, slowly but surely makin' my way up there to the preacher. And when I got up there, I was just cryin' . . . I just felt like lettin' all the pain out . . . I let it out like a girl do, you know? My life never been the same.

These are the voices of spiritual individuation: the journey, the illumination, and the ownership of experience that becomes an adolescent's personal spirituality.

You can continue to help your son or daughter by welcoming their conversation, encouraging them on their quest. The thing is, we never know when these spiritually moving moments may unfold or may already have unfolded for a young person. Sometimes children, teens especially, keep the experiences to themselves or only share them with friends they know "get it."

Nature primes teens for the surge, but to most fully engage it, teens need encouragement and practice. They need to develop ease with the nature of quest energy and the curiosity and urgency it brings. They need a vocabulary to articulate and integrate their experience to align the lessons as new spiritual coordinates with their inner compass.

Many teens gladly share their story, but only with certainty that it will be viewed as real, precious, and significant, as it truly was in her own path. Your teen needs to feel that she will be understood, that she's not in danger of an adult "not getting it," or "not getting her," or being vulnerable for sharing.

Teachers and school counselors often ask, "What should I do when I see this?" A studio art teacher in a secondary school in the Southwest put it beautifully when she explained: "In my work, I always meet the student where he is. So just the other day a student's drawing clearly was expressing a spiritual struggle. I asked him to tell me about it and asked him what it felt like, and how he was making sense of it. I gave him room to talk about what you are calling his 'spiritual quest' just intuitively because that was where he was. I didn't talk about anything from my own religion, just supported him."

A Parent's Privilege: Facilitating Adolescent Spiritual Individuation

In spiritual individuation, there are three essential components that build upon one another to create a lifelong infrastructure for spiritual living. Spiritual individuation calls upon the teen to, first, recognize quest energy as spiritual in nature and see or locate themselves on a journey of spiritual individuation; second, to deliberately practice a way to open themselves toward transcendence; and third, to embrace the internal experience of transcendence as a response or guide to the nagging questions or hunger of quest.

Whether or not the adolescent has been prepared in the first decade, the work arises and can be facilitated by a caring adult with encouragement, wisdom, and respect. Personal spirituality is the outcome of spiritual individuation and it is always on the teen's own terms, without command or demand ever being issued from the adult. But adults can engage with thoughtful questions that support each step of the teen's self-discovery. Simply by offering new words, ways to describe the feelings, you can help your adolescent identify the pangs of quest hunger:

Do you sometimes feel edgy, frustrated, like a feeling of wanting more, or trying to get going? How would you describe your feelings?

I've noticed that sometimes the old usual things or way of doing things can seem irritating. You already sense there's something more, so keep tuned. In time, you will feel "the something more" on your own terms.

Do you feel that something inside might be bubbling up for your attention—saying, "Pay attention to me"? Do you feel pulled inward in anyway?

Acknowledging quest energy as rising up from inside helps support this natural process and helps your teen understand it as normal and important. For the adolescent it is a huge relief to understand these bubbling visceral feelings, have a name for them and a way to see them as part of their personal big picture. You can then share, "This quest hunger may be very helpful to spur you on in your spiritual wondering, moving you along your own path of discovery about spirituality."

As parents and professionals who work with youth, we can locate the adolescent in the individuation process. In some settings, a ritual can be honored or invented that embraces the hard work of quest; being unclear on the challenge at hand makes focus on the work more difficult. When you talk with your adolescent about the spiritual quest, you are speaking to the transcendent self, supporting awareness of the inner seat in "command central" from which the developmental work is conducted.

Now that you are a teenager your brain is wired up to ask more and want more. It may take some questioning and testing out along the way, but eventually it comes together.

This challenge could be a valuable opening for a deeper look into the world. If we pay attention, sooner or later, life shows up and points the way.

Your higher self has a clear view of things, as way to start to answer important questions that come up for you. You can ask your higher self for guidance and direction.

This feeling might be about "coming into your own" on the big important things in life—it may happen little by little, and then it may all come together eventually. There is not a rush, and you don't need to have answers, just respect the feelings and honor the questions. You are a mythic quester, on a road of discovery.

This entire book honors and regards this profound work of spiritual life. I have shared with my own teenage children this chapter as a source of information, an arrow in their quiver on the road of trails ahead. If you feel that your teen might be empowered by the information as it's presented here, available for them to read on their own, consider this book itself a way into a conversation between you.

Meditation, prayer, collective spiritual practice, and ritual all open up the teen to the experience of the transcendent presence. Adolescents, if introduced, can learn to open themselves up or prepare themselves to better connect with the transcendent presence. Whether or not teens adopt a transcendent practice is up to them, naturally, but if they do, they are empowered with a vehicle for journeying. Given the chariot and the choice, teens can build a road to the transcendent presence. The spiritual path is authentic and of their own intention, fueling the individuation process.

Inviting adolescents to describe their experience, if they so wish, helps to embrace the reality of the transcendent presence. Together you can reflect on the nuances of lived experience.

How do you listen for your higher self—how do find your inner compass when you have a big decision to make?

How do the holidays make you feel? When we share the holidays together, somehow I feel a brightness between people that is like the field of love, or is the field of love.

You're welcome to join me while I meditate, or find a place on your own, in your time and space. You might find that your inner world starts to be more a part of everything, less isolated and cut off.

If it's been a while since you prayed, well, I can say that I just start. Even if it is awkward and does not carry much feeling at first, once the momentum builds inside myself, it becomes whole and full, all by itself.

Integration is the crucial work of bringing home the transcendent relationship into a guided way of living (putting the front brain–back brain connectivity into action). Integration looks different in different teens and in the same teen at different moments. Some teens have a question and get an answer through a deepening of faith, the question propelling a more intense connection with the higher power. Other teens wrangle and struggle and then *boom*, get a clear sense through an experience or a prayer or a meditation.

We can honor teens and listen with utmost respect, as they trace their daily lives, challenging choices, and school pressures back to the framework of the transcendent relationship. An honest and open discussion with a teen can go like this:

Teen: I think that Melissa is truly mean. She ignores me in the hallway if she happens to be walking with the popular kids, or her other friends. She'll just do this quick wave, and then she turns and walks right by me. I mean, what did I do to her?

Parent: What does your heart say? When you call on your higher self and connect with your transcendent relationships, what do you sense? What does the inner dialogue tell you?

Your teen may find her way to something along these lines below, but if not, listen and explore the thoughts as they are shared, and perhaps introduce these conclusions as possibilities to consider:

Teen: I looked within and my heart says that I do matter, and that I am loved. This is Melissa's mistake, not mine. I didn't do anything wrong to deserve the meanness. And, I just need to keep being who I am.

This capacity to call on the higher self and connect with the transcendent relationships, once set up, will be a source of strength, guidance, and decision making for your teen.

In Spiritual Individuation the Adolescent Digs Deeper for Personal Meaning

Psychologically, the transition from first decade to second decade brings a shift from a strongly parent-centered, parent-guided experience to one in which the emerging teen takes ownership and control of the experience. That is the journey of identity development and individuation in general, and spiritual individuation follows that same path. Your teen sets out to experience her reality, really claim it, and then, in later adolescence or early adulthood, attempts to reconcile it with the reality offered up by you and her community. To some degree for every adolescent, this first requires separation, then integration to make things whole.

Teens each have their own work to do in coming to a spiritual understanding that holds meaning and purpose for them: this is the essence of personal spirituality. They must make the journey personal in order to set up a life of value that includes identity, and contribution to the larger good. They need to grapple with questions of moral or ethical behavior involving choices they face and the consequences. They need to practice bringing a spiritual lens—their higher self and the transcendent relationship—to events of the day.

This essential self-knowledge is gained through the developmental challenges and tasks of the second decade. A strong identity emerges as they come to know and accept themselves in all ways: gender, sexuality, personality, tastes, appetites, and interests. All of those "selves" need support. All the things we know from basic psychology are still true: Teens want to love and be loved; they want to connect. And now, the science of spirituality and psychology tell us that they want to transcend. In order for all that to happen they need to accept themselves and feel accepted.

Abraham Maslow, a founder of humanistic psychology and seemingly quite spiritual, in his seminal book, *Religions, Values, and Peak-Experience,* observed that identity development could not be whole if the spiritual piece was missing. "Isolating two interrelated parts of a whole from each other, parts that need each other, parts that are truly 'parts' and not wholes, distorts them both, sickens and contaminates them. Ultimately it even makes them nonviable."

As we'll see in the chapters ahead, a partitioned self creates a spiritual split for the teen, who can feel deep inner conflict over who he knows himself to be and who he feels he is expected to be, or must be, to be accepted by friends, family, or community. Race, ethnicity, religion, sexual orientation, emotional challenges, or learning differences: by absorbing hateful messages, these become infinite sources of unworthiness in the mind of a teen, and in that split the spiritual self becomes disconnected. The congruence of these different aspects of identity—the student, the friend, the athlete or artist, the family member, the seeker, the doubter—creates the spiritual bedrock for the developmental tasks of adolescence. A doctoral student once told me, "As a teen and young adult, I first had to come to know and love myself as a Black woman to then know myself and feel I was part of the universe." She speaks for all adolescents in that regard. To feel a part of the loving universe, they must be able to know and love themselves, and accept themselves and feel accepted.

The Quest and the Prize: Spiritual Individuation

Teens are willing to struggle with life's big questions. The quest is meaningful to them. When they understand that the answers to those questions aren't simple or quick, they're willing to keep searching, to engage in the conversations. Too often, just when the going gets rough, we leave teens to "figure it out"—to find their way through the woods without a compass, decent walking shoes, or much else of true value in their survival pack.

Alone and unmet in their struggle, this can be a particularly turbulent time for that novice 747 pilot. As one high school girl told me after a talk at her school, "It's a relief to know I don't need to know the answer immediately."

Especially in a performance-oriented culture where kids are expected to find the right answers fast, it can worry them when the questions defy a quick answer. We want our kids to know that sometimes the questions you spend your whole life thinking about are the most important, and that it's okay not to know the answer right away. Spirituality gives us the space to sit and hold the uncomfortable, to understand moral nuance, ambiguity, and our ultimate potential. These big questions are not SAT fill-in-the-right-bubble questions. We need to support their search for the deeper explorations.

I interviewed a former residential dean from an Ivy League college. He had seen so many sophomores melt into crisis without even a hint of inner knowledge, neither a thread of strength nor tools to navigate an inner storm. He explained that his students had done so much outer pleasing, racing to curry the awards and favor of other people, that they had not cleared time or allowed their intentions to turn inward for building a strong inner self.

Confused, unprepared, and unmet in his spiritual burgeoning, a teen's struggle is often misunderstood. Research suggests that a significant portion of teens who are depressed do not have a biologically based medical depression, but have developmental depression originating in the struggle for spiritual individuation and responsive to spiritual support. And in the chapter ahead, we'll look more closely into the teen's experience of developmental depression and how parents can meet them and help them through it.

10

DEVELOPMENTAL DEPRESSION AND SPIRITUAL AWAKENING

An Epidemic of Suffering Among Healthy Teens

Kaitlin was nineteen, a sophomore at an academically rigorous college in New England who was majoring in philosophy, and an intense thinker who had been a gregarious, positive person during freshman year. From Plato and Aristotle to Nietzsche and newer voices in science and philosophy and theology, her course readings and discussions covered the nature of reality and of good and evil, whether God exists or ever did, and whether there is "something greater" in our lives. Kaitlin enjoyed the big questions and found them intellectually stimulating. To her surprise, however, in the autumn of her sophomore year these philosophical questions about meaning and purpose suddenly began to nag her in a deeper way.

The questions became more than an academic exercise for her. She ruminated on the existential question of reality and meaning: What really was her "purpose on earth"? What was the "point of it all"? Even the question of whether she believed in an ultimate divine presence seemed unanswerable: How could you not know whether you "believe in God," and yet how could any intelligent person pin something so profound on mere belief? The unsettling self-inquiry drove her into a dark, brooding frame of mind. It began to affect her physically. She couldn't get out of bed to go to class in the morning. She broke up with her boyfriend of over a year. Finally, unable to pull out of the slump, she arranged to see a psychotherapist near campus.

The therapist quickly determined that Kaitlin met the clinical criteria for major depressive disorder (MDD) and told her that she would need to take the rest of the semester off from college if she were not in treatment. Kaitlin started regular psychotherapy along with antidepressant medication. Four months into spring semester, she was functional but still felt empty and adrift. She went home for summer break to live with her father on the coast of Maryland, where she felt surrounded by love and encouragement and warmth—yet still she struggled. Then one afternoon something changed.

"I was walking along the ocean, headed out along the dock, and saw the light sparkling on the water," Kaitlin says. "Suddenly it all became clear to me. Of course there is the creator, and the world is bright and full of love—there is spirituality in everything!"

She felt a sense of peace, a calm reassurance that came from both within and beyond her, an uplifting sensation of sacred connection and certainty. It wasn't a matter of belief or nonbelief; her experience was real and she knew it to be true. In that moment, she says, her intellect ceased to ignore her intuitive sense of spiritual connection with the "something greater." She started to feel reconnected, awakened to a sense of oneness with the universe and the sacredness in all things, all moments. She remembered having felt something similar as a child, but now the feeling emerged as a visceral answer from a hard-fought phase of dark doubt and questioning. Although Kaitlin continued to heal in stages over time, she identified the turning point in her depression as that moment on the dock. Something in the illuminated water, beyond its picturesque beauty, had moved her, buoyed her up, and held her in a loving space.

Kaitlin's downward spiral is not unusual for adolescents. It is common, in fact, as is the existential quest that led her there, and the breakthrough that awakened her spiritual connection. Much of what we see as the Sturm und Drang, the suffering and confusion of adolescence, has long been understood by ancient cultures as spiritual awakening endemic to puberty. As we've seen across time and geographical divides, diverse cultures have provided coming-of-age rituals that engage the adolescent's emerging hunger for meaning and connection and for answers to the same questions that nagged Kaitlin just as they have challenged philosophers, theologians, and all of humankind for thousands of years.

The value of a human life. Not just anyone's: *your* human life. The purpose of your whole being. Your value. And the point of the entire world around you. This is the core work of spiritual individuation—the quest. It is hard and challenging, and everything—heart and soul, literally—is on the line. Quest has a side that is hard going, a road of trials with very little light to show the path at times: confusion, discouragement, disillusionment, despair. Total darkness at moments. This is the hard side of quest that is, in the most basic sense of the word, depressing. Everything about the quest that we explored in the previous chapter takes work, and this work at times can be very painful and may feel to be without light or promise. This is depression—often not an illness, but the type that arises from the natural struggle and sometimes suffering that fuels the individuation process. This is where a rough bump of life is first felt in a semiadult way. The adolescent is biologically primed and prepared—the connections booting up between front brain and back brain—to start coming to terms with the complex map of reality that is taking shape for him.

College counselors, youth ministers, and psychotherapists often tell me that a large part of their work involves meeting a teen in the midst of a "dark night of the soul." The teens are struggling with family issues, confronting tough moral contradictions, overwhelmed by loss or change or something that they have done that has "changed everything" for them. Sometimes this depressive struggle is prompted by an event that sets in motion a deep, serious reflection on life's ultimate purpose. Or a depressive struggle may seem to start spontaneously, without so much as a tap from the outside. Either way the issues are fundamental to spiritual individuation. Too often we don't hear the doubts, questions, or dark thought patterns as spiritually significant; we look at them as standardized symptoms of a medical depression when in fact these "symptoms" are signs of the emerging capacity for spiritual quest, moral complexity, and transcendent attunement. This is serious business, this turmoil and distress, yet it doesn't fit neatly into the clinical criteria for purposes of diagnosis or insurance. Nor have there been many treatment or prevention models to guide clinicians, parents, teachers, and youth advocates.

The conventional conceptualization of depression—especially around developmental depression in adolescents—is incomplete. Western medicine largely views depression exclusively as an illness: a chemical imbalance, illness related or the result of psychological dysfunction or deficit. I see otherwise. The new science of spirituality shows that adolescent depression is something more: a natural aspect of the quest that is inherently developmental—and spiritual.

Common Misperceptions About Adolescent Depression Put Healthy Teens at Risk

There are many paths to depression, some of them medical—a chemical imbalance, for example—but in adolescence, depression is only sometimes an illness. Far more often it is part of the hard work of individuation. At home, at school, in their online lives, and in their inner lives, adolescents struggle to come up with a road map for living the rest of the week and the rest of their life.

The common conceptualization of adolescent depression solely as an illness is perilously insufficient to the teen's long-term mental health and thriving. As we'll see shortly, the effectiveness of our response to an adolescent's first depression experience is crucial. If we reflexively treat depression as a medical illness, wait for it to get "bad enough," and then medicate for symptoms but overlook the adolescent's spiritual needs in the struggle for individuation, research shows that the risk is very high for a subsequent, more severe depression. Medication may lift the emotional and physical expression of symptoms of developmental depression, but when the medication stops, most studies show that there is not a lasting gain. By contrast, if depression is treated as a developmental opportunity, the adolescent learns to engage distressing situations and come through to the other side. But ignoring the developmental challenge not only leaves our adolescents to fall between the diagnostic cracks, but worse, abandons them on the precarious edge of a lifetime risk of depression.

On its own, developmental depression is an opportunity for growth—an opportunity of a lifetime. It is an initiatory taste of adult suffering, which compels the adolescent to seek and find a way toward personal purpose, existential meaning, spiritual connection, and guidance. But if it is not met as such, developmental depression can quickly devolve into a downward spiral, a deeper and then different breed of depression, which is deeper, painful, and takes longer to treat, and more often with medication.

Whether a medical cause is absent or ambiguous, or whether the depression is considered "low level" or more acute, our response can nonetheless address the developmental factors inherent in the process of individuation. This developmental approach is critical for a teen's present and future health and well-being because, as we'll see shortly, successive bouts of depression set a trajectory for continued recurrence of depression with greater severity through adulthood.

As previously noted, a strong body of scientific literature shows that adolescence is the window of onset for depression: a period in which a mix of genetic, biological, psychological, and developmental factors create a heightened vulnerability for depression. What has been overlooked, however, is that when depression occurs in adolescence, the same forces that create the window of onset create the window of opportunity for deep inner growth.

Depression in Teens Has Been a Medical Puzzle Missing a Piece

Depression in adolescents is widely discussed in our culture, but actually not well understood by the science of mental health. Depression is so pervasive and yet so varied, that it cannot be pinned down by a singular model. Decades of research by top research teams highlight the elusive nature of depression. For instance, studies show that on average if the same patient goes to visit two qualified mental health professionals, the likelihood that the patient will get the same diagnosis has been shown to range from 66 percent to as low as 28 percent.

Part of the reason for the uncertainty in diagnosis is that some symptoms are so general that they could reflect any number of underlying conditions, while more specific symptoms can vary significantly between people, presenting many different faces, or clinical subtypes, of depression. According to the standard *DSM-5* diagnostic guide, a diagnosis of major depressive disorder (MDD) is based upon someone having a few from the basket of common symptoms, but even those common symptoms routinely vary from one person to the next. Not every severely depressed person is so fatigued that they can hardly get out of bed; some are superachievers meeting the mark every day, while hiding their feelings—and crying themselves to sleep at night or self-medicating with alcohol or drugs. You and your best friend might well show different symptoms when depressed. We do know that symptoms of depression are fairly consistent between biological relatives. For instance, if a mother gets anxious or does not eat when depressed, her child is more likely to do the same. And, for the individual, a new bout of depression tends to look the same way and presents with largely the same symptoms as in past depressions. Despite these potential consistencies, the range in clinical presentation of depression makes depression hard for mental health professionals, as well as scientists, to pin down.

Research suggests that while about 20 percent of adolescents may have a case of MDD before their midtwenties, an additional 30 to 40 percent of adolescents have a *subthreshold* (moderate) level of depression, less severe than major depression, but still very distressing to the teen. Taken together, these rates mean that *the majority of adolescents suffer meaningfully from depression at some point.*

Subthreshold depression shows in symptoms such as low mood, decrease in self-esteem, edginess, and a spinning round and round rumination of thoughts. Although subthreshold depression is diagnostically described as a relatively moderate level, it nonetheless interferes with a teen's happiness, relationships, and the work of normal daily life. We know this because these teens are just as likely to seek out psychotherapy as a teen with major depressive disorder.

We also know, based upon a study of a sample of 1,700 adolescents in Oregon led by Peter Lewinsohn at the Oregon Research Institute, that about 35 percent of the time, subthreshold depression goes along with subthreshold levels of a second condition, such as anxiety or substance abuse. A case of subthreshold depression typically is dragging a lot of other things with it. Research puts the risk for developing a secondary full-blown disorder at 2.5 to six-fold among adolescents with subthreshold depression, the same risk of a comorbid condition as if they had major depression.

Especially in adolescents, depression does not always look like a low, withdrawn sadness or a retreat inward. An edgy-style depression in a teen often can be mistaken for defiance, conduct problems, or oppositional behavior.

However incomplete the conventional diagnostic picture may be, one avenue of study has given us a very important piece of the clinical picture of depression in adolescents. Research on lifetime occurrence and progression of diagnosed depression shows that the first experience of depression most often occurs in adolescence. That being the case, then the way that an initial episode of depression in adolescence is treated and resolved has a significant bearing upon the risk for subsequent episodes of depression throughout adulthood.

In a process called "kindling," which Kenneth Kendler tested in his twin studies on depression, each successive episode of major depression makes us more sensitive to being triggered again. After the first episode of depression, if the teen does not develop a more resilient way of coping with negative life events, a subsequent episode is more easily ignited by stress that previously might not have been enough to trigger depression. Kendler goes on to show that by the time someone has had three episodes of major depression, it does not take a major life event to push them into depression; the tendency for depression has become a reactive sensitivity in their nature. Whether someone who suffers depression in adolescence grows resilient or grows particularly sensitive to depression is in large part shaped by the inner work done in response to the initial depressive episode in adolescence.

This means that in the initial struggle with depression, teens face a "gateway" to adult coping with the rainfall of life's unwanted events. They establish a stance in living, a relationship to life's bumps. Adolescent depression is set up to answer the question: Will the hard times be met with resilience or with deepening hopelessness, and perhaps recurrent depression? This is all based upon the outcome of individuation: *Who am I? Who am I going to be, given this challenge or loss? What am I really here for? How am I going to understand and engage the bumps in life?* The more resources a teen has for resilience—and spirituality is a significant one—the better equipped she is to understand and engage those bumps.

The research data and our evolving understanding of spiritual development and adolescence call for a new, more flexible, variable, and nuanced model of adolescent depression. We need a more discerning understanding of depression that enables us to conceptualize a developmental depression in which transcendent opportunity has been blocked or foreclosed upon. The fact that spiritual awakening co-occurs with such a robust protective effect during a biologically timed window of onset for depression suggests that we are looking at a shared underlying process, essentially two sides of the same coin. We will see in the data in a moment that depression can be viewed as foundationally spiritual in nature, with a potential spiritual resolution. We know from Alcoholics Anonymous and research into spiritually engaged treatment approaches for substance abuse and eating disorders that the transcendent faculty can support healing and recovery.

For parents, a teen's developmental depression is the cue to lean in, not out of your teen's path, as they do this vital work to set up their way of being, their road map for living. We'll look at ways to engage your teen shortly. But first, given the importance of adolescence as a gateway to the lifetime course of resilience or recurrent depression, it merits a careful look from science.

The Emerging Picture: Science Supports the View of Developmental Depression as a Normative Process

Recent science offers a fresh view of depression as a developmental process, especially in light of what we know about natural spirituality, its development, and its relationship with mental health in adolescence. As we know from the science of the spiritual brain and the adolescent surge:

- Natural spirituality burgeons by 50 percent in adolescence. The transcendent faculty is kicking in during this window of genetic expression.
- Once spirituality surges, harnessing it into a transcendent relationship is more protective against depression than anything known to medical or social sciences.
- Spiritual individuation helps build relationships based on commitment and love and work based upon calling. This is a blueprint for a life of thriving, meaning, and purpose.

As the adolescent brain boots up with a surge in the transcendent faculty, the resulting quest can deliver moments of great and surprising brightness and illumination. It can also prompt shocking moments of despair. A synthesis of the research makes two critical points. First, that developmental depression is strongly linked to spirituality. This kind of depression is an expression of the large spiritual questions that confront the teen and the increased spiritual capacity that the teen is just learning how to handle. Developmental depression, rather than being an inconvenience or something teens need to just "get over," is an indicator that your teen's spiritual faculty is coming on line—prompting the quest that propels spiritual individuation. Second, developmental depression, contrary to the outward appearance of a teen as withdrawing from experience, is more precisely the experience of being highly attuned, open to experience—and unmet. Developmental depression is a prompt to get the back of the brain—the "experiencing brain"—talking to the front of the brain, the "interpreting brain."

I shared some science in chapters 2 and 8 from my collaboration with Myrna Weissman on her study of three generations: depressed grandmothers, depressed parents, and now the grandchildren who are growing up. Our collaboration together started by looking at her sample of teens over a ten-year period. These were teens in the second generation who initially were heading into the window of risk for a lifetime course of depression. The study then followed them for over another decade, into adulthood. By examining more than twenty years of data produced by Weissman and her team, we saw the intertwined path of spiritual development with the lifetime course of depression, from the window of risk through middle adulthood. Looking very closely, we learned some stunning things that rewrite the book on adolescent depression.

Our analysis of the data, subsequently published in the leading psychiatry research journals, showed clear patterns of the relationship between spirituality and depression over the life span:

- Highly spiritual young adults (mean age twenty-six) had in common a past history of depression during adolescence. They were 2.5 times more likely than young adults with lower levels of personal spirituality to have been depressed at some point in the decade from age sixteen to twenty-six. It appears that depression opens a path for spiritual growth that, if taken, can lead to a deeply cultivated, lasting personal spirituality.
- Those people who considered themselves highly spiritual at age twenty-six, were, in the forthcoming decade of mature adulthood (the decade leading to their mid-thirties), 75 percent protected against recurrence of depression, and 90 percent protected

against recurrence if they were at high family risk to begin with. Loaded with genes predisposing them to depression, and growing up under the rain cloud of family depression, spirituality was all the more significant in its protective benefits.

- In MRI studies, the same region of the brain to show cortical thinness in the families at risk for depression instead showed thickness if there was a sustained personal sense of spirituality or religion being highly important over the past five years. The same regions to show cortical thickness in these study participants—highly spiritual Catholic and Protestant women— also have been shown by other labs to be thicker in experienced versus novice meditators.

- EEG data on the same highly spiritual participants who have recovered from depression showed the same wavelength of high-amplitude alpha (associated with meditative states) as found by other labs in studies on people who recovered from depression through SSRIs like Prozac. This also was the brain wavelength found in a study of meditating monks, again showing multiple practice roads to transcendence. It appears that the physiology underlying spiritual individuation through depression may be "jumped" by SSRIs, at least as long as the medication is being taken.

- High levels of the neurotransmitters dopamine and serotonin, and their constituent components, have been associated with a sense of transcendence. Lower levels of the same neurotransmitters (and constituent components) have been associated with depression and related comorbid disorders.

This means that the sixteen-year-olds in Weissman's sample who struggled through depression and arrived into a strong personal spirituality had a greater likelihood of a lifetime of resilience. It would appear that through spiritual engagement they actively shaped their sensitive brains in a way that was neuroprotective against recurrence of major depression. Taken with the EEG findings, it may be that their spiritual engagement "trained" their brains to access a resting state of spiritual connection and oneness, much like an actively meditating monk.

Given that subthreshold depression is so widely common among teens, it makes great sense to seriously question whether the illness model really applies well here. Is a 45 to 70 percent rate of some level of depression really an epidemic of medical illness? Or, might subthreshold depression, based upon its rates and the related science, more accurately be seen as a normal developmental process, that only if ignored, untreated, and unsupported tends to slip into a more severe and debilitating major depression?

My own clinical perspective, based upon the data and listening to teens, is that many, perhaps even the majority of adolescent depressions, are the hard work of quest, holding potential for spiritual individuation that makes the teen stronger and more resilient for the rest of adult life. Nearly every adolescent suffers from developmental depression at some point; it's the general rule of growth, not the exception. The opportunity for spiritual individuation usually comes with hard work, doubts, dangling questions of ultimate significance, emptiness, and dark emotions. In a severe depression, medication may help, as long as the individuation work continues. For some it may be moderate to mild in that they are challenged but not overwhelmed by the developmental demands. Perhaps they have spiritual resources already well developed or at least emerging enough to help them manage as they go. Whatever the degree of challenge and depressive experience, research shows that the lifetime course of depression can be strongly affected by the spiritual developmental work of adolescence.

Taken altogether, research supports the idea of a common physiology underlying depression and spirituality. Put simply, the very same biological propensity for depression can be harnessed, engaged, and guided instead for spiritual awareness and transcendence.

With this understanding, developmental depression can be understood as a crucial opportunity, a developmental imperative for spiritual growth that should be acknowledged and engaged, even honored as part of the rite of passage through adolescence into adulthood. Neurologically, psychologically, and spiritually, spirituality and depression appear as two sides of the same coin.

Illness vs. Normative Developmental Struggle: Our Understanding Guides Our Response

If we consider that the majority of adolescents experience at least a subthreshold depression, then we have to consider that this is normative; it is not an illness, but rather, very often part of a common developmental process. For those adolescents particularly prone to depression due to family risk, depression appears not be a deficit, but reflects a sensitivity and attunement that can be harnessed. The closest we have gotten as a culture to acknowledging developmental depression is in the casual reference to "teenage angst" among adolescents in high school. A type of depression diagnosed as a form of adjustment disorder is called "sophomore slump" because it typically hits the older adolescent in the second year of college, give or take a couple semesters, when the pressure to perform, pick a major, and declare a career path meets a developmental gap: the student's search for identity and individuation hasn't yet found firm ground. It's difficult for students to make huge decisions when they are still figuring out who they are to themselves.

The mental health field differentiates between various types of depressive conditions short of major depression, identifying abnormal or excessive reactions as emotional or behavioral symptoms that can be linked to a specific stressor as "adjustment disorder" or "situational depression." Again, however, the frame of reference is "disorder," when, in fact, science tells us that a heightened experience of *everything* is the norm not only for the adolescent brain and body, but spiritual faculty, as well.

Like any test, developmental depression pushes the adolescent brain to use all of its resources. As such, developmental depression becomes an opportunity for growth. A teen's questions and struggle reflect an opening. As one high school boy said after an assembly on this subject:

"For me, it's not the questions that are depressing. It's when I don't ask them that I get depressed."

Our interview studies offer a glimpse of the work of developmental depression:

> "I mean, what's the point of it all? You work hard in high school to go to college. Work hard in college to get a good job, and make money. So then what? So your kids can do the same and start it all over again?"

> "I want to know if there is a God, not because it would be nice, but because I want to know the truth. Only if it's true will I base the rest of my life upon it."

> "Does it matter at all that you exist? That I exist? Not at all. What does any of it matter?"

These are profound questions, not necessarily symptoms of illness, and not just a passing uncomfortable phase to be tolerated. We need to take teens at their word—hear their questions and observations as what they are: valid existential concerns, developmental in nature, and not necessarily symptoms of chemical imbalance, deficit, or disorder (a completely different kind of depression). Our role in their process is simpler than we think: we don't need to have answers to their epic questions, only support their own exploration.

In sum, when you overlay the common symptoms of depression with common moods and behaviors of adolescents, the picture that emerges would suggest that the vast majority of adolescents have some type of passage through depression: it is the norm. Very few teens slip through the crucial individuation work of the second decade without a period of darkness, or struggle for meaning and purpose. A teen's experience with depression (no matter what kind) becomes the runway to adulthood: how they lift off creates a trajectory for continued struggle—or thriving.

Kindling for Spiritual Resilience: The Goal of Treatment for Developmental Depression

Now that we have looked at adolescence as a gateway to either resilience or to recurrent suffering, let's return to the idea of "kindling" or the way that a pattern of emotional experience sensitizes us and predisposes us to experience more of the same. We know that kindling occurs in the context of depression. Kendler's data showed that the more depression recurs, the easier depression is triggered from one time to the next.

Science also shows us that the reverse is true, too. A resilient response to negative or unwanted moments builds greater resilience for the next time. In the face of stress or challenge or loss, a resilient view says: *Go into life, not out. Go deeper, find meaning, view the unforeseen opportunities here, step farther along the path, open a new or different door.* This is the reverse kindling for spiritual resilience, which is associated with thriving. The voice in the moment is: *I would never have chosen this, but I'll move through it and be open to what there is for me to learn.* And in retrospect, deriving the meaning in the experience: *I would never have chosen this, but if this hadn't happened, then I would have never found this person or found my way to do this unimaginable new work or find this leg to my journey.*

Ken Pargament found that when we face difficult times, resilience is strongly associated with a sense of *collaborative* relationship with God or a guiding universe, or of "being in the hands of" our higher power. In this collaborative relationship the feeling is that we do as much as we can do, ask for guidance or help, and in that two-way transcendent dialogue find support through hardship; if not the wished-for "answer to a prayer," then some sense of supportive, guiding presence. Under extreme circumstance, such as illness, injury, or others over which we have little or no control, the collaborative relationship encompasses a feeling that in spiritual terms is described as "surrender"—not so much giving up as giving over. *I'm praying for a miracle, but I'm ready to accept what is. I've done all I can do; it's in God's hands now.*

The more the teen has set up the personal transcendent relationship, the more resilient, emotionally and physically, they are likely to be when they confront illness, loss, and bereavement—all the things that eventually come our way in life. The spiritually resilient voice says: *This is part of my purpose and calling and my path*. Spiritual surrender is not the fatalism that operates from a premise that life is simply a game of chance and one's life has no meaning, value, or purpose. Resilience that comes from spiritual awareness says: *I have value, and my life has value, whatever the circumstances*. And that's the real potential of developmental depression, whether in adolescence or midlife of any life passage: it presents the opportunity to deepen spiritual awareness. No matter how spiritual you may already be, a descent into pain or depression holds the potential for new growth and opportunity. That understanding alone can be the first step toward firmer ground of resilience and recovery.

Pargament's and other studies show that in depressing circumstances, even when people don't see the opportunity, per se, those who feel this collaborative relationship with the transcendent often feel a deep-down *okayness*, rather than deep-down despair. *Even if it's not the way I wanted it or planned it, I am full and life is full*. This is hugely reassuring and helpful to the struggling teen.

Studies also show that a preoccupation with personal control in the face of unwanted life events that are not controllable leads to recurrence of depression, anxiety, stress disorders, and addictive consumption of food, alcohol, and tobacco. The perfectionistic voice inside says, *If I'm smart enough/fast enough/good enough, I should be able to fix this*. Or retrospectively, the illusion of control leads to self-assigned groundless guilt: *If I had fixed the situation, then nobody would have suffered*. This is a heavy dilemma for the already burdened teen.

A collaborative relationship with the higher power sees value and fullness when the world is not as the teen had anticipated or wanted. Her inherent worth, personal meaning, and calling persists, challenged but resilient under stress.

The field of positive psychology frames these ideas in this way: positive emotions and strategies have a cumulative value as a resource. The more you build, the deeper your reserve for resilience. Indeed, a growing body of research shows that strong personal spirituality builds greater grit and optimism in the face of adversity.

With this understanding of depression as a gateway to a spiritual way of living into struggle, and developmental depression as a common mark of adolescent spiritual individuation under way, we can use the spiritual lens to see more deeply into the teen's struggle and see how quickly the struggle can turn suddenly from manageable to overwhelming.

Three Faces of Developmental Depression

Your teen doesn't sit down at the kitchen table with a list of symptoms pinned to his shirt. Your troubled son or daughter may not be likely to pull up a chair to start a clarifying conversation about the meaning of life. But you can listen for the depressive echo of a deepening inner struggle in a teen's harsh, critical, or dark view of himself or others, or in comments or behaviors that suggest a sense of worthlessness, hopelessness, or futility, or a general and pervasive negativity or anger.

"I can never do anything right. I don't know why I even bother."

"I don't know what's wrong with me."

"I'm such a loser."

"I know I'm hard to be around—even my friends can't stand me."

"It doesn't really matter whether I exist or not—I could drop dead tomorrow and it wouldn't change a thing for anybody."

"I hate myself."

"They're all idiots. It makes me sick to even have to be in the same building with them."

"You all are such losers. Everyone is a loser."

As we'll see in the following three snapshots of developmental depression, a dark passage may be triggered by an external event, or it may arise from within as the developmental surge and quest hit a point of overwhelm for the teen.

Cory: I'm not good for anything else.

Cory was sixteen and a starter on the travel soccer team when he suffered a serious injury in practice one day that took him out of play for the season and raised a serious question about future participation in competitive field sports. After surgery and initial physical rehabilitation, the injury appeared on the mend, but his future as a competitive athlete was not. His doctors doubted whether the injury would ever heal strong enough to resume the intense physical demands of the sport. At first Cory seemed angry, but then shifted toward being withdrawn at school and reclusive at home. Negativity set in around his feelings for school and even his teammates. It was a precipitous drop in his grades that prompted his parents to seek help.

The injury was painful, but what ultimately brought Cory down was that he felt he had lost everything—everything that defined him. He couldn't play the sport he loved—the thing that made him feel most alive and part of something that mattered. And because his life—his social relationships, his sense of self, his mental and physical discipline—had revolved so heavily around his sport and his team, when he ceased to be a part of the team, he did lose it all. At the very developmental moment when his world of peers and performance beyond family became his raison d'etre, Cory's injury yanked it all away in a split second.

Whatever else this loss was in practical and even social and emotional terms, it was, more deeply, a crisis of individuation. To feel worthless, without a sense of self and "without a home"—the place where you belong—is a lonely, depressing place to be. Individuation, and specifically spiritual individuation, helps you see that you are valued as a human being and you have a home with all people and can find new ways of being.

How teens develop during these tastes of adulthood, their first run of unwanted events, sets a pattern for how they deal with events that are beyond their control and shake their outward identity. For Cory, his new reality amounted to an ego death: a shocked discovery that new circumstances had stripped him of everything that previously defined him to himself. In the context of adolescence, with identity and individuation still a work in progress, that loss can feel like an annihilation of the self; the new reality can be empty and frightening. However, Cory's immediate loss is an opportunity for spiritual individuation. With direct parental support, Cory can arrive into a more profound sense of who he is, his purpose in life, and what really matters and endures.

This can happen to any teen: the one who moves to a new community or new school and is overwhelmed by the challenge to start over; the one whose family is struck by a crippling financial loss that changes everything; the one who loses a parent or close friend. Yet depression is always a knock on the door, and the ability to open the door can lead to a vital and expanded life.

Kendra: Whose life is it anyway?

How can you be depressed when you got everything you wanted? That was the question that stuck in Kendra's mind, not only because that's what her parents and friends were saying, but because that's what she was saying to herself. She had been the quintessential superachiever in high school with a spotless GPA, stellar accomplishments in a staggering roster of extracurricular activities, a circle of admired and admiring friends. Most important, she had earned top scores on her college entrance exams and gotten into her dream school. It didn't get any better than this! Then barely into her freshman year, after returning from winter break, she tanked. Overwhelmed by anxiety, then depression, she had a frightening view of herself going under. Not only lost, but perhaps most shocking: inexcusably *failing*.

How can you be depressed when you got everything you wanted?

Here is how. Under so much pressure through their school years, especially high school, to perform and strive for outer accomplishments, to fill that CV and get those reference letters for college admissions, high-achieving kids often have to set aside the deeper quest and genuine work of individuation. Exactly as described by the Ivy League dean, they feel they have to devote themselves to making the grades, doing the clubs, staying up late to get homework done and getting up at 6 A.M. (or earlier) to catch the bus or the ride to school.

The outcome? An older adolescent in college or elsewhere who wakes up one morning to the unfinished business of individuation: the developmental energy of surge and quest was channelled into meeting external expectations while the deep inner work of the self—coming to know one's own deepest purpose and passion—was put on hold.

If spiritual individuation and the normal quest for meaning, purpose, and transcendent connection is unmet, the core is not built. As with Kendra, the developmental task left hanging can give way to enormous anxiety and depression. Some students drop out or take medical leave to address the depression; others simply redouble their efforts to silence the inner quest and accomplish the performance goal that's been set out for them. Diplomas are no cure for depression, however, and developmental depression left unresolved in adolescence increases the risk of major depression in the years ahead.

Whether it is Cory's identification with outward success or Kendra's tidal wave of hunger for more but not knowing where to turn, sooner or later, quest propels the need for spiritual individuation. Continually denied, the teen may seek to escape or numb the pain with substance use or emotional withdrawal. For Max, who suffered deep rejection as a gay boy in an oppressive high school culture, sleep was his escape.

Max: I am unacceptable.

Max, a gifted dancer from an early age, suffered deeply from age twelve to sixteen because he was gay in an unaccepting community. In his large high school he was constantly teased and taunted. He was miserable as he struggled to find a sturdy sense of self, connection, and accomplishment in such a hostile environment. Most school days he would go to the football field and lie underneath the bleachers to sleep in the middle of the day, searching simply for peace, he told me some twenty years later. He felt stuck, trapped in his misery, and he prayed. He was a person of great faith and he prayed and he prayed and he prayed to feel God and to feel connected to the world. Day after day he didn't feel that connection, but he had a deep and persistent faith. He would not quit. He told me that he prayed every day from age twelve, thirteen, fourteen, fifteen, sixteen.

Finally when he was sixteen, his mother, long divorced, remarried, and his stepfather, a minister and a hugely empathetic man, came to him and said, "I see this depression day in and day out, and it pains me." His stepfather and mother together joined him in prayer, embraced him with complete acceptance and love—and it was, Max said, that "bolt of love" that ignited Max's spirit. At one point, they engaged in a prayerful religious ceremony of "laying on of hands." Max can still remember the feeling, through this sacred ceremony, of his mother's love. "I felt the tenderness of my mother's soul aware of mine for the first time in years." He also felt the love of his stepfather, as they recited verses of love and compassion from the Bible.

In this healing, loving ritual, he says, he heard something crack and felt the armature of suffering fall away. In the flash of that transcendent moment his experience of connection was greater than his suffering, and it marked a turnaround in the sense of deep isolation that had dogged him for so long. The years ahead were not without trial, but he never again felt alienated from a spiritual presence, he says. He has never lost the feeling of existing in a sacred space. Max describes that moment as the rebooting of his spiritual life and feels that the spiritual connection through his family, the field of love, is what lifted his depression.

An identity crisis triggered by change or challenge, an individuation process stalled out, or a rejection that denies a teen's core being: these are just three of the many faces of developmental depression as it shows up in our teens, calling for our attention.

On a Troubled Front: Parent as Spiritual Ambassador

A parent's role as spiritual ambassador—the embodied guide on the ground introducing a child to the spiritually attuned life—is especially important for the teen who struggles with developmental depression. As we saw earlier, research has found that from early childhood, a child's relationship with God or a universal spirit is imbued with the attributes of their parents. Through adolescence, as well, to the degree that parents are unconditionally loving and accepting, teens perceive God or their higher power to be so. Studies show that parents' unconditional love supports their teen's sense of a higher power that "I can turn to in times of difficulty," one who gives direction and offers guidance.

When it comes to helping an adolescent with developmental depression, ambassadorship means showing, not directing. Parents can share from their own spiritual discovery through adversity, which may include depressive experiences. You can describe these difficult passages as a source of growth on the human journey: hard-going but eventually generating valuable insight. How was working through these periods life changing for you or other people you know? Perhaps your work yielded a deeper sensitivity to other people, compassion—for them and for yourself.

Depression or an inner struggle may have been a crucial knock on the door, to shed a destructive habit and awaken to a better way of life. This gives a ray of hope and purpose to depression. The transcendent relationship opens an awareness of a spiritual world. If honored and engaged, the outcome of depression can be a lifelong deepening of the transcendent relationship, spiritual awareness. Research also shows that the transcendent relationship remains a lifelong guide and source of resilience through illness, loss, death, divorce, or relationship crisis, as well as through depression.

As parents, our spiritual ambassadorship has a profound impact on our teens, especially those who are struggling through developmental depression. We can adapt our approach to respect the teen's journey of quest and individuation, while at the same time acknowledging a particularly difficult passage. As spiritual ambassadors for our teens in distress, we can:

- Remember this is epic work. See the teen as emerging, in effortful work—essentially climbing up a steep hill for a view. Praise the teen and highlight the hard work. Stop yourself when all you want to say is "just deal with it" or "get over it" or "get your act together." A teen hears these with the emotional volume turned high.

- Refer to the struggles of others, particularly those who are annoying, in "learning terms," which inherently involves compassion. Our teens need to hear us as loving, and not judging, others—and them, of course—as lesser or flawed human beings.

- Be transparent about your own spiritual individuation, as it continues through the seasons of your own life. Acknowledge, "I have hit an impasse, I do not know exactly where I will land, but I do feel buoyed up, that life is full, or perhaps that God is by my side." This is the most helpful and generous gift a parent can offer, their own act of "becoming more."

- Start and end each day with an expression of appreciation for being alive and being a family, for the opportunity to support one another through the most challenging life struggles and acknowledge learning and growth.

- Pray, meditate, or do collective spiritual ritual in front of your adolescent. Even if they say "you are weird," the practice will in time not seem weird, and it will be there for your teen when it is wanted and needed.

- Set an example and meet adversity or challenges with an expressed intention to "hear the knock at the door and open it."

Developmental Depression Says: *Ask the Questions, Invite the Conversation, Engage*

With a more nuanced understanding of depression and recognition of the spiritual individuation process under way in every adolescent, we can be more helpful to our teens who struggle. Teens with developmental depression can greatly benefit from a psychotherapist who integrates spiritual development into mainstream models of treatment. As a field, psychology has only recently started to see "teen angst" and "sophomore slump" as developmental depression, but the expertise is increasingly becoming standard. The American Psychological Association publishes the journal *Spirituality in Clinical Practice,* and several professional books have been written on spiritual work in mainstream treatment, as spiritual orientation to treatment both outside of any religious traditions as well as within specific religious traditions. It is essential that parents, teachers, counselors, and others recognize developmental depression and the positive support that a teen's natural (not imposed) spirituality can give.

Medication can be very helpful or essential if the pain is too strong or the teen is in danger of self-harm or potentially harming others. Medication may be effective for some teens in supporting them as they do the hard work to pull themselves out of a total deep dive. The solution is not medication alone, however. Medication taken in conjunction with psychotherapy and parental support is a *both-and* (not an *either-or*) approach to long-term growth and health. When medication is removed, the teen can relapse. Parents need to watch to see that the medicated teen who starts to feel better does not skip the inner work of spiritual individuation necessary to develop the strong central core that will direct adulthood. Medication alone is not sufficient to build a lifelong infrastructure for the spiritual life.

Adolescents struggling with developmental depression are grateful to feel understood, not alone in an epic battle of meaning. Often adolescents start to feel much better through the combination of loving parental support and interest, and a spiritually oriented psychotherapy. A teen may benefit from even a relatively brief (say, two to four months) developmentally focused treatment, often in tandem with a personal spiritual practice that resonates and invokes the transcendent presence.

In the midst of treatment, we can still support teens in their own work toward spiritual individuation by creating an environment that supports it. Beyond psychotherapy, we can encourage spiritual engagement through contemplative practices, involvement in a spiritual community, community service, and open conversations about the moral issues and spiritual struggles that arise in everyday life for teens.

We looked at some of these options for all teens in the previous chapter, but in the face of depression a few that are particularly relevant for the depressed teen include meditation and prayer, religious communal prayer and ritual, mindfulness practices, yoga, Transcendental Meditation (TM), as well as many other more traditional forms of contemplative practice rooted in religion that have been found to have positive effects on aspects of mood and perception. Research suggests that meditation clears and strengthens the neural pathways for spiritual experience. Practices that help us "re-envision" the world, perceiving beyond our habitual framework to a broader view of reality, also have been shown to expand spiritual awareness.

Prayer is powerful. As we've seen in the science throughout earlier chapters, the most consistent, recurrent, and important scientific predictor of health and mental wellness in teens is captured in the research statement: "I turn to God for guidance in times of difficulty." Teens who learn how to pray, particularly from a parent or loved one in the field of love, have a stronger sense of the transcendent relationship, which can relieve the feelings of isolation and helplessness that are often part of developmental depression.

My lab conducted a series of studies to explore the potential interface between mindfulness, adolescent spirituality, and developmental depression. We set out to learn, first, whether mindfulness might be a gateway to spirituality for adolescents. Second, whether the summation of research on mindfulness showed potential positive effects in ameliorating developmental depression. The findings were dramatic: religious practice and (nonreligious) mindfulness practice both contributed equally—in different ways—to teens' spiritual development. And depressed adolescents with severe symptoms derived over twice the benefit of mindfulness as age peers not struggling with acute depression and anxiety.

In the collaboration with the Maytiv Center for Positive Psychology, we looked at a sample of 436 Jewish early and middle adolescents in Tel Aviv, Israel. Some of the students were quite observant of traditional Judaism and others were not observant. Eleanor Cobb and Ariel Kor analyzed the data on the students' tendency toward mindfulness and/or religious practice and observance. They also looked at the extent of each student's personal spirituality, measuring a sense of spiritual discovery, daily spiritual experience, and transcendent relationship.

The surprising findings showed that the conceptual schism between mindfulness and spirituality did not exist for the teenagers. Adolescents who were both mindful and whose families practiced religion showed the highest level of spirituality of all. Religious practice plus mindfulness add up to more spiritual awareness and engagement. Mindful teens (with little religious practice) and religiously observant teens (with less mindfulness) both were equally spiritual, equally connected with the transcendent relationship, felt a sense of spiritual discovery, and felt daily spiritual experience. The teens represented two different ways of arriving into personal spirituality. They both got there in equal measure. The lowest levels of spirituality in adolescents were found in teens whose families did not have a religious practice and were not mindful.

From our lab at Columbia University, Teachers College, doctoral student Sarah Zoogman together with Simon Goldberg and William Hoyt, from the University of Wisconsin, Madison, worked to come up with a definitive assessment of just how helpful mindfulness is for youth. They ran the first meta-analysis covering twenty peer-reviewed scientific studies on mindfulness and adolescents to determine how much it helped and for whom it was most helpful.

For profoundly depressed adolescents in mental health settings, with severe symptoms of depression and anxiety—the kids who need it most—mindfulness by far brought the greatest benefit. These teens were already in treatment, so mindfulness was tested for an added benefit beyond usual treatment, as a compliment (not instead of treatment). Adolescents with severe symptoms derived over twice the benefit of mindfulness as age peers not struggling with acute depression and anxiety.

Spiritual community gives struggling teens the benefits of the expanded field of love or social engagement system, shared spiritual values, unconditional acceptance, and communal prayer and spiritual activity. As we learned in chapter 5, the tendency for mirror neurons to prompt synchronization between brains among participants during religious ritual in turn makes all participants more primed to experience transcendence. This means that teens' potential for transcendent experience is enhanced by the group's heightened neurodyanmic, a benefit for the developmentally depressed teen.

The field of love also emerges as a rich resource for the depressed teen and for adults in the tough position of wanting to help but feeling helpless to do so. Depression affects an entire family, after all—siblings included—with what I call "family bystander stress," until the depression is acknowledged and named: "Ah, George is actually depressed; he doesn't hate me." "Telling Carla to 'just look on the bright side' may have no traction—maybe I could ask, 'Is that the depression talking?'" "I wonder if you are depressed—is something troubling you, knocking at the door right now for you? There may be something valuable on the other side of that door." Extended family, teachers, coaches, and clergy can often connect with a teen with deep empathy that helps the teen feel accepted, loved, and part of the "something larger" that has spiritual meaning.

So how do we as parents open the conversation? Or, as one parent rephrased the question, "How do you get a wall to talk back?"

The teen says: "That's stupid." "I don't care." "You have no idea what I'm going through." "Everybody is totally shallow." "Nobody understands."

As a parent, you can respond directly to specifics of your teen's experience, or you might share from your own experience to show that these strenuous inner struggles are normal and we can access spiritual experience and spiritual practice, as resources to help us through. Some ways into that conversation:

"Your experience is your own, of course, but I can tell you that I did go through an angry (or sad, or hopeless) period when I was in tenth grade. And I'm here to listen—you can vent or dump or share anything and it's safe to unload with me."

"The majority, over two-thirds, of teens get depressed at some point. It means that you're working on life's big questions and they are naturally tough. It hurts because the questions are that big. It doesn't mean that you're sick, or zoned out. You're facing the big point of life. I won't tell you what to think or do, but I am here to listen."

"My dad died years ago, but I still talk to him sometimes when I'm feeling down or I don't know what to do."

"Sometimes when I'm feeling overwhelmed, or I'm worried about something, I just go out and sit and watch the sunset, or sit out under the night sky. Even just a few minutes like that can help me feel calmer."

Side by side, offer your teen the chance to join you. To a teen, if a parent says that your pain is real—*I know it*—then the developmental slump suddenly is not a dark, frightening and all-encompassing Times Square for the rest of life, but a place to move through and from which to learn on the way to a life that feels like home.

11

HEALING THE SEVERED SPIRIT

Two Portraits of the Adolescent Struggle for Spiritual Wholeness

f we really listen to teens we can start to hear their spiritual struggle and the emergence of spiritual development. Where we used to hear other things—moodiness, or moral infractions, or pathologies—we can hear them at work on spiritual individuation. We've talked about the principle work of adolescence as spiritual awakening, individuation, and integration into all realms of living. This involves two major developmental tasks. One, the teen must connect head and heart knowing in order for their spiritual and analytical faculties to inform one another. Two, they must integrate all parts of their being—their varied selves as social, emotional, intellectual, and sexual beings—into a whole self, with spirituality at the developmental hub of command central.

We also know that even as our teens separate from us, they need our support for this epic inward journey. They don't always get it, whether because parents intentionally disavow or unwittingly neglect their natural spiritual quest. Whatever the reason, when support is absent, the two major ways that the spiritual individuation process goes awry are (1) when heart knowing is quashed, basically discredited as a legitimate source of perception; or (2) when parts of a teen's identity become split off and hidden, essentially disaggregated from the whole.

The following two stories take us into each of these experiences of the severed spirit for a better understanding of the teen's painful reality. These stories also show how the spirit can heal once the adolescent is made whole. Marin's story of a deep depression shows the impact of quashing spiritual knowing. Kurt's is a case of disaggregation, in this case spirituality cut off from his emerging sexuality. A so-called unacceptable part of himself was forced into hiding. We see how healing and recovery are possible when the adolescent feels supported. We can help a child make the bridge between head and heart.

The most common so-called disorders of our time can be reframed from a view of spirituality development. For girls, this is depression, as told in the case of Marin. For boys, there is another very common, clandestine form of suffering that is told in the story of Kurt. What we habitually speak of as pathology or morality might more fundamentally be understood through an awareness of the clear story of spiritual development.

Marin: Unearthing Long-Buried Gifts of Spirituality

Marin, now nearly thirty, shared with me in interviews and writings the story of what she now understands as her struggle with developmental depression in high school, which, unaddressed, devolved into a major depressive episode in her freshman year in college. She has vivid recall of what she describes as a debilitating "descent into darkness" that began in her midteen years at home, and which she sees now as a spiritual sojourn much like the "dark night of the soul" that spiritual writers have long described. Aspects of her story reflect characteristics that commonly distinguish girls' spiritual journey through darkness.

I am not sure when the sadness arrived, but it must have been when I was about fifteen years old. It came with increasing frequency until by the end of my freshman year in college I was officially depressed at seventeen. I could catalog a host of reasons for my descent into the darkness. I had a family history of depression and there was, of course, my own awkward passage through teenagedom and its attendant identity crises.

I recall the heaviness in my limbs and how holding up a pencil or my own head seemed impossible. Or the day my mother asked me to vacuum and how I felt as if I were being asked to climb out of a deep hole and up a steep mountain. The cotton in my head left little room for clear thoughts as I ruminated over social slights and felt unworthy of my companions. I spent most of my time under my bedcovers and tried to make sense of the barrage of images that would haunt my dreams. It was the equivalent of a psychic flu, where everything was coming out of me all at once, with no way to manage it, no ability to keep it at bay. I remember feeling so weepy that I pictured myself as a willow tree, cursed to spend my days by a riverbank of sorrow, hunched over in endless despair. I was mourning a life I had yet to live, but somehow already knew I did not want to lead. I knew something was wrong, but I had no words for it.

Yet, because Marin was still succeeding academically with straight As, nobody noticed or asked her why she seemed remote and withdrawn. In high school Marin had sensed she wasn't the only one struggling this way, but the other girls seemed to come in and out of their dark moods. Her "mood" never seemed to pass; she had to consciously work to rise above it to function like everyone else. A few months into her first year at an all-women's college, she knew she was no longer unique. Her initial visit to the campus health clinic resulted in a brief chat, followed by a diagnosis of depression and an immediate prescription for an antidepressant; there were no offers for extended conversation beyond management of the medication. Her inner experience was not the topic at hand. Developmental depression wasn't mentioned either. Her depression was viewed strictly as an illness. The need for medication was "a serious wake-up call," she says. She soon discovered that most—and at times nearly all—of the girls on her dorm floor had also been diagnosed as depressed and were taking medication for it.

> It was as if we had synchronized, not our menstrual cycles, but a deeper waning and descent to a depth none of us was prepared to understand or navigate. There was the former model who put on forty pounds and started dressing "ugly." The "disappearing" girl who we all knew, but said nothing about her extreme gym work-outs and no-eating habit. And my favorite, the one who started writing poetry and wore all black—black beret, lipstick, and nails. We were clearly not coping well, each in our own way. The suffer-ing was very real. It was as if everyone's rudders were inoperable, and we were lost out to sea.

Like many girls, Marin was left to do the inner work on her own, with-out a guide.

> My own story was one of *learning to find my way back home.* I be-gan to pray, to listen, and to interact with the disturbance within me—the depression. It was telling me that things had to change, and in a way I grew to embrace it as a loving presence. While I disliked that it would not let me function in the real world, I ap-preciated its invitation to get to know my spirit and forge a dif-ferent way of being. It was a voice that insisted I stop the constant striving and instead begin to accept myself and trust in my own gifts . . . to hear my voice. I do not know when or how this turning point came about, but I experienced it as a form of Grace, and understood the grief and destruction as necessary for my rebirth.

Bit by bit, as part of this reflective process, Marin confronted memories of family life in the shadow of her father's brooding negativity. Her daily experience of her father had been that he was brittle, often critical, and, in ways, hurtful, not just to her but to her mother and her siblings, as well. She realized now how her father's "utter denial" of her intuitive sense and spiritual compass required at the time that she dismiss her own reality.

I knew my father always loved me, but he could be very unkind at times. . . . He would distort reality in such a powerful way. My reality did not exist. And he would say also that my optimism was a distortion—that I didn't know what life was about like he knew. I was considered "emotional" and like a Pollyanna, a naïve girl, and my belief in God or the universe was the ultimate betrayal of sanity.

He had dismissed Marin's ways of knowing—heart knowing specifically—as "unscientific." He criticized her quest for meaning and spiritual purpose as frivolous. Along with her deepening desire to connect with life's higher good, Marin had felt an emerging sense of spiritual perception; this intuition could have been her guide through the spiritual quest, but her father denied her foremost way of knowing. The effect was discouraging and eventually debilitating; she felt cut off from the spiritual equipment to know herself and set a direction in the world. Her inner instrument went silent, such that she could not respond with the heart to answer the painful questions of meaning, purpose, or even the point of life. Her once bright inner sense of knowing yielded to her father's nihilism, sending her further and further downward into a disaggregated inner life, lost in depression.

At no point in her years of spiritual struggle did Marin find spiritual support from family, school, psychotherapy, or community. Alone, she wrestled with her depression until, midway into her college career, help came from an unanticipated place. Marin spent her sophomore summer

on a scholarly trip to assist a team of archaeologists—three distinguished
women scholars—digging in a remote area on an island off the coast of
Scotland. Their collegial spirit and their astonishing use of intuitive as
well as technical skills had impressed her. She had been deeply moved
by the trust the archaeologists showed in her as they assigned her to important duties and mentored her. "They took me seriously during a time
when I typically felt underestimated or dismissed," she says.

> I had met my spiritual mothers: three radical archaeologists who
> inoculated me with their wisdom. . . . They taught me that import-
> ant things existed beneath the surface and could be accessed. . . .
> One day on a walk through the desolate countryside, one of them
> came to a halting stop and said with absolute certainty that the
> ruins of an ancient watchtower were directly beneath her. Out came
> a shovel, and soon after a stone wall was unearthed.

Marin was shocked by the certainty the team accredited to intuition,
and that they would expend resources on a dig based upon this inner sense
of certainty. Knowing of the heart was considered valuable, actionable,
and essential to the work of intellectual inquiry. Her heart knowing had
value. She had value. The world had value. Depression says that nothing
is important; the archaeologists were saying that everything is important. The women's on-the-ground wisdom struck Marin as a larger, spiritual truth she could take forward. "They were telling, literally showing
me: Everything is alive. Even the forgotten things. Even the buried
things—and maybe those are the most important things."

Marin dug deeper in her quest, rediscovering heart knowing through
contemplation, yoga, and meditation. In time, her search brought her
closer to the sound of her own inner voice. That inner wisdom led her
to change her course of studies from premed—which she had pursued
under pressure from her father—to history, which she realized resonated
deeply for her. It was in her studies of the foundational texts of Eastern
and Western thought that she realized that "the deep questions and

answers of existence lay within our spiritual life," she says. In her studies she found that this difficult and often discouraging path had been
well traveled by the great prophets, who had undergone a separation,
disillusionment, a dark night of the soul, and returned with profound
insight and enlightenment. "They took on their struggle earnestly and
through it forged a faithful relationship with a guiding principle of
abundant love in the universe," Marin says. It was a journey she could
envision for herself. Spirituality now was in the director's chair, presid-
ing over what was for Marin real, valuable, and truthful.

As Marin became more actively engaged in her spiritual exploration
through continued study and contemplation, she experienced the healing that naturally existed within. She stopped "waiting for the darkness
to abduct me" into a deep depression again. She turned to cultivating
her spiritual dimension, having discovered that her depression was, at
the heart of it, a spiritual quest.

> The way I interact with my spirit is through nature and I believe
> God talks to me through nature all the time—not just out in the
> country but in the city, too—everywhere. The oneness comes
> through, the synchronicities come through. . . . You can take that
> idea, an attitude, and have it be anywhere. I believe that what those
> archaeologists were telling me was that nothing is insignificant.
> It reframes everything from a loving perspective.

Marin was able to find her way forward, not through her parents, but
through her direct, personal two-way relationship with God. As I mentioned earlier, when parents are unavailable for whatever reason to provide the loving connection to the field of love, some children are able
to access it as Marin eventually did: through a direct, felt, transcendent
relationship with their higher power, or through the spiritual guidance
in nature, or with others who offer a heartfelt, supportive presence that
honors what is good in life. In Marin's case, she drew from all three:

her direct conversations with God through what she describes as her inner sacred self, through her archaeologist "wise women" mentors in the field, and through spirituality revealed in nature in her everyday experiences.

Marin's story features a significant challenge: As she was listening to her inner instruments, hearing wisdom, and feeling the transcendent presence, the surrounding adults—her father, most notably—told her that the heart is not a source of knowing.

After a painful descent into depression, ultimately she persisted, recaptured her innate gift of heart knowing and, having since benefited from years of treatment and meaningful psychospiritual work, is now particularly reflective and articulate in sharing her story. She has regained her birthright, a sense of validity in a strong personal relationship with her higher power, no longer dependent on validation from others.

Depression is now epidemic among females, with rates twice as high among girls as boys. At the same time we know that spirituality is particularly protective against depression in girls. We also know that with the onset of physical puberty, this protectiveness *increases by 50 percent*. That fertility in girls is associated with spiritual awakening is echoed in a myriad of indigenous traditions. Among the Navaho, for example, the newly menstruating girl sits in the peaceful solitude of the spirit hut, where she comes to know her augmented spiritual capacity. Marin's case shows us what all too often happens to girls. Like Marin, their spiritual capacities and awakening spiritual sense are quashed. Without this central organizing factor for understanding life, when they face developmental depression, girls do not have their own spiritual resources to call on. Rather than developmental depression being a means to the end of spiritual individuation, it becomes a persistent downward spiral. As a culture, we harm girls by silencing the knowing of the heart, the spiritual perception of girls that burgeons with adolescence.

Marin's story also shows us a tremendous opportunity. If a father or a mother is positive and interested in an adolescent's evolving capacity for spiritual perception, it becomes a ready resource to meet hard existential questions. This inner dialogue supports a teen's spiritual individuation and preempts a downward spiral of unanswered questions, of feeling unrooted, of doubting her capacity to understand and know life. A girl's sense of direct knowing becomes a vital source of strength.

Kurt: Hidden Boy

Kurt was the youngest of five children in a fairly observant religious family and the shining star of his high school. He was the picture-perfect teenage boy by the external standards of his community: handsome, popular, an honor-roll regular, a star in the school musicals, a drum major in the band, junior class president, and graduating senior year with honors. He was also a teen leader in his church, roundly admired by young and old. That was how everyone knew him—everyone but Kurt himself. His "real" identity was one he kept hidden through his entire adolescence because part of it—an addiction to pornography—was a dark secret he felt he couldn't share.

A friend had introduced him to porn when he was eleven, and he had quickly become a habitual user even as his involvement at church intensified. "Pornography became a big part of my life . . . eleven until really late into my twenties," Kurt says. In his church, at age twelve a boy is formally recognized as part of a lay "priesthood" with special responsibilities and service commitments, and that transition only intensified his inner conflict.

> [Pornography] was something that really wasn't in harmony with what I believed and it became a real trying fire for me as I progressed spiritually. Getting introduced to pornography at eleven and at twelve getting that priesthood, I had a lot of really mixed feelings about spirituality. It had always been something I just had just believed, and then I had this thing that came and just

confronted it. Then I was given responsibility on top of that. It really was a hard thing for me to understand, to deal with.

His pornography use put him at odds with what he believed to be right and wrong, but part of the early thrill of it was simply that he was sneaking around his parents' watchful eye to do it. When they began to suspect that he was using the family computer to visit sites he shouldn't, they took the computer cord with them to work each day. Kurt rode his bike to the nearby computer store and used his allowance to buy a cord of his own, making sure to unplug in time for his parents' arrival home.

Kurt's illicit activity began as natural sexual curiosity and a quest for independence. These aren't bad impulses, to be curious about what a woman's body looks like, what sexual intercourse looks like, or to want to be independent and figure things out on your own. To be sneaky is not a value to be encouraged, but it is a common way of individuating. Kids want to push off and separate, but they want to do it knowing that, somehow, they remain in the zone of your protection and regard. Kurt was pushing off but quickly dropping out of that safety zone, away from his core of being, and out of sight from adults. As he began to experience his inner self as split—the acceptable, celebrated self versus the unacceptable, hidden self—he began even more determinedly to separate from his family. His budding spiritual self had no place for sexuality. Although Kurt's parents had discussed adolescent concerns such as drugs and alcohol with him, at no time did they discuss sexuality or pornography. In fact, there had never been any meaningful discussion with his dad or mom, or any other adult, about questions of sexuality, and certainly not healthy sexuality as an expression of, or a conduit for, the spiritual self. His parents sensed something was going on—that's why they hid the computer cord. But that was as far as they were prepared to go.

As he moved further into adolescence, his clandestine habit and his outwardly exemplary life as a leader in school and church created a deep internal rift—a spiritual split. Developmentally, his capacity for spiritual growth and development was opening wide. But instead of processing life's big questions—*What is my own view of sexuality? How does that align with my sense of divine purpose? What is love and how do we show it?*—in a way that included a healthy sexuality through his developing spiritual faculty, the "hidden piece" that troubled him most was off-limits for spiritual inquiry.

By thirteen or fourteen, the split between the Kurt everyone knew and the Kurt that he knew himself to be was clear to him.

> It was pretty entrenched by that time as far as pornography goes, and pornography and masturbation became a big part of my daily living . . . I became really good at compartmentalizing because you want to live up to duty, you want to live up to God, and at the same time my adolescent mind really enjoyed this other part. . . . I was still going to church every Sunday, still going to church-related activities with my peers during the week, and I was still very much immersed in a spiritual community. But I had this other part of me that was "if you really knew me you wouldn't like me," and that became very entrenched. It was very, very deep. Probably one of the deepest wounds I carried for a long time was that belief that if you really could know me you wouldn't like me. And I took that to God—*God, if you really knew me you wouldn't like me, you wouldn't love me.*

To feel unlovable to your higher power is a very cold place. Split and unworthy before his higher power, he naturally hid from the people he loved most. His secretive self grew to claim more and more of his life. Kurt tried not to think about it all because when he did, he felt hopeless and more isolated than ever.

> It was like having the floor ripped out from under you. There was nothing to stand on. It's as if everything you thought was real all

of a sudden is not only not real, but a complete lie. Part of me believed that God loved me, part of me connected to that and knew that, but part of me also knew that God wouldn't love me if he knew me. So it became very easy to disconnect from God during this period of my life. God felt distant, God felt like across the country. He felt like someone I could make a phone call to but who wasn't necessarily with me in the room healing me in life.

Over the course of three years, his relationship with pornography had become more than a sexual activity; like alcohol or drugs, it had become a buffer to the normal, painful challenges of adolescence, a numbing agent from hunger for connection and meaning.

For my fourteen-year-old brain, from my understanding of life, sex became this way to disconnect; it was a safety thing. It was very easy, very safe. I wasn't vulnerable, didn't have to feel anything. . . . I was running from life. Life hurt just in general because I was so sensitive to it. When you have that release, that orgasm, and it blows out your receptors and things start to come back in, you're just really sensitive to anything that isn't that numbness and so now things start to really be hard to deal with because any sort of difficulty, any sort of resistance, gets blown way out of proportion. Now it's like having an open wound—anything that touches it is too much, *gotta numb this, gotta hide this, can't expose this.*

It wasn't even about the sex. It was about getting through that to what I wanted. That's hard for people to understand because they say it's a sex addiction, that you're addicted to sex. But the pornography becomes such an object, it's like a TV remote, like a light switch, it's the keys to your car. It isn't about that woman in the picture, it's about what that provides, how you get through to that. It's not about a person at all, not about connection at all, it's about getting to what you want, getting to where you feel good about yourself, getting to where you don't have to feel this anymore, whatever it is you're feeling, and that's the drive. That is what pornography taught me, the lie that it taught me: that there is a way to not feel pain, a way to make it go away. That there's a way to make anything uncomfortable not exist, and what that does is it cuts off your capability, because now you have no reason, no reason to try to do something. You can't love, you can't hate, you can't connect to people in any sort of way because you can't feel anything. And you're so used to not feeling anything that if you do feel something you immediately classify it as bad. That was my experience. I was so disconnected from what it meant to be human.

On a walk with his father to church one day, as they strolled by a used-car dealership, his father had delivered a birds-and-bees talk. He warned Kurt not to be tempted to marry just so that he could have sex. It was a talk about what sex *wasn't*—a reason to marry—and not what it *was* or *could be*: a joyful expression of intimacy in the context of love and a spiritually whole and integrated life. Or, at the very least, that it could be the subject of a father-son conversation about Kurt's own questions and inner conflict. Instead, the message he took from his father was that sex is bad and marrying for sex is bad. Young Kurt took it a step further. If sex was bad, pornography was worse, and these thoughts evolved into an understanding of his sexuality as a bad thing, or, as he put it, "really outside of my human experience as God intended."

For all adolescents the spiritual map within becomes the map of lived relationships in life. For Kurt, his sexuality—including his use of pornography—was off the map, period.

"It was so shaming yet it was such a part of me," he says. "I was engaged with my sexuality but not in a way that I would ever admit was part of my identity. It's like this is a part of me, but not a part of me that I would ever consider owning or ever consider thinking how God can touch this part of my life."

Eventually Kurt discovered that his father and older brothers routinely used pornography, too. He confronted them about it—the whole question of the moral contradiction it presented with the family's professed religious values—but those conversations went nowhere. He tried talking with church counselors and got nowhere. By age fifteen he recognized that his pornography use had become an addiction, but his stellar success in high school was all that showed and all anyone cared about. As a compartmentalized life it was quite successful. However, in terms of a spiritually integrated life it was going from bad to worse. The larger his life, the deeper the divide became.

> I was very normal as far as how I looked to other people. But I felt very different, very unloved, very much again like if people knew me they wouldn't like me. Looking back, I was engaged with a lot of people and doing a lot of things, but I never really connected to people.

By the time Kurt was nineteen he concluded that he was on his own with his problem. "I understood it as 'this is something you can't involve God in because He can't help you. He can't help your brother. He can't help your dad. This is something outside of that.'"

Let's look at this through the lens of the transcendent self as the central organizing and integrating force of the psyche, through which we know the world and ourselves. Kurt was fully cut off from his inner resources of his own natural spirituality, which for him had once included a relationship with God. The center of his developmental web had been annihilated, leaving the other faculties flailing. He was truly on his own to deal with how a failed spiritual self should manage a bad, out-of-control sexual self, with no help to build a unifying command central. Even as he lived a celebrated teen life on the outside, Kurt felt isolated and despairing. A severed spirit invariably cuts us off from those who love us. Kurt was disconnected from a God he loved and the love of God as he had experienced it as a young boy. *If you knew me you wouldn't love me.* That's as lonely as it gets.

The independence, stoicism, and "manliness" we expect of our adolescent boys and which they are driven to by their own cultural "rules of masculinity" can cause deep loneliness. It is self-reliance taken to a punishing extreme, to the serious detriment of boys. The "hidden boy" is every boy who hides a secret about himself in a dark, hidden space where he feels unworthy or not accepted by others, unacceptable in his own mind. This secret, split-off piece of himself might be about aspects of sexuality that he has learned to view as unacceptable: he might be gay or sexually curious or experimenting. Or, his secret may be that he suffers anxiety or depression, believes himself physically or intellectually inadequate, or in some way can't measure up to "be a man" in ways he has come to believe a man must be. It could be that he's hiding alcohol or drug use, or other high-risk behaviors. When a boy takes his secret into hiding he is psychologically sneaking down into the dark, silent cellar of his self. Anytime the higher self is silenced or cut off this way it cannot evolve as an instrument for direct knowing; we must be truthful in who we are to know our spiritual nature. A boy can't fully develop a well-integrated, whole, and healthy identity when a foundational part of it is hidden away. Most important, disconnected from his transcendent self, a boy is spiritually isolated, banished to a place where he feels that God cannot possibly be with him.

To be of any use to boys, we must align spiritually with the male journey. We must acknowledge the reality of where they live, which is in a culture that has long celebrated physical strength, sex, and stoicism as masculine ideals and is only slowly evolving to acknowledge boys' fuller emotional lives. In this environment domination is still more celebrated than service or contribution. Anger is considered masculine; emotional intimacy and vulnerability are not. Sexual conquest is encouraged and sex without emotional intimacy is unquestioned. Pornography has become an acceptable backdrop for sexual coming-of-age. When we place boys in this environment and then back out on them spiritually, we abandon them to live in a painful, unworthy place, emotionally and spiritually isolated.

I've shared Kurt's story at length because we so rarely hear from boys inside this experience, and the porn experience is becoming increasingly common and intense for our preteen and adolescent boys. Kurt's insightful perspective a decade later is invaluable to us as parents, teachers, and youth advisers who want to support boys.

We know that Kurt's spiritual struggle is not a sidebar to this experience, but central to it, and that, ignored, the spiritual split surfaces later, prevalent among heavy pornography users and men with sexual addictions. A recent study led by my doctoral student Ariel Kor surveyed a broad and diverse sample of more than 2,300 men, many of whom struggled with addiction to pornography. The findings showed that pornography addiction was curtailed by religious observance only when it sustained personal, existential, and spiritual fulfillment. As in Kurt's case, empty religious observance—absent meaningful personal spirituality—does not protect boys and men against feeling out of control and obsessed with pornography.

We fail boys when we fail to discuss sexuality, spirituality, and the virtually unavoidable presence of pornography in our society, and especially in male culture. Thirty-five percent of Western Internet downloads are from pornography sites, and many boys are not internally equipped to arbitrate their inevitable chronic exposure to pornography. The average age of first exposure to pornography on the Internet is eleven, the same age Kurt first experienced it. Young boys trying to grow spiritually while feeling aroused by a pornographic culture are unable to reconcile the two parts of themselves. Our religious faith communities can help young men deal with pornography if they help boys use spiritual values to understand themselves as sexual beings, and to bring any relationship with a consuming sexuality into the same open conversation. We do not want to send boys into hiding.

What Kurt needed more than anything was for someone to engage him and ask, *Well, where is relationship in your sexuality? Where is spirituality and meaning in your sexuality?* He needed to be asked more generally about sexuality in conjunction with his inner spiritual life: meaning and purpose, relationships. But when he sought out adults, they shrank away from the conversation.

Eventually, a failed marriage engagement moved him to confront his addiction and see it as a field in which he could purposefully cultivate his faith and a connection to God in a way that would support his recovery from addiction. Kurt eventually did for himself what he had needed someone to do with him at a much younger age: put spirituality and sexuality in the same room; let his personal spirituality inform his sexuality and relationships. What would have helped Kurt? He now reflects, "I would have liked to have been asked, '*What does your higher self feel about sexuality?*'"

I believe there are a lot of boys with a dark and unacceptable part of themselves that could be reintegrated if someone could lovingly sit by their side, accept them without punitive judgments, and help them understand their struggle and their search as part of the process of spiritual growth.

Sexuality is just one aspect of self that can become severed from command central, leaving boys to hide. We need to support their spiritual development so they can bring that light to all manner of hidden things, integrate all facets of life under a command central of spirituality. Kurt eventually accomplished this within his religious tradition and a loving relationship with the woman he later married. No matter what the secret may be that sends them into hiding, the split self can be healed for all boys with sensitive and spiritually present parenting. The spiritual map and mentoring help a boy develop his personal spirituality as an added resource in meeting the demands of adolescence and eventually manhood.

The opportunity here is for parents to reintegrate all parts of the self into a dialogue with the child's higher self, back under command central. All parts of us are valuable and good: our minds, our bodies, our sexuality, our urges and desires. We can embrace and discuss all of these pieces of our self and integrate them as important pieces of the whole self. Our spiritual life, as command central, can help us accept and find a positive place for these impulses, and parents can support and encourage this process by talking frankly, by not shaming, and by helping the child look within to his higher self for understanding.

However the severed spirit manifests, we can support a teen's path to wholeness by honoring the developmental task of spiritual awakening, individuation, and integration into all realms of living. The teen benefits from even a small bit of support and guidance and can be shattered by a perceived parental disavowal of their felt spirituality, or the severing of their spirituality from the rest of their being. We may not always know the specific nature and the depth of the teen's inner struggle—in fact, most often we won't—but regardless, we can commit to supporting teens' spiritual exploration and emergence, knowing that in wholeness lies healing.

12

PARENTHOOD

The Spiritual Awakening

A few years ago when my children were young, a fellow mom and I struck up a conversation over coffee and found ourselves talking about how motherhood changes us. She said she had never done particularly well in school or found work that was meaningful to her, and she was shy and unconfident around people. Then she had a baby and she arrived into herself. She started to feel easier in the world, more confident and capable. She turned to me and said, "Being a mother just fills you up and makes you powerful, and big, and strong, and you can do anything."

At some point when you arrive into parenthood, you know you have arrived into something much bigger. Planned or unplanned, joyful or heavy with uncertainty, it is a threshold passage in the deepest sense.

"It's like you become a whole new person," the mother of a young son told me, echoing sentiments I have heard from parents many times.

A child is "a wake-up call from the universe," says Thompson, father of a teen daughter and son. "You hear people say, 'My life changed because of an X-ray,' or 'I was in a horrible accident,' 'I got sick,' 'I lost all my money,' or whatever it was, and that can be a transformative event, but those are extreme. It doesn't have to be that way. . . . A child is the universe saying 'It's time to reconnect with this.'"

Much has been written about adult psychological development, most of it centered on age-related passages tied to career or the parenting shift from full house to empty nest. Spiritual development at midlife hasn't received as much attention; it is usually seen as a solitary initiative aimed at personal growth, or inner peace. My purpose in this book has been to map the spiritual development of children and adolescents. Central to that has been to show the profound and integral role that parents play in shaping a child's spirituality. With that understanding, now we can look more closely at the parallel story of parenthood. We can see how *our* spiritual growth as parents can progress in tandem with our children's spiritual development.

The arrival of a child in our lives awakens us spiritually, whether we call it that or not. Haven't we all, upon becoming a parent, felt the "something more," experienced something difficult to describe but very real stirred by this new being in our lives? Many parents, particularly fathers, have told me that they "did not believe in anything" until their child was born. Parents of infants born with serious medical complications or of children with other special needs have shared with me how their child's struggle has tested their faith or perhaps drawn them deeper into a sense of sacred purpose, or a partnership with God. Some who were ambivalent before feel drawn into that spiritual dialogue for the first time. The journey into parenthood launches a spiritual opportunity for every parent. It is an awakening of our own transcendent capacity that is every bit as vital for us as our children's spiritual development is for them.

Once we become parents, we are forever changed. No matter how your child comes into your life—by birth, by adoption, through parenthood, or grandparenthood, or the synchronicity of friends or strangers—your love for a child opens the field of love. To the degree that you cultivate the field in the ways we've discussed—unconditional love, actively engaging the child in spiritual reflection and contemplation, conversation and right action in everyday life—the field becomes your child's spiritual reality, your family's spiritual reality, and your own.

The Pilgrimage of Spiritual Parenthood

Parenthood is a spiritual pilgrimage however you travel the path. Imagine the solitary monk making his way to the mountaintop in search of enlightenment: The hard work and austerity, the steep climb with its trials and setbacks, uncertainty in place of control, the disorientation as the self or ego dissolves into a spirit that is no longer self-centered but now exists for something larger and more precious than the self—your child.

Now adjust that picture for the realities of parenthood. Relieve the monk of his solitude and hand him the diapers, the strollers and car seat, the laundry, the shopping list, food prep and meals, team snacks, carpool duty, bath time, bedtime, story time, and tuck-in. Toss in fevers, rashes, and projectile vomiting. Add showing up at work during weeks, even months, without sleep, too tired to remember where you put your coffee. But somehow the exhaustion, trials, and wear of parenting do not make us less, they make us more. Parenting is an erosion of vanity and of the illusion of control. Through struggles and trials and soul searching, we become clear about what matters and what really doesn't.

"Parenting is an offering of the self in your entirety," a Unitarian minister said in her Sunday sermon, offering a lovely down-to-earth definition of the parenting version of ego death. "It is an enlarging of your own self-definition to include another, a softening of your boundaries, making them more porous so that another person can move easily in and out. Becoming a parent is when a gift of life has been offered and received, when love quietly moves into our lives and takes over."

When we work to bring the child's awareness into our larger map of reality we see the world through their fresh eyes and inherently spiritual perspective. We grow by both leading and listening to them. The chop-wood-carry-water years of early parenthood leave little time for solitude, but give us many opportunities to ground ourselves in our own natural spirituality, as well as our child's, to share the journey and to grow alongside them. Our child's earliest spiritual assets can reawaken our own capacities for radical love, unitive empathy, and connection to our spiritual compass.

Catching spirituality from our child can wake us up. We recognize our significance and purpose. The world looks different in all ways, from our own parenting interactions to how we experience the world. Mothers and fathers have told me:

"She gives off joy, just pure joy. It's contagious. I feel it, too."

"No more existential questions. This face: this is the point of life."

"She looks at me, watches me. She makes me want to be a more loving person."

"My heart feels full. Even when I'm exhausted or frustrated, I feel this steady love."

Becoming a parent lets you experience the world in a new and open way. This new openness, combined with supporting your child's natural spirituality, gives you the opportunity to think about, experience, and develop your own spirituality. It's okay to give yourself permission to take the time to get to know your own spirit, as you support and encourage your child's.

In these ways, the child shepherds the spiritual realignment or reawakening of the adult. In the field of love, spiritual awareness and the search flow both ways between parents and children.

Parenthood's Three Spiritual Rites of Passages

Parenting by its very nature gives us transformative opportunities, which offer up the possibility of opening us to our spirituality, a clearer sense of our place in the universe, perhaps a spiritual partnership with a higher power. Three spiritually transformative passages unique to parenthood expand our ground of spiritual engagement by first breaking us open to an awareness of our vulnerability and loss of control, then introducing us to the resources we need to forge our selves anew, deeper and stronger, for the journey of spiritual parenting.

Control: Less Makes Us More, Surrender Makes Us Stronger

From the moment of your child's arrival into your life, from cradle to college, parenthood requires our surrender. In our first hours of parenthood we lose forever our assumptions about "driving the bus" of life. We are now, possibly for the first time in our well-ordered adult lives, not in control.

As a Type A personality, Linda meticulously planned and executed her life, from her wedding to writing her birth plan and distributing copies to family members. Once labor began, the baby's position and timing called for different responses, and the illusion of control vanished.

> It was like he was saying, "Okay, Mom, you're really cool but you can't plan everything out. I'm gonna be fine but you have to stop trying to control everything." That's been a good lesson. . . . Sometimes it's okay not to have a plan. Which is good for me to learn, you know?

We no longer control all the details: not when we leave the house or what time we arrive where we're going. And especially not the more important matters of health or biological endowments unique to our child. In the loss of control, parents often feel they are somehow *less*—I hear this a lot from mothers. They show up to a meeting or coffee with smashed sweet potatoes on their shirt, or so tired they sometimes can't complete a sentence. They feel a total breakdown of physicality, and they feel less: less competent and effective, less organized, less presentable. In truth, parenthood—even at its messiest and most complicated—is the very definition of ego death, a surrender of control and vanity that actually makes us *more*. Releasing control leads to spiritual awakening, as we tune into the natural rhythm of the world, open our own hearts to transcendence. Our children dispel the illusion that we can ever be in control and on top of it all. In letting go, we free ourselves to discover a buoyant current to carry us.

Help Needed: Parenting Is Bigger Than Parents

For the first few hours of parenthood, we are absorbed completely in our infants; everything we want or need is right there in their eyes. As soon as we go to change a diaper while looking for a new onesie, we realize: we also need an extra arm. Maybe two. Asking for help, which goes along with ceding control, is a big adjustment for most parents, especially with our perfectionist, you-can-do-it-all societal expectations. But we learn. We learn to ask for help and come to rely on it for everything from babysitting to housecleaning to pizza delivery. We turn to just about any parent in the park for help or conversation, when previously we may not have visited with "strangers." We use all the help we can get. Help with the deeper challenges of parenthood calls for more than practical solutions, though. When we find ourselves thin on patience, lost, or questioning whether we have what it takes to be a "good" parent, strapped for the courage or confidence we wish we could summon in difficult moments, where can we turn?

Bill, the father of two young children, spoke to me of turning to his spiritual community when he realized that he needed help with the challenges of parenthood.

When I doubt most that I can do it—and I often doubt that I can do it—my faith becomes my rudder and the thing that keeps the boat from tipping over. I have to go to church because it is the only day in the week where I can pull all those emotions and all of those fears into some kind of coherence that is bigger than me. I find solace and comfort in it. For me to be in the trenches every day with these kids, doubting that I know how to raise them successfully, makes it all the more important for me to reach out to

something divine, something transcendent of the day-to-day mi-
nutia; something that is beyond me that confirms in myself that I
can do it, that I'm doing it well. The church is the structure for
me. It's not like I go to church to have an "aha moment." It's just
more that I feel more [at] peace with myself; I feel resolved about
that which I want to do [better].

Bill found the spiritual fortification he needed in connecting with
the divine. It was a vital experience of peace and serenity in the midst
of the emotional turbulence brought about by being a new parent.
Bill's example is just one of many I have heard from fathers and mothers who have discovered spirituality for the first time or returned to
religious roots, deepened their transcendent relationship with the higher
power, or turned to spiritual communities for support.

Connection: The Field of Love Expands

In my premotherhood days, for five years I saw the same woman at the
grocery store checkout. She was always very cold and curt, dismissive in
a way that made it clear she just wanted to move on to the next person.
But the day I showed up with baby Isaiah in my arms she lit up with a
huge smile—she wanted nothing more than to talk and laugh with me
and my baby.

The field of love expands exponentially with children. Every contact and connection is an opportunity for understanding human-to-
human communication, and understanding the world from a new
perspective.

Martin, a gay dad, shared a story of vacationing in Eastern Europe
with his partner and their six-month-old baby. As they paused to relax
in the park square one day, an older woman stared at him and his partner disapprovingly, eyeing them up and down. As the two dads struggled to fit the baby into a carrier, they needed a third set of hands and
asked her for help.

She focuses on our son and her face lights up. [As she] asks for him, she picks him up and she holds him and she falls in love with him. She then looks back to us, this gay couple, as if to say, "I get it."

Martin and his partner have two children and the dads continue to see the world of others open this way.

The kids have been inadvertent ambassadors for us in the world, and there are rewards that have come because of that. We've met wonderful people and we've had great experiences with people who we'd never have thought that we would have been friends with. . . . People reach out to you.

Whether it is a crabby grocery-store employee, estranged family, strangers with prejudices—children with their open hearts and frank questions can tear down walls and let the adults in.

As the father of two adolescents said to me, "It's like your heart is walking around with them. The child takes your heart into places that you have let it go. Having a child makes your heart open and vulnerable to the world."

The Child Awakens the Parent: Come Grow with Me!

As we've seen, parenting the young child often reawakens our own natural spirituality. In addition, our imaginations are reactivated and our minds are reawakened. Purposefully connecting with our child as we share stories and meals, meet animals, talk, walk, and climb hills opens up our own heart knowing. We start to feel unitive empathy—a connection to all of life. We hear the voices in nature and those speaking to us from the pages of books and in imaginative play with our children. Our capacity for imagination can come as a surprise, especially to parents whose work demands, whether by choice or need, have taken them far from the richly creative spirit of childhood.

Danielle embraced her firstborn child, Noah, in the world of story. He simply loved their story times. "He looks me in the eye and says, 'Mommy, will you tell me a story?'" Danielle relates. Every night she would make up long, long stories and she asked Noah to name the characters. Giddy with laughter and with a light in her eye, Danielle told me one of their stories.

Noah named the protagonist Pooper Pipper and his cousin, Poop Poops, and they had a dog called Messa. As our story went on and on over weeks and months, eventually he made more and more characters who all together went on elaborate adventures. I always thought that they were people, but after several months he said, "No, Mommy, they are animals!" Pooper Pipper was a mouse! Poop Poops a dog. Bacha and Bocha cows, and Treelow a fox. There was one human, Freeza, a boy, who was their guardian. They were all going on adventures, discovering magical bears in the forest and climbing mountains.

As I listen to Danielle telling me the details of the story, I suddenly realize that she is herself journeying through the majestic, imaginative world.

I remember we were hiking up a mountain and there was a clearing with a magical flower. They want a petal, so they have to ask permission to pick the flower. Then they bring the flower back to his house. At the end of each story, Pooper Pipper goes to bed—he tells the story to his parents of the whole day, what he did and found. Whether he finds a magical bean, or chases an animal, or something follows him. One day Pooper Pipper laughed and followed Poop Poops the dog. The dog was barking at a rock, so Pooper Pipper lifted the rock, and under it was a tiny little person, and then many tiny people, a whole world under the ground. Someone found purple magical flowers.

Danielle shared with me how her long walks in nature with Noah during a vacation in the hills of North Carolina inspired her unfolding story.

We played in big rivers, which for the story I made into beautiful little streams, just trickles of water that come alive. In the story then we'd go hiking up a mountain, discover delicious creeks of cold water that you splash on you—and something magical would happen.

As she spoke, Danielle moved fluidly between two expeditions with her son: in North Carolina, and into the imaginative world where nature has the power to speak. Danielle's eyes were wide and bright with enthusiasm and excitement as she told the interwoven stories. The reality that undergirds both worlds for mother and son is the field of love. Here, Danielle and Noah hike, splash, and step more deeply into the world to discover their spiritual reality.

In raising her children (she now has two sons and a daughter), Danielle says she "follows their lead." She watches each of her children to find out who they are as individuals, as young souls, and where to meet them.

It's not about you or what you are going to turn them into. How can I help them be who they are, to be the most complete? Why are they here? What do they need to do to fulfill their meaning? It slows you down so you can listen. You think: *This is who you are.* They are all so different. This is how I am growing. There is nothing else in the world that can teach you what it means to be human. It's like watching a flower unfold in incredibly slow motion.

Adolescence and Midlife: Shared Passage

The emergence of spiritual awakening in our adolescents matches a window of spiritual seeking in parents during what Carl Jung called "the second half of life." For the parent, this midlife "surge" (similar in so many ways to that of adolescence) typically arrives at a time when developmentally, we have fully lived the external life of accomplishment and material goals, and we're ready to focus inward. This shift inward is the crux of the "midlife crisis," developmental depression "take two:" feelings of emptiness, restlessness, and dissatisfaction. For some, this passage is not experienced as a crisis at all, but as a questioning and wonder, and openness to the "something more." This looking inward, reflecting not just on life's meaning but on *our* life's meaning, is a natural process for adults and can be a deeply meaningful meeting place with our teen. Active, engaged listening without judging or pushing an agenda can put both parent and child at ease as they explore.

"The ultimate meaning of my life? Well, I have thought a lot about that lately, too. You're starting out on your road, and I'm taking stock while I still have time hopefully to make my mark in this world. In a way, we are in a similar boat, figuring out our ultimate meaning and purpose. I would love to share notes."

"Yes, your question is very important. What is our purpose? Sometimes I look at my strengths, and see if I have used them to inspire and help others. Are there moments of *aha!* for you, when you sense that you're using your strengths in some way that feels more than a talent—in a way that makes you feel life is full?"

"I don't know where your inner compass guides you regarding the ultimate point of it all. But for me, speaking for myself, being a source of love has a lot to do with it. Sharing love. That I

love you and your mother—that just touches my deep inner wisdom as true and strong. I know this family is real and right."

Essentially facing a second round of spiritual individuation, we have
skin in the game. For many of us it is a natural time to look inward. For
some of us this inward journey will be familiar, for others it will be less
so. Whether or not we face roadblocks or open highways, memories of
ethical and loving messengers, or quite the opposite, the second half
of life gives us the opportunity to plunge deeply and find our bedrock
of reality and to build a spiritual life. Being open to our own spiritual
nature also allows us to meet our teen authentically, with the best we
have to offer.

The Most Important Thing

My own father took the time to do this with me. When I think back on
it, it would have been really easy to hear my adolescent big questions as
"just a stage" and dismiss them, but instead he honored them. He would
set aside his work, get a cup of tea, and sit down on the floor on our car-
pet with the Midwest sun shining in, and he would never end the conversation. Of the hundreds of things that I might have brought up in a
week, not everything got this kind of interest. The dance, the clothes,
winning the race, whether the grade was an A or A-minus—such
matters did not even turn his head. But start talking about what's the
point of life, and he was riveted. He sat. He listened, really listened. To
him, the journey was of the highest importance. It's about the inner life.
It's about finding meaning and purpose and relationship.

My father's whole life was about inner life. He didn't claim to know
the answers. He'd say, in a judicious, academic tone, "Many cultures, many
people, have had many answers. Many people have tried to answer this
question."

So when I'd ask these questions, the response would be *Yes*, this is
the question! An open question is valuable. Does it matter? *Yes*, that's a

very important question. He would never close the inquiry, end the quest. He'd say, "Yeah, a lot of people have thought about that through time and I don't have an answer for that." Then he'd talk about his own journey. "For me, I need work that gives me meaning, makes me tick, and relationships that are built on love and trust." He spoke of the type of work and love that is part of something more.

Often, if he'd had an experience that he himself was processing—a vivid dream, for instance—he would share, sitting there on the floor.

I remember he sat there the week after his mother died. I was about nine and I remember him sitting down with me and sharing. "I had a dream this week, and Grandma Ellie was in it." The dream was raw and unprocessed: "In this dream, Grandma Ellie was wearing an outfit, an everyday gray suit. Grandma Ellie normally dressed up in elegant clothes, but here she wasn't; she was in this everyday suit. We were walking down Grand Avenue in Des Moines, the central thoroughfare, where we went many times, with a sense of her beside me. I took it to mean that she was my mother and would always be my mother and would continue to walk beside me, in whatever sense that is."

He was always the doubting academic. It was the week of his mother's death. I felt as if in sharing this dream, he'd given me the most important thing in his life. That experience became a template for me, now with my own kids and in my own work: next to listening, our journey as the parent is the greatest thing we have to share. My father's telling of his dream was a lovely shared moment, both of us at the cusp of grief and trying to figure it out together. He didn't have an answer and I didn't have an answer, but we knew it was important and we were leaning in. He let me into the relationship, embrace, and sustenance of inner spiritual life, into the reality of symbolic life. It was a sacred moment. It was as intimate and real and just as important as life gets.

13

SEVEN RIGHT THINGS

Opportunities for Spiritual Parenting

The parents I talk to on the soccer field, at pickup, at schools, at scientific conventions, over coffee, and in my clinical and wellness practice often come around to the same question: *What can I do?* This question comes from parents of varied traditions and origins, as well as those who do not ascribe to any religion, and from people who consider themselves to be spiritual and those who identify as being nonspiritual. Parents are looking for ideas and approaches to help their children build a spiritual life:

How do I help my child's spirituality grow? Can I make her spiritual? How do I keep them from losing their natural spirituality?

What if I am uncomfortable with religion? I'm spiritual but not religious—how do I teach that? How do I talk about it? Where do I start?

In this chapter, I discuss seven strategies that you can use on your own terms to encourage your child's spiritual growth. You are the foremost expert on your child. The thousands of moments shared with our children create a multitude of lessons, and often the greatest teaching moments arrive unplanned and unbidden. Consider them a gift. Breathe and trust. It's not that we said the perfect thing in a grand moment that changed our child's life. We just need to open our hearts and try. Parenting—and spirituality—is not a scorecard. Think of it as a tidal wave of love that we are learning to surf. What works is when day after day we show up ready to try—spiritually, emotionally, and physically present—to feel and move with an open heart.

We can create the space and time for spiritual conversation or activity, but spiritually meaningful moments often cannot be planned. Life offers us opportunities, some that we can anticipate, others spontaneously; it's up to us to recognize them and point out the view to our children. These opportunities may arise in the happiest of times: a birth, a wedding, a special family dinner, or in recognition of a personal milestone or turning point. But hard times all the more urgently call us and our children to reach deeper for courage, or calm, or compassion needed to meet the moment. A child is snubbed at school or feels humiliated by a teacher; a family member or friend is hospitalized or ill; a disturbing news event rouses a child's concerns about the world or perhaps has him question his own choices—these are moments primed for spiritual reflection.

"How generous and kind of the gentleman behind the counter to ask after your brother. Usually we come here together as a family. He really cares. That's the point of life."

"Look, that little bird is building a nest in the top of our porch! She sees you each day and must know this is a safe and loving place to raise her babies. Let's come out each day and say hello and cheer her on!"

"Isn't it a miracle that Daisy Dog was brought to the Humane Society just when you came to find your own true dog? You found each other."

You do not need to study spirituality or know the science of spirituality to be an effective resource for your child's spiritual awakening. You do not need to have formal religious training or even have your own spirituality figured out 100 percent. You just need to be willing to share your own experiences, engage authentically with your child, and have the utmost interest in and respect for her own direct experience with spirituality. The status of your own spirituality—stable, nonexistent, or growing—is not a worry here. These conversations are not about measuring up to some spiritual standard or ideal, either as a parent or as a child. Spirituality's very nature is abundant love that cannot be measured or assessed for adequacy! This isn't a test; it's a conversation, a process, an opening, an embrace.

Your own inner compass as a parent is the ultimate checkpoint for how to spiritually parent. There is no expert in the world who has as deep a knowing of your child as you do. For your own exploration and consideration, here are seven right things, to be added to your store of opportunity, knowledge, and creativity, so that you are poised with more material in the moment.

1. Speak: Use Spiritual Language Daily

"Use your words," we tell our young children time and again, insisting that they use language to express their most intense emotions—as if that is something we all do quite easily as adults. However, we know language is important, not only to communicate to others about our experiences, but also to process those experiences ourselves. It can be difficult to find the words for spiritual expression and transcendent experiences. But it's important to connect language with our experiences, even those that are difficult to articulate or hard to understand. Once we identify the language to go with our spiritual life, we can start to use those words to express our spiritual selves more fluidly.

Each of the following words, and the spiritually significant ideas they represent, can become a part of your child's spiritual vocabulary if you use them: field of love, direct knowing, heart knowing, head knowing, inner compass, spiritual compass, culture of love versus culture of judgment, feeling part of the oneness, synchronicity, sanctity, connection with spirit. You might also invent your own language, or find renewed guidance in the language of your own religious tradition.

This language may feel unfamiliar at first, but it will flow more easily as you get used to articulating your experience and listening to your child's; direct spiritual language is optimal for holding these experiences. When you use these words, you help your child connect with the felt experience. You're educating your child about his own inner life by giving him a way to find meaning literally and symbolically through language.

Using spiritual language in daily settings is a way to point out to our children when their everyday acts and interactions reflect a spiritual quality. For instance, rather than assuming they held the door for an elderly person just to be polite (following the rules of common courtesy), you can help them see the act as an expression of who they are and how they relate to other people. We can purposefully "catch them being compassionate" (or loving, or generous, or thoughtful) so they can see themselves that way.

"So, you decided for yourself whether or not to take the ice cream from the school fridge, even when the other kids said it was okay. You listened to your inner compass!"

"John's mother told me that every child in the class made fun of him when his nose was running—everyone but you. Your heart knowing and natural compassion made all the difference to John. He came home and told his mom about it."

"I saw you pick up that little ant on a tissue and take him to the backyard. Your love and respect for the spirit of every living being is so beautiful. Look how you care for sacred life. You inspire me!"

2. Share: Transparency and the Voice of Spiritual Experience

In our busy world, we can be so quick to express our impatience, disappointment, or unhappiness to our children. Whether or not we articulate these emotions precisely, they often pick up on our tension or negativity. Each of those moments (and countless others throughout the day) invite us to be transparent, to show how we call on our spirituality to work through challenges. Let your child see and hear how you use spiritual experience as the path through which you resolve daily problems, hold relationships, and understand life events and circumstances. Show your child that spirituality can be a resource, and how it can be supporting:

"It made me sad when Sharon behaved the way she did, but I sat and reflected on the situation and what felt deep down like the right thing to do, and realized I could forgive her in my heart and let it go."

"The slow service at that restaurant was so frustrating! I was going to leave a bad tip just to make the point, but then I realized—the waiters were overwhelmed, and I could either leave a bad tip and add to their bad day, or show a bit of compassion."

"He would never have found out my mistake was what created the problem, but I couldn't just sit quietly and let the blame fall on someone else. My higher self knows the right thing to do."

"I was so angry about what he said that I took a moment and went for a walk to calm down and reconnect to all that is good in the world."

Frame these as spiritual problems and not simply as moods. This is especially important when talking about large and difficult challenges such as losing a job or illness and death. Treat challenges and setbacks as a spiritual opportunity.

"Losing my job right now puts us in a bind financially, but the most important thing is that we have each other. As a part of our family, I feel that love and it helps me find the energy and optimism to keep going."

"Grandmother's death was a blow to all of us. Nothing changes the fact that she's gone, but I've found that 'keeping someone's memory alive' is actually real in the field of love. When we hold people in our thoughts they stay present to us. They are actually with us."

"Sometimes I pray just to thank God for all the blessings in my life, and sometimes I pray because I could use some help. I personally don't think of God as a fixer, but I do pray for the courage and wisdom to find the answers."

Transparency is an intentional willingness to show our children how we resolve daily frustration, painful events, ethical problems, and difficult decisions through our own spiritual relationship. This process is possible whether or not you're a fan of religion and even if you've never thought of yourself as spiritual. Start where you are. Don't feel a need to fish for a sentence from this book to use if it doesn't seem genuine. A heartfelt, authentic relationship with your child is the best vehicle for sharing spirituality. Your language may be *Let's go fish by a lake,* or *Let's take a breather,* or *Let's take a walk,* or *Let's call in the dog.*

There's no pressure here. The point is that you are to share authentically from your experience and to practice feeling deeply into the bigness of life. Your child will see you listening to life as a spiritual opportunity.

We can delight in the world and appreciate it out loud:

"The sunrise is so utterly beautiful. I feel I could take a photo of it every morning. What a treat to live on earth."

We can express gratitude for being alive:

"I just look at you running alongside your brother, and the two of you laughing, and I feel so fortunate for being your mother. I feel grateful every day for you and your love for each other."

We can apologize:

"I'm sorry that on this beautiful day I was so snappy and jumpy. You were kind and good, and I feel that I wasted the day for us together. So I made a little prayer asking for forgiveness for squandering the day, and I hope that you went on to have a happy rest of the day without grumpy Mommy."

Tell your child your own spiritual story. It doesn't have to be perfect or noble; the power comes from it being real and yours. You can explain that you had moments of doubts, or share stories about the times that you've heard or felt a sacred presence, and about times of darkness and abject doubt when God felt very far away. You can share about your times of suffering through which you lost or found your sense of worth.

The point is to send your child the message that you consider this journey to be sacred, even if it doesn't make immediate sense all of the time.

If we are not perfect, but are works in progress who live our lives to learn, then our children tackle life as a process of learning, spiritual awakening, and discovery.

"Let your life speak," the Quakers say, encouraging us to listen to our heart knowing. Pay attention to our inner compass. Act on that higher guidance to create a life of meaning and purpose. When you share openly of your spiritual journey in conversation with your child, you also let your life speak in another way. You become a reassuring voice to your child or teen: *You can do the work, you can make the unique journey that is yours to make.*

3. Connect: Meet Them Where They Are

From the backseat of my SUV, Isaiah, age eight, spoke in a tense tone I had never heard before.

"Mommy, Charlie says that you are not my real mother. You are not my mother at all. My name is not Miller. And I am not Jewish." He looked at me for an answer, wide-eyed and anxious.

I was surprised by his desperate concern. Isaiah was well aware that he was adopted and that we considered his pathway to us to be the greatest thing in the world—a miracle.

"Isaiah, remember how Mommy prayed for Isaiah, and Daddy prayed for Isaiah, and Grandpa Henry and Grandma Harriet prayed for Isaiah? Everyone prayed for Isaiah," I said to him.

Isaiah paused, his anxiousness still lingering in the air, this response of mine somehow falling short. "Yeah, yeah," he said, then urgently, "but what about the woman who gave me up? What about her?"

Now I understood the desperation in his tone. This question had come earlier than I had expected, but I always knew it would eventually be asked: *Why did she leave me?* As a psychologist, I knew this vulnerable and tender question marked a crucial moment of crisis, and its resolution would lead to a deep sense of value, meaning, and purpose and of the nature of the world.

I paused and took in a huge breath, unsure how to answer.

Isaiah did. From the backseat, with sudden gusto and certainty, "Oh, I know! Yeah! God whispered in her ear and said that you were crying for me."

Sure enough, the child knows the answer to big questions right from the source. I am so glad that I did not preempt with the adult version of "She was young and the country had just faced a tough time. She wanted you to be taken care of." Isaiah found the deeper answer.

Spirituality is a way of living, an experiential space. It is a lived reality, so it is a way of being with hardship. It is a way of being with joy. Spirituality is a way of being in the world that informs every moment. So meeting kids where they are means you hear about mean gossipy girls at school and have a spiritual perspective on it. Meeting them where they are means hearing about the real disappointment of being cut from the team and have a spiritual perspective on it. The things that are so real and feel so big to them are not separate from spirituality. You can meet them where they are in a way that is authentically informed by spiritual values—the spiritual clock is always ticking.

A teen's passion—whether it's running, writing, basketball, or friendships—is a wonderful place to meet them, and to explore the spiritual dimension of their experience. *Is it wrong to want to win? What if things I write make people mad? I didn't make the cut—it's not fair!* Your enthusiasm for your teen's ability to investigate these kinds of questions through personal talents and interests is a light on the path to spiritual awareness.

Meeting your child where he is also means a willingness to tolerate doubt and questioning about spirituality. Following a talk I gave in Tennessee on spirituality in teens, I received a moving letter from a youth program pastor who explained that he didn't believe in "beating traditions of faith into adolescents," but instead chose to "be supportive of their quest to find meaning for their lives." With this "meet them where they are" philosophy guiding the youth group at his church, the group had grown dramatically in the number of teens attending. Even more impressive, he said, was "the level of spirituality and contentment that our kids seem to express during this rough stretch of adolescence is astounding." He continued,

> Some of the stories that these students share and the truthfulness they use while expressing their life experiences is more than enough to bring tears. So, it's because of some of those stories that I decided that in the ministry work that I do, for the rest of my life, I will seek to know the person, first. Their knowledge of the church's doctrine and customary actions is important to the church, of course, but I strongly believe in following Jesus, not just knowing about Him. It is vastly more important that we seek to give youth more depth and transparency as opposed to giving them a surface-level masquerade. And when we do this, the effectiveness is life altering.

Meeting your child also includes being present with love and interest to hear spiritual questions or hear about experiences that are unfamiliar or unsettling. When you just don't know the answer, appreciate the moment.

Our child might ask:

"Does God love people even when they're harming others?"

"Why is that man sleeping on the street?"

"Why did Jennifer's mother die? Are you going to die?"

Unprepared, our inclination may be to hedge around painful questions or the simple fact that we don't know the answer. But they aren't asking you for answers, really; they are working. The ideal takeaway is to help the child learn to engage life on spiritual terms, to lean into a spiritual understanding of the world. They are asking questions that cut right to the core of life—hard questions about life and death, right and wrong. Instead of feeling anxious or avoidant or guilty and unable to respond, we can see it as an invitation back in, a call to engage. We need only encourage the conversation, the openness and exploration of the idea, and be willing to listen with the same openness and curiosity that accompanies the question.

> "When I was a child I wondered that, too. I am so happy you are sharing these thoughts with me."

> "Wow, you bring such important questions to the family. You help us think about the big positive reasons we are all here alive together!"

> "You are so right that the things we do really matter. How I treat you and your brother and the homeless man all matter."

Your child may share a moving spiritual experience of great significance to her: that a grandparent came to her in a dream, that she had a strong sense of the joy and love, or that she had an intuition about something that happened or will happen. These experiences are almost always bright and positive and important to the child's long-term sense of self and spiritual grounding. You do not need answers; just honor the moment as bigger than you:

> "Wow, that is a moving and wonderful experience."

> "Such joy and love! Please, will you tell me more?"

> "That sounds very important and I am so grateful you shared it with me."

> "Grandma has always loved you and still loves you. Loves you everywhere you go."

"I still remember that when I was a child, I had an experience in some ways similar. May I share it with you?"

"It really is the point in living to embrace these special bright gifts, these experiences. You may reach back to this special moment the rest of your life."

4. Teach: Build a Spiritual Practice Together

Practice brings our attention to spirituality in a consistent way. When parents and children practice together, it brings this consistent spirituality even more strongly into the field of love.

Family practice can be praying or meditating or sharing a ritual or ceremony together. Regular practice together as a family paves a pathway for the child that endures a lifetime. The pathway is permanent. It will be there for your child in times of developmental change and challenge.

Invite your children into your space, whether you're meditating or praying, so they see your deliberate spiritual practice and purposeful creation of opportunity for spiritual insight, refocus, and growth. A gratitude practice every Sunday, an appreciation practice, a healing practice in which we apologize to one another and fix things are all shared practices. The common thread here is teaching a deliberate way to handle life, and of constructing life with a spiritual infrastructure.

In addition to practice, family rituals have great importance: Christenings, namings, and new baby parties bring families together and actively honor the field of love for the new child; bringing out Grandma's punch bowl for New Year's links us to past generations. Around the Christmas tree we can share a tale from our own childhood holidays, or add an ornament saved for forty years. All of these are ways of bringing the child into our own practice of spirituality.

5. Nurture: Embrace Relationships with Animals and All of Nature

One day as I was walking down the street, a Buddhist nun with a shaved head and long robes approached and exclaimed, "Greetings! Greetings!" and with a great joy, "How are you, little one?!" She was talking to my dog, Penny, whom she saw directly as a soul. I understood because that is just how we feel about Penny at home.

Bring the living world to your child by delighting in the relationships of nature. Live with animals, whether as indoor pets or familiar outdoor "neighbors" you come to know. Talk with animals. Actively engage in the sanctification of nature by openly celebrating it and its contribution to your family and the world we live in. Listening to trees, thinking that the wind has something to show you, knowing that the weather is not separate from who we are: part of the universal oneness is having respectful and loving relationships with nature and animals. Children can learn that all living things are our teachers; we can learn from their wisdom, judgment, and sensibilities.

In Michael Thompson's book, *Homesick and Happy*, he writes,

Nature is so much bigger than all of us, any of us, that it makes you feel small and therefore puts your life in perspective. There is no question that the sunrise, the sunset, the stars in the night sky reminds you of your place in the world, and that leads to reflection . . . being in Nature focuses you.

Give your children long peaceful moments to know firsthand a relationship with nature.

6. Care and Repair: Tend the Field of Love

Family needs to be explicitly established and supported as a sacred part of life, a blessing to every person. Express these ideas aloud to your children: *I am so fortunate and blessed to be your mama! Our family is a source of light to me every day. Our love is the most important thing. How can we bring our love to the world?* In terms of spiritual development, acknowledging and embracing family as sacred gives your child a spiritual place to live in, every day. From this "spiritual home base" the child moves into the world. Supporting spirituality at this core—at the family—primes your child to see the rest of the world as inclusive and loving, and to bring those feelings to the world, as well.

Researcher Marshall Duke and colleagues at Emory University have shown that children are more likely to thrive when they have a grasp of being an important part of a lineage, what they term the "intergenerational self." This sense of belonging to a chain of ancestors is often transmitted through stories.

Children want to understand their place in the family, both physically and spiritually. Family history in general is very important, to explain to children what came before. Many families also tell a "creation myth"— in other words, the story of how the child entered the field of love. This isn't myth in the sense that it is fiction; it is myth in the sense that it is full of meaning and symbolism and explains the child's arrival and place in the world in a new way.

Here is my creation myth as told to me as a child by my mother:

When my maternal grandmother, Harriet, was in her late sixties she developed a very aggressive form of cancer. Her prognosis was poor. She went to the best treatment center available to her at the time, and, once exhausting the treatment regiment, the oncologists said her chances were very slim. My mother told me that she had wanted to give grandma "a little something more to live for"—so much so that she conceived me years earlier than she and my father had otherwise planned. Grandma was a woman of great faith and intense love of her family. When her cancer suddenly reversed, the doctors were stunned and wrote up the case in a medical journal as that of a religious woman overcoming great odds. Grandma Harriet lived another thirty-eight years, and met her great-grandchildren.

Part of the sanctification of the family is showing that family is part of something larger, something beyond the purely physical. Understanding family as sacred involves showing how family is intertwined with spirit. Narratives are a wonderful way to communicate this vital thread in family.

> "Your great-grandmother could only bring one suitcase from Ireland, and she packed her Bible with this note on the front page from her own mother. So we use it on special holidays."

> "Family was the most important thing to Grandpa, which is why he always insisted we have dinner together. On his birthday we all come together to celebrate him and the love that makes us a family."

> "Your grandma never had shoes growing up because her family was too poor. This is why we donate shoes and clothes to those who need them—everyone needs to feel protected."

> "Our family escaped from a country where they could not pray. All they wanted was for this moment, to be here in safety as a family, praying out loud. So we pray right here out loud, and we appreciate what they did for the family."

Cultivate your child as a link in the family chain. For example, my youngest child, Lila, stands before her school class each year on Hanukkah. She teaches about this Jewish holiday to the other children, most of whom are of other faiths, and then lights a menorah. She explains that her "great-great grandmother carried the menorah from Russia, then gave it to her great-grandmother in Iowa, who gave it to Grandma Margo, who gave it to my mom, who gave it to me." Without fail, children and teachers alike are absorbed and moved by the universal power of spirituality passing through the generations.

Sanctification of the family also happens when we acknowledge with gratitude each person in the family and the specialness of being a whole. Sunday family dinner, Shabbat dinner, or special Tuesday pizza night can start with a shared embrace of gratitude, a prayer of thanks, or a family act of appreciation for one another. Hug! Cheer! Shake hands and say, "I love and appreciate you," or "Thank you for____."

An agnostic couple I know who have four young children conduct a gratitude ceremony together every Sunday. Each child draws a picture or writes (if they can) a heartfelt statement of gratitude on a little piece of paper. All the notes are put in a bag, and the family members take turns pulling them out, sharing them with the family, and asking the original author about each note.

As we've said, a child's spirituality is to a large extent held in the family relationship. So when the family relationship changes in some way—for example, through divorce, remarriage, or a new baby—we need to acknowledge this and give the field of love explicit attention, honor, and care. In addition, parents—people in general—aren't perfect; we make mistakes. When we do, forget trying to hide it from your child. Any change or disruption in the family is an opportunity to reconnect and communicate.

"As your father, I apologize that I have not been very attentive to your feelings and those of you mother. I apologize first to you and Mom, and then I also apologize to the whole field of love that holds our family. I want to fix and make stronger than ever this big love between us all."

"The family, and our field of love, is the most important part of living, and it holds the life itself that keeps us going. I am so sorry that I yelled at you from my own anxiety and concerns about work. I want you to know that what is real and important is you, our love as a family, and the presence of spirit that flows through our strong love as family. Our family comes first. May I lead us in a meditation to repair it so that we are closer than ever?"

"Grandma has passed—it's been two weeks. Still, I feel her here with me and with you. Perhaps you might have a sense of her by your side. Or she may come in a dream. Grandma's love for us is right here in the family field of love, always."

"Baby Ruthie is born! We have just added a big splash to the field of love. She loves you, and you love her. She loves Mommy, Mommy loves Ruthie, and of course, always you. Love grows everywhere with one more!"

7. Strive: The Inspired Life

The long line at the post office was filled with people doing the usual post-office thing—exchanging glances and rolling their eyes, simmering with hostility at the delay. I could see that the clerk behind the counter—all alone at a rush time—was incredibly angry, glaring and steaming at each customer who approached her window. Then it was my turn.

Suddenly she blurted out, "I've had the worst day ever." I said, "The worst day ever? I'm so sorry you had the worst day ever." In a flash, the shift of energy and intention in the crowd was palpable—where there had been a simmering hostility by exasperated customers and the clerk's defensive hostility back, suddenly those in line changed from a position of anger to understanding. People stopped glaring, smiled in sympathy, and quietly tidied the line instead of leaning impatiently forward. I witnessed a sudden manifestation of the culture of love by a line of people whose response said, *Let's encourage this soul on earth, this postal clerk who is alone, whose job is beyond demanding and situation infeasible.* Everyone banded together to encourage and uplift the clearly overburdened clerk.

In our culture, sometimes the bar for behavior and ethics is so low that it's barely above what's legal, and often doesn't register as human. Spiritual values say there's a much higher bar ethically than that which is demonstrated in the everyday bare-minimum standard. Instead of operating from the perspective of "floor ethics," the bottom of what's barely acceptable, we instead can talk about "ceiling ethics"—how high we can go. I call this approach the spirituality of inspired living, which is the ethic through which we connect in the universe to one another and to a higher presence. The spirituality of inspired living is always present, always available to us. It posits that people are good, that we are ready to live optimally, to spread love and understanding, like those people in line in the post office. We can demonstrate these ideas and live these ethics actively every day for our children. The inspired life sees transcendence in each moment, opening life to much more.

The inspired life honors our deep inner compass: knowing the true standard is so much higher than just what's allowed and living that truth. It's not just making do with the customary rules of the school or the workplace; it's imagining how life could really be instead.

We often talk about right action: going out of our way to help people or working at homeless shelters. But there is another form of right action and that is to repair the world, fix things; in the Jewish tradition this is called *tikkun olam*. If I lose my temper with the cashier at Starbucks, it means apologizing. Go back and, awkward as it may feel, say, "I'm sorry." Apologize. Fix things. The more we do it, the easier it becomes, and it starts to feel good.

The year Leah was born, the garden shop delivered a tree for outside her window. It was a pink flowering azalea, a very young tree. But that first spring there were no flowers at all until May, and then just a few tiny buds up at the top. I was disappointed and thought to send it back, but decided to give the baby tree one more year. The following spring there were a few more buds, but they were black! I debated having the tree pulled up and replaced, but Leah was now one year old, and I couldn't help but think of the little tree as a parallel budding life. Obviously, I would not have replaced Leah. So I kept the tree, which I named Azalea, and talked to her, and each season a few more flowers came. I could sense that she was trying, but there were never many flowers.

Last winter, Isaiah, who is now a teenager, saw that a neighboring young tree had bent in the snow. He straightened the little neighbor tree by tying a line to the nonflowering Azalea. Isaiah and I thanked Azalea, and then did not check during the remaining cold months of winter. Come spring, it was quite a sight. Nonflowering Azalea had sprouted five new branches exactly opposite the line she held for her little neighbor. She had never produced flowers, but she was willing to grow new arms to balance and hold the other tree in the field of love. She is a dignified, quiet hero whom I love.

Our opportunity for the inspired life is always right here, right now. You don't even have to wait for your child to get home from school or wait for mealtime or bedtime. Life as right actions becomes a prayer, a lived dialogue in the two-way relationship expressed in and through the transcendent other—the spirit in other people and all living beings. In this sense, every moment of daily life is a spiritual opportunity—for both you and your child—to encourage, uplift, or turn anger into a moment of humor and connection. Sometimes the worst situations open into spiritual opportunities.

The moments begin at home, between you and your child. By example and by listening with an open heart and mind, embrace your child's natural spirituality. Encourage your children to feel a part of the "something larger" and to tune in to the inner life for reflection and guidance; to meet their everyday actions with their highest self—to decide what kind of soul on earth they want to be. Help them to reach out to someone at school who is having a hard time, to look past unfashionable clothes or a bad attitude, and look into another's eyes and ask, "How are you doing?" While you're at it, do the same for that crabby colleague at your office. Ask what he is thinking or curious about; ask how he is.

The culture of love spreads very quickly. As we cultivate a world of opportunity for those around us, people will want to jump in, like the people in that post office. Together we raise the bar and create the inspired life. Just as the child reawakens parents to natural spirituality, children can reawaken our culture to our natural spirituality.

We can let our children really affect us, change us by reminding us of who we really are. As a society we can cultivate our collective spirituality, knowing that it is real and important. By being open to these ideas, these values, and being aware of how we live them, we can change our world. It starts with each child, and his or her spiritual birthright: the spiritual child.

A colleague and friend of mind is an obstetrician who delivers babies several times a week. She is intensely dedicated to her work and is present at all hours of the night during deliveries. By 5 A.M. each day she is commuting hours to inner-city hospitals. Recently I saw her and asked, "Hey, what's new? Have you delivered the new Dalai Lama?" To which she smiled and replied, "Yes, they all are."

Acknowledgments

From Lisa:

Many people shape a child, each with unique and powerful contributions. *The Spiritual Child* thrives from being influenced by numerous people, each with talents and expertise that have been beyond fathomable.

My deep appreciation goes to the many contributors who so generously shared from their own lives and spiritual experiences to inform this book through my years of formal research, field interviews, conversations, and correspondence.

Teresa Barker, your elegant crafting of the writing for *The Spiritual Child* brings these fifteen years of research into a beautiful flowing journey for caring parents to read. You are an artist in the truest sense, through your keen mind, passion, and elegant prose.

Nichole Argyres at St. Martin's Press: You are a brilliant, ingenious editor with intense commitment to the very finest quality of books. *The Spiritual Child* reflects your vision, editorial investment, and great regard for the reader's experience of each word.

This book was born because of the wisdom of the St. Martin's Press publishing leaders who from the beginning believed in its possibility: Sally Richardson (who even helped create the title) and George Witte. Also, my deep appreciation to the late Matthew Shear.

My gratitude to the outstanding team at St. Martin's Press, who work extremely effectively together. Heartfelt appreciation, and awe, really, to the ingenious marketing team, Laura Clark, Karlyn Hixson, and Scottie Bowditch, and highly effective publicity team, Tracey Guest and Allison Frascatore.

Great delight and appreciation to the creative people who helped produce such a beautiful book: Lisa Pompilio, Michelle McMillian, Elizabeth Catalano, Lisa Goris, and Helen Chin. Also to the focused and capable copilot in all affairs, Laura Chasen.

David Kuhn at Kuhn Projects, you are an inventor of culture. I came to you with fifteen years of research and the deep desire to share the best that science has for children. You explained *The Spiritual Child* to the publishing field, with full awareness of the impact of science on culture. David, you are an alchemist of ideas.

Elizabeth Shreve, you are a publicist extraordinaire! My gratitude for your brilliant vision, strategic insight, and highly capable execution! You have spearheaded an outstanding, far-reaching, publicity plan.

Every child is a spiritual child. Three spiritual children, whom I am honored to mother, are Leah, Lila, and Isaiah. This book is dedicated to you. Your loving brightness, your natural spirituality, inspires every day of our lives. I hope that you grow up in a world where natural spirituality is understood to be the core of humanity.

Philip, you have been heroic and supportive from the beginning, through graduate school, the long academic pathway, and now day after every day. Your deep love is the bedrock of my life.

Mom and Dad, thank you for being spiritual parents. To Mark, a true and loyal sibling, and to your dear family. The Miller family all. To TC students, generations of teams in my lab, faculty, and administrators who collaborated in growing this new field. Alice for reading. Always GFs. YC, MA, and JBS, lifelong friends.

My mentors who continue to guide: Martin Seligman, Myrna Weissman, Carol Dweck, Len Sperry, Scott Richards, Gary Weaver, Bob Lovinger, Ron Young, Susan Nolen-Hoeksema, Paul Rozin, Tom James, Bill Baldwin, Susan Fuhrman.

My fellow scientists, thank you for your collaboration over the years, for sharing witness of our awe-inspiring Universe.

In deepest gratitude to sacred Creator.

From Teresa:

My gratitude to Lisa for asking me to partner with her on this book and this journey; to my mother, Maxine, and my father, George, whose open hearts and everyday spirituality infused my childhood and remain a cherished living legacy; to Dolly for her special light and love; to my transcendent friends, Leslie, Kathy, Sue, Margaret, Elizabeth, and Wendy; to my husband, Steve, for his love, patience, and support, and to our inspiring next generation, Rebecca, Rachel, Aaron, and Lauren, and my granddaughter, Leyna; to Holly and Bob, Michael and Theresa, Catherine, Benny, and others whose generosity, wisdom, and humor continue to touch my work and life, and to my extraordinary agent, Madeleine Morel.

Notes

Introduction

5   *Optimism was shown to be teachable*   Martin E. P. Seligman, *Learned Optimism: How to Change Your Mind and Your Life* (New York: Knopf, 1991).

5   *emotional intelligence (EQ)*   P. Salovey and J. D. Mayer, "Emotional intelligence," *Imagination, Cognition, and Personality*, 9(3), (1990): 185–211; see also P. Salovey, A. Woolery, and J. D. Mayer, "Emotional Intelligence: Conceptualization and Measurement," in *The Blackwell Handbook of Social Psychology*, ed. G. Fletcher and M. Clark (London: Blackwell, 2001), 279–307; see also J. Mayer, M. Brackett, and P. Salovey, *Emotional Intelligence: Key Readings from the Mayer and Salovey Model* (Port Chester, NY: Dude Publishing, 2004); see also Daniel Goleman, *Emotional Intelligence: Why It Can Matter More Than IQ* (New York: Bantam, 1995).

5   *genetic determinants of human behavior*   Dean Hamer and Peter Copeland, *The Science of Desire: The Search for the Gay Gene and the Biology of Desire* (New York: Simon & Schuster, 1994); see also Dean Hamer, *The God Gene: How Faith Is Hardwired into Our Genes* (New York: Doubleday, 2004).

6   *two radically different "mindsets"*   Carol Dweck, *Mindset: The New Psychology of Success* (New York: Random House, 2006).

7   *Then in 1997*   K. S. Kendler, C. O. Gardner, and C. A. Prescott, "Religion, psychopathology and substance use and abuse: A multimeasure, genetic-epidemiologic study," *American Journal of Psychiatry*, 154(3), (1997): 322–29.

8   *Our own research*   L. Miller and M. Gur, "Religiousness and sexual responsibility in adolescent girls," *Journal of Adolescent Health*, 31(5), (2002): 401–06.

8   *while personal devotion is highly protective*   L. Miller, M. Davies, and S. Greenwald,

"Religiosity and substance use and abuse among adolescents in the National Comorbidity Survey," *Journal of the American Academy of Child and Adolescent Psychiatry*, 39, (2000): 1190–97; see also L. Miller and M. Gur, "Religiosity, depression, and physical maturation in adolescent girls," *Journal of the American Academy of Child and Adolescent Psychiatry*, 41(2), (2002): 206–14.

10 *A significant percentage* Gallup.com, "Religion," (2013); see www.gallup.com/poll /1690/religion.aspx.

10 *Today, more than one-third* Ibid.

10 *Two-thirds of Americans* Ibid.

12 *It is no surprise that* Fetzer Survey on Love and Forgiveness; see www.fetzer.org /resources/fetzer-survey-love-and-forgiveness-american-society.

13 *In 2010, the Fetzer Institute* Ibid.

13 *A Religion and Social Trends* Gallup.com (May 6, 1999), "As Nation Observes National Day of Prayer, 9 in 10 Americans Pray—3 in 4 Daily"; see www.gallup.com/ poll/3874/nation-observes-national-day-prayer-pray-daily.aspx.

19 *my edited volume* Lisa J. Miller, ed., *The Oxford University Press Handbook of Psychology and Spirituality* (New York: Oxford University Press, 2012).

1. Birthright

27 *around the world* P. L. Benson, P. C. Scales, A. K. Syvertsen, and E. C. Roehlkepartain, "Is youth spiritual development a universal developmental process? An international exploration," *Journal of Positive Psychology*, 7(6), (2012): 453–70.

28 *Using a classic twin-study* K. S. Kendler, C. O. Gardner, and C. A. Prescott, "Religion, psychopathology and substance use and abuse: A multimeasure, genetic-epidemiologic study," *American Journal of Psychiatry*, 154(3), (1997): 322–29.

28 *Neuroscientists including* A. Newberg, "Transformation of brain structure and spiritual experience," in *Oxford University Press Handbook of Psychology and Spirituality*, ed. L. Miller (New York: Oxford University Press, 2012), 489–99; see also M. Beauregard, "Neuroimaging and spiritual practice," in *Oxford University Press Handbook of Psychology and Spirituality*, ed. L. Miller (New York: Oxford University Press, 2012), 500–13.

37 *flourishing, healthy, thick portions of the brain* L. Miller, R. Bansal, P. Wickramaratne, C. Tenke, M. Weissman, and B. Peterson, "Neuroanatomical correlates of religiosity and spirituality: A study in adults at high and low familial risk for depression," *Journal of the American Medical Association, Psychiatry*, 71(2), (2014): 128–35.

37 *regulates our levels of cortisol* T. E. Seeman, L. F. Dubin, and M. Seeman, "Religiosity/ spirituality and health: A critical review of the evidence for biological pathways," *American Psychologist*, 58(1), (2003): 53–63; see also E. A. Dedert, J. L. Studts, I. Weissbecker, and P. G. Salmon, "Religiosity may help preserve the cortisol rhythm in women with stress-related illness," *International Journal of Psychiatry in Medicine*, 34(1), (2004): 61–77.

43 *In a study of spiritual individuation* L. Miller, M. Davies, and S. Greenwald, "Religiosity and substance use and abuse among adolescents in the National Comorbidity Survey," *Journal of the American Academy of Child and Adolescent Psychiatry*, 39, (2000): 1190–97.

44 *Along with other forms*   L. Miller and M. Gur, "Religiosity, depression, and physical maturation in adolescent girls," *Journal of the American Academy of Child and Adolescent Psychiatry*, 41, (2002): 206–14.

2. The Science of the Spiritual Brain

55 *was there a landmark twin study*   K. S. Kendler, C. O. Gardner, and C. A. Prescott, "Religion, psychopathology and substance use and abuse: a multimeasure, genetic-epidemiologic study," *American Journal of Psychiatry*, 154(3), (1997): 322–29.

56 *not just one part*   K. S. Kendler, C. O. Gardner, and C. A. Prescott, "Clarifying the relationship between religiosity and psychiatric illness: The impact of covariates and the specificity of buffering effects," *Twin Research*, 2(2), (1999): 137–44.

58 *One meaningful body*   C. R. Cloninger, D. M. Svrakic, and T. R. Przybeck, "A psychobiological model of temperament and character," *Archives of General Psychiatry*, 50(12), (1993): 975–90.

59 *spiritual philosopher Ken Wilber*   Ken Wilber, *Integral Spirituality: A Startling New Role for Religion in the Modern and Postmodern World* (Boston, MA: Shambhalah Publications, 2006).

61 *identified three core components*   R. L. Piedmont, "Does spirituality represent the sixth factor of personality? Spiritual transcendence and the five factor model," *Journal of Personality*, 67, (1999): 985–1013.

63 *Together with Mark Leach*   R. L. Piedmont and M. M. Leach, "Cross-cultural generalizability of the spiritual transcendence scale in India," *American Behavioral Scientist*, 45, (2002): 1886–89.

63 *among the Filipinos*   R. L. Piedmont, "Cross-cultural generalizability of the Spiritual Transcendence Scale to the Philippines. Spirituality as a Human Universal," *Mental Health, Religion and Culture*, 10, (2007): 89–107.

65 *What we found*   L. Miller, M. Davies, and S. Greenwald, "Religiosity and substance use and abuse among adolescents in the National Comorbidity Survey," *Journal of the American Academy of Child and Adolescent Psychiatry*, 39, (2000): 1190–97.

66 *In a five-year qualitative study*   B. Kelley, A. Athan, and L. Miller, "Openness and spiritual development in adolescents," in *Research in the Social Scientific Study of Religion*, ed. R. Predmo, 18, (2007): 3–33.

66 *A biological surge*   L. Miller and M. Gur, "Religiosity, depression and physical maturation among adolescent girls," *Journal of the American Academy of Child and Adolescent Psychiatry*, 41(2), (2002): 206–14.

67 *The Colorado team found*   T. Button, M. C. Stallings, and S. H. Rhee, "The etiology of stability and change in religious values and religious attendance," *Behavioral Genetics*, 41, (2011): 201–10.

68 *The Minnesota team*   L. Koenig, M. McGue, and W. Iacono, "Stability and changes in religiousness during emerging adulthood," *Developmental Psychology*, 44(2), (2008): 532–43.

72 *"Human spirituality is deeply rooted in relationship"* George E. Vaillant, *Spiritual Evolution: How We Are Wired for Faith, Hope and Love* (New York: Broadway Books, 2008).

73 *Research from Bruce Greyson* B. Greyson and S. Khanna, "Spiritual transformation after near-death experience," *Spirituality in Clinical Practice*, 1(1), (2014): 43–55; see also *The Handbook of Near-Death Experiences: Thirty Years of Investigation*, ed. J. M. Holden and B. Greyson (Santa Barbara, CA: Praeger, 2009).

74 *This is a clinical observation* P. S. Richards, M. H. Smith, M. E. Berrett, K. A. O'Grady, and J. Bartz, "A theistic spiritual treatment for women with eating disorders," *Journal of Clinical Psychology*, 65(2), 2009: 172–84; see also P. S. Richards, "Honoring religious diversity and universal spirituality in psychotherapy," in *Oxford University Press Handbook of Psychology and Spirituality*, ed. L. Miller (New York: Oxford University Press, 2012).

74 *There is also emerging science that points to the heart* R. McCraty, M. Atkinson, and R. T. Bradley, "Electrophysiological evidences of intuition: Part I—The surprising role of the heart," *Journal of Alternative and Complementary Medicine*, 10(1), (2004): 133–43.

75 *A meta-analysis published* T. B. Smith, J. Bartz, and P. Scott Richards, "Outcomes of religious and spiritual adaptations to psychotherapy: A meta-analytic review," *Psychotherapy Research*, 17(6), (2007): 643–55.

76 *Mindsight* Daniel Siegel, *Mindsight: The New Science of Personal Transformation* (New York: Bantam, 2010).

3. The Nod

81 *Weissman's core findings* M. M. Weissman, V. Warner, P. Wickramaratne, D. Moreau, and M. Olfson, "Offspring of depressed parents 10 years later," *Arch Gen Psychiatry*, 54(10), (1997): 932–940.

88 *The data was clear* L. Miller, V. Warner, P. Wickramaratne, and M. Weissman, "Religiosity and depression: Ten-year follow-up of depressed mothers and offspring," *Journal of the American Academy Child and Adolescent Psychiatry*, 36, (1997): 1416–25.

88 *The data showed that if* M. Jacobs, L. Miller, P. Wickramaratne, and M. Weissman, "Family religion and depression in offspring at high risk," *Journal of Affective Disorders*, 136(3), (2012): 320–27.

91 *the power of the parent* P. Granqvist and L. Kirkpatrick, "Religion, Spirituality and Attachment," in *APA Handbook of Psychology, Religion, and Spirituality (1): Context, Theory, and Research*, ed. K. Pargament, J. Exline, and J. Jones (Washington, DC: APA Press, 2013), xxvii, 139–55.

98 *we tend to internalize* L. Miller, M. Weissman, M. Gur, and P. Adams, "Religiosity and substance use among children of opiate addicts," *Journal of Substance Abuse*, 13 (2001): 323–36.

4. A Soul Arrives

104 *the "sanctification" of family*   A. Mahoney, K. Pargament, et al., "A religion and the sanctification of family relationships," *Review of Religious Research*, 44(3), (2003): 220–36; see also A. Mahoney, "The Spirituality of Us: Relational Spirituality in the Context of Family Relationships," *APA Handbook of Psychology, Religion, and Spirituality (1): Context, Theory, and Research*, ed. K. Pargament, J. Exline, and J. Jones (Washington, DC: APA Press, 2013), 365–89.

105 *a series of elegant studies*   Paul Bloom, *Just Babies: The Origins of Good and Evil* (New York: Crown, 2013).

106 *Brielle and Kyrie Jackson*   http://www.lifenews.com/2014/06/20/their-rescuing-hug -stunned-the-world-now-the-twins-are-all-grown-up/.

106 *a natural set of social-cognitive assumptions*   Justin L. Barrett and Bonnie Poon, "Cognition, Evolution and Religion," in *APA Handbook of Psychology, Religion, and Spirituality (1): Context, Theory, and Research*, ed. K. Pargament, J. Exline, J. Jones (Washington, DC: APA Press, 2013), 221–37.

108 *in their book,* Super Brain   Deepak Chopra and Rudolph Tanzi, *Super Brain: Unleashing the Explosive Power of Your Mind to Maximize Health, Happiness, and Spiritual Well-Being* (New York: Harmony, 2012).

109 *a study of 479 five-year-olds*   Anat Shoshani and Ilanit Aviv, "The pillars of strength for first-grade adjustment: Parental and children's character strengths and the transition to elementary school," *Journal of Positive Psychology*, 7(4), (2012): 315–26.

122 *nonlocal mind as an aspect*   S. Schwartz and L. Dossey, "Nonlocality, Intention, and Observer Effects in Healing Studies: Laying a Foundation for the Future," in *Oxford University Press Handbook of Psychology and Spirituality*, ed. L. Miller (New York: Oxford University Press, 2012), 531–47.

122 *As the healer started to work*   J. Achterberg, K. Cooke, T. Richards, et al., "Evidence for correlations between distant intention and brain function in recipients: A functional MRI analysis," *Journal of Alternative and Complementary Medicine*, 11, (2005): 965–71.

125 *Buddhist thought holds that*   http://www.sgi.org/buddhism/buddhist-concepts/one ness-of-self-and-environment.html.

131 *a child initiated discussions*   C. Boyatzis et al., "Parent-child communication about religion: Survey and diary data on unilateral transmission and bi-directional reciprocity styles," *Review of Religious Research*, 44(3), (2003): 252–65.

5. Field of Love

137 *the neurological wiring of the* social regulation system   Stephen W. Porges, *The Polyvagal Theory: Neurophysiological Foundations of Emotion, Attachment, Communication, and Self-Regulation* (New York: W. W. Norton, 2011).

138 *transcendence is prominent*   George Vaillant, *Spiritual Evolution: A Scientific Defense of Faith* (New York: Broadway Books, 2008).

138 *from accepting and loving parenting*   W. N. Bao, L. B. Whitbeck, D. R. Hoyt, and R. D. Conger, "Perceived parental acceptance as a moderator of religious transmission among adolescent boys and girls," in *Journal of Marriage and the Family*, 61(2), (1999): 362–74.

139 *when parents and children invoke*   G. Brelsford, "Divine alliances to handle family conflict," *Psychology of Religion and Spirituality*, 3(4), (2011): 285–97.

141 *passes through our neurological wiring*   Andrew Newberg, *Principles of Neurotheology* (Burlington, VT: Ashgate Publishing, 2010).

142 *The Art of Possibility*   Rosamund Stone Zander and Benjamin Zander, *The Art of Possibility* (New York: Penguin, 2002).

143 *a natural "sanctification" of family*   A. Mahoney, "The Spirituality of Us: Relational Spirituality in the Context of Family Relationships," in *APA Handbook of Psychology, Religion, and Spirituality (1): Context, Theory, and Research*, ed. K. Pargament, J. Exline, J. Jones (Washington, DC: APA Press, 2013), 365–89.

143 *the brain literally perceives*   J. A. Coan, H. S. Shaefer, and R. J. Davidson, "Lending a hand: Social regulation of the neural response to treat," *Psychological Science*, 17, (2006): 1032–39.

144 *transmission of spirituality from parent to child*   S. Hardy, J. White, Z. Zhang, and J. Ruchty, "Parenting and socialization of religiousness and spirituality," *Psychology of Religion and Spirituality*, 3(3), (2011): 217–30; see also K. C. Leonard, K. V. Cook, and C. J. Boyatzis, "Parent-child dynamics and emerging adult religiosity: Attachment, parental beliefs, and faith support," *Psychology of Religion and Spirituality*, 5(1), (2013): 5–14.

145 *When spirituality is transmitted*   L. Miller, V. Warner, P. Wickramaratne, and M. Weissman, "Religiosity and depression: Ten-year follow-up of depressed mothers and offspring," *Journal of the American Academy Child Adolescent Psychiatry*, 36, (1997): 1416–25; see also S. K. Spilman, T. K. Neppl, M. B. Donnellan, M. Brent; T. J. Schofield, and R. D. Conger, "Incorporating religiosity into a developmental model of positive family functioning across generations," *Developmental Psychology*, 49(4), (2013): 762–74.

147 *Ritual conducted by one person* Andrew Newberg, *Principles of Neurotheology* (Burlington, VT: Ashgate Publishing, 2010).

156 *any committed loving source*   D. Zhang, Y. Barton, and L. Miller, "Psychological adjustment among left-behind children in rural China," submitted.

157 *cynical people have*   E. Neuvonen, M. Rusanen, A. Solomon, T. Ngandu, T. Laatikain, H. Soininen, M. Kivipelto, and A. M. Tolppanen, "Late-life cynical distrust, risk or incident dementia and mortality in a population based cohort," *Neurology*, 10, (2014).

157 *We know from Harold Koenig*   H. Koenig, L. George, and P. Titus, "Religion, spirituality and health in medically ill hospitalized older patients," *Journal of the American Geriatric Society*, 52(4), (2004): 554–62.

6. The First Decade

164 *medical schools show her video*   G. Fox, "Teaching normal development using stimulus videotapes in psychiatric education," *Academic Psychiatry*, 27(4), (2003): 283–88.

166 *ritual creates a special bond*   Joseph Campbell with Bill Moyers, *The Power of Myth* (New York: Random House, 1991).

169 *When we talk about educational curricula*   E. J. Tisdell, "In the new millenium: The role of spirituality and cultural imagination in dealing with diversity and equity in the classroom," *Teachers College Record*, 109(3), (2007): 531–60; see also L. Miller, "Present to possibility: Spiritual awareness and deep teaching," *Teachers College Record*, 111(12), (2009): 2705–12.

171 *When we neglect*   Nancy Eisenberg and Janet Strayer, *Empathy and Its Development* (New York: Cambridge University Press, 1987).

7. The Six Spiritual Strengths

179 *children made more spontaneous spiritual remarks*   Chris J. Boyatzis, "Parent-child communication about religion: Survey and diary data on uni-directional transmission and bi-directional reciprocity styles," *Review of Religious Research*, 44(3), (2003): 252–65.

185 *this "sanctification of family"*   A. Mahoney, "The Spirituality of Us: Relational Spirituality in the Context of Family Relationships," in *APA Handbook of Psychology, Religion, and Spirituality (1): Context, Theory, and Research*, ed. K. Pargament, J. Exline, and J. Jones (Washington, DC: APA Press, 2013), 365–89; see also K. Kusner, A. Mahoney, K. Pargament, and A. DeMaris, "Sanctification of marriage and spiritual intimacy predicting observed marital interactions across the transition to parenthood," *Journal of Family Psychology*, 28(5), (2014): 604–14.

188 *Native American system*   Bobby Lake-Thom, *Spirits of the Earth: A Guide to Native American Nature Symbols, Stories, and Ceremonies* (New York: Plume, 1997).

192 *The biggest mistake* "Tricycle Talk with Rita M. Gross," *Tricycle*, February 29, 2012; see http://www.tricycle.com/blog/tricycle-talk-rita-m-gross.

192 *a child as young as age six*   L. Heiphetz, L. Spelke, and M. Banaji, "Patterns of implicit and explicit attitudes in children and adults: Test in the domain of religion," *Journal of Experimental Psychology*, 142(3), (2013): 864–79.

202 *A dream often brings*   C. G. Jung, "Dreams," *The Collected Works of C. G. Jung*, ed. S. Shamdasani (Princeton, NJ: Princeton University Press, 1974), vols. 4, 8, 12, and 16.

8. Window of Awakening

209 *personal sense of spirituality are 80 percent less likely*   L. Miller, V. Warner, P. Wickramaratne, and M. Weissman, "Religion and depression: Ten-year follow-up of depressed

mothers and offspring," *Journal of the American Academy of Child and Adolescent Psychiatry*, 36(10), (1997): 1416–25; see also L. Miller, P. Wickramaratne, C. Tenke, and M. Weissman, "Religiosity and major depression in adults at high risk: A ten-year prospective study," *America Journal of Psychiatry*, 169(1), (2012): 89–94.

209 *60 percent less likely to become heavy substance users or abusers* L. Miller, M. Davies, and S. Greenwald, "Religiosity and substance use and abuse among adolescents in the National Comorbidity Survey," *Journal of the American Academy of Child and Adolescent Psychiatry*, 39(9), (2000): 1190–97.

209 *Girls with a sense of personal spirituality are 70 percent less likely to have unprotected sex* L. Miller and M. Gur, "Religiousness and sexual responsibility in adolescent girls," *Journal of Adolescent Health*, 31(5), (2002): 401–06.

210 *Individuation is the process through which the adolescent forms an aware core self* Erik H. Erikson, *Identity and the Life Cycle* (New York: International Universities, 1959; New York: W. W. Norton, 1980 reissue).

211 *Spiritual individuation is the personal determination of spiritual views* James Fowler, *The Stages of Faith: The Psychology of Human Development and the Quest for Meaning* (New York: Harper & Row San Francisco, 1981).

213 *the adolescent brain grows rapidly and gains gray matter* J. R. Giedd, J. Blumenthal, and N. O. Jeffries, "Brain development during childhood and adolescence: A longitudinal MRI study," *Nature Neuroscience*, (2), (1999): 861–63.

215 *This pronounced gap between the teen's felt surge* B. J. Casey, R. M. Jones, and T. Hare, "The adolescent brain," *Annals of the New York Academy of Science*, 1124, (2008): 111–26.

216 *the teen's own personal practices or habits of living* R. E. Dahl, "Adolescent brain development: A period of vulnerabilities and opportunities," *Annals of the New York Academy of Science*, 1021, (2004): 1–22.

216 *neural fibers in the prefrontal cortex can override* Y. I. Sheline, J. L. Price, Z. Yan, and M. A. Mintun, "Resting-state functional MRI in depression unmasks connectivity between networks via the dorsal nexus," *Proceedings of the National Academy of Sciences of the United States of America*, 107(24), (2010): 11020–25; see http://www.ncbi.nlm.nih.gov/pmc/articles/PMC2890754/.

217 *a different intersystem experience when imbued with transcendence* J. H. Jang, W. H. Jung, et al., "Increased default mode network connectivity associated with meditation," *Neuroscience Letters*, 487(3), (2011): 358–62.

221 *"A 'Portrait of 'Generation Next,'" reports that* Pew Research Center; see http://www.people-press.org/2007/01/09/a-portrait-of-generation-next/.

221 *A related Pew Forum report* Pew Research Center; see http://www.pewforum.org/2009/04/27/faith-in-flux/.

223 *Madeline Levine in her book* Madeline Levine, *The Price of Privilege: How Parental Pressure and Material Advantage Are Creating a Generation of Disconnected and Unhappy Kids* (New York: HarperCollins, 2008).

224 *Luthar portrays the developmental path* S. Luthar, S. H. Barkin, and E. J. Crossman, "I can therefore I must: Fragility in the upper-middle classes," *Development and Psychopathology*, 25, (2013): 1529–49.

227 *William James, in 1904*   William James, *The Variety of Religious Experience: A Study in Human Nature* (Seven Treasures Publication, 2009 reprint; public domain work).

227 *Geppert showed spirituality as a consistent force in recovery*   C. Geppert, et al., "Development of a bibliography on religion, spirituality and addictions," *Drug and Alcohol Review*, 26(4), (2007): 389–95.

227 *The fMRI research of our team and other labs suggests*   H. Kirk, J. Downar, and P. R. Montague, "Interoception drives increased rational decision-making in meditators playing the ultimatum game," *Frontiers in Neuroscience*, 5(49), (2011).

227 *63 percent of addicts in recovery from cocaine dependence claim*   P. M. Flynn, G. W. Joe, K. M. Broome, et al., "Looking back on cocaine dependence; reasons for recovery," *American Journal on Addictions*, 12, (2003): 398–411.

228 *acknowledgment of spirituality*   Anne Fletcher, *Sober for Good: New Solutions for Drinking Problems—Advice from Those Who Have Succeeded* (New York, Houghton Mifflin, 2001).

9. The Quest

234 *Steinberg speaks of the "exquisitely sensitive" adolescent brain*   Laurence Steinberg, *Age of Opportunity: Lessons from the New Science of Adolescence* (New York: Houghton Mifflin Harcourt, 2014).

235 *Erik Erikson*   Erik H. Erikson, *Identity and the Life Cycle* (New York: International Universities Press, 1959; New York: W. W. Norton, 1980 reissue).

247 *Katz describes one African community's spirit-based culture*   Richard Katz, *Boiling Energy: Community Healing among the Kalahari Kung* (Cambridge, MA: Harvard University Press, 1982).

250 *students who were involved in community service and/or religious community*   S. Hardy, M. Pratt, M. Pancer, et al., "Community and religious involvement as context of identity change across late adolescence and emerging adulthood," *International Journal of Behavioral Development*, 35, (2011): 125–35.

251 *the general ecology of school is even stronger*   M. Regnerus, C. Smith, and B. Smith, "Social context in the development of adolescent religiosity," *Applied Developmental Science*, 8(1), (2004): 27–38.

252 *the teen has a hand in fostering relationships*   A. Desrosiers, B. Kelley, and L. Miller, "Parent and peer relationships and relational spirituality in adolescents and young adults," *Psychology of Religion and Spirituality*, 3(1), (2011): 39–54.

266 *Abraham Maslow . . . in his seminal book*   Abraham H. Maslow, *Religions, Values, and Peak-Experience* (New York: Viking, 1970; reissue: Penguin, 1994).

10. Developmental Depression and Spiritual Awakening

272 *it is part of the hard work of individuation*   S. N. Ghaemi, "Feeling and time: The phenomenology of mood disorders, depressive realism, and existential psychotherapy,"

Schizophrenia Bulletin, 33(1), (2007): 122–30; see also N. Mascara and D. Rosen, "Existential meanings role in the enhancement of hope and prevention of depressive symptoms," *Journal of Personality*, 73(4), (2005): 985–1013.

272 *risk is very high for a subsequent, more severe depression* D. N. Klein, S. A. Shankman, P. M. Lewinsohn, and J. Seeley, "Subthreshold depressive disorder in adolescents: Predictors of escalation to full-syndrome depressive disorders," *Journal of the American Academy of Child and Adolescent Psychiatry*, 48(7), (2009): 703-10.

273 *precarious edge of a lifetime risk of depression* D. S. Pine, E. Cohen, P. Cohen, and J. Brook, "Adolescent depressive symptoms as predictors of adult depression: Moodiness or mood disorder?" *American Journal of Psychiatry*, 156 (1999): 133–35; see also J. Fogel, W. W. Eaton, and D. E. Ford, "Minor depression as a predictor of the first onset of major depressive disorder over a 15-year follow-up," *Acta Psychiatric Scandinavia*, 113, (2006): 36–43.

274 *likelihood that the patient will get the same diagnosis* R. Freedman, D. A. Lewis, R. Michels, et al., "The initial field trials of DSM-5: New blooms and old thorns," *American Journal of Psychiatry*, 170(1), (2013): 1–5.

274 *a subthreshold (moderate) level of depression* D. M. Fergusson, L. J. Horwood, E. M. Ridder, and A. L. Beautrais, "Subthreshold depression in adolescence and mental health outcomes in adulthood," *Archives of General Psychiatry*, 62, (2005): 66–72.

275 *35 percent of the time, subthreshold depression* P. M. Lewinsohn, S. A. Shankman, J. M. Gau, and D. N. Klein, "The prevalence and co-mordibity of sub-threshold psychiatric conditions," *Psychological Medicine*, 34, (2004): 613–22.

275 *each successive episode of major depression makes us more sensitive to being triggered again* K. Kendler, L. M. Thornton, and C. O. Gardner, "Stressful life events and previous episodes in the etiology of major depression in women: An evaluation of the 'kindling' hypothesis," *American Journal of Psychiatry*, 157(8), (2000): 1243–51.

278 *showed clear patterns of the relationship between* L. Miller, "Spiritual awakening and depression in adolescents: Two sides of one coin," *Bulletin of the Menninger Clinic*, 77(4), (2013): 332–48.

278 *Highly spiritual young adults* L. Miller, P. Wickramaratne, C. Tenke, and M. Weissman, "Religiosity and major depression in adults at high risk: A ten-year prospective study," *America Journal of Psychiatry*, 169(1), (2012): 89–94.

278 *75 percent protected against recurrence of depression* Ibid.

279 *families at risk for depression instead showed* L. Miller, R. Bansal, P. Wickramaratne, C. Tenke, M. Weissman, and B. Peterson, "Neuroanatomical correlates of religiosity and spirituality: A study in adults at high and low familial risk for depression," *Journal of the American Medical Association, Psychiatry*, 71(2), (2014): 128–35.

279 *the same wavelength of high-amplitude alpha* C. E. Tenke, J. Kayser, L. Miller, V. Warner, P. Wickramaratne, M. M. Weissman, and G. E. Brudner, "Neuronal generators of posterior EEG alpha reflect individual differences in prioritizing personal spirituality," *Biological Psychology*, 94(2), (2013): 426–32.

279 *High levels of the neurotransmitters dopamine and serotonin* N. Perroud, "Religion/Spirituality and Neuropsychiatry," in *Religion and Spirituality in Psychiatry*, ed. P. Huguelet and H. Koenig (New York: Cambridge University Press, 2009).

281 *two sides of the same coin*   L. Miller, "Spiritual awakening and depression in adolescents: Two sides of one coin," *Bulletin of the Menninger Clinic,* 77(4), (2014): 332–48.

295 *For profoundly depressed adolescents in mental health settings, with severe symptoms of depression and anxiety*   S. Zoogman, S. B. Goldberg, W. T. Hoyt, and L. Miller, "Mindfulness Interventions with Youth: A Meta-Analysis," *Mindfulness* (New York: Springer, 2014); see http://link.springer.com/article/10.1007/s12671-013-0260-4?no-access=true#page-1.

12. Parenthood

326 *during what Carl Jung called*   Carl Jung, *Memories, Dreams, and Reflections* (New York: Random House, 1961).

Index